Cambridge Series on Judgment and Decision Making

Inside the juror

Inside the Juror presents interesting and sophisticated work on juror decision making from several traditions – social psychology, behavioral decision theory, cognitive psychology, and behavioral modeling. The authors grapple with crucial questions, such as: Why do jurors who hear the same evidence and arguments in the courtroom enter the jury room with disagreements about the proper verdict? How do biases and prejudices affect jurors' decisions? And just how "rational" is the typical juror? As an introduction to the scientific study of juror decision making in criminal trials, *Inside the Juror* provides a comprehensive and understandable summary of the major theories of juror decision making and the research that has been conducted to evaluate their validity.

D0898373

Inside the juror

The psychology of juror decision making

Edited by

Reid Hastie
University of Colorado

CAMBRIDGE
UNIVERSITY PRESS

Published by the Press Syndicate of the University of Cambridge
The Pitt Building, Trumpington Street, Cambridge CB2 1RP
40 West 20th Street, New York, NY 10011-4211, USA
10 Stamford Road, Oakleigh, Melbourne 3166, Australia

First published 1993
First paperback edition 1994

Printed in the United States of America

Library of Congress Cataloging-in-Publication Data

Inside the juror: the psychology of juror decision making / edited by
Reid Hastie.
p.   cm. – (Cambridge series on judgment and decision making)
ISBN 0-521-41988-3 (hc)
1. Jury – United States – Decision making.   2. Jury – United States –
Psychological aspects.   I. Hastie, Reid.   II. Series.
KF8972.I57   1993
347.73'0752 – dc20
[347.307752]   92-5018
                                                                    CIP

A catalog record for this book is available from the British Library.

ISBN 0-521-41988-3 hardback
ISBN 0-521-47755-7 paperback

Contents

Series preface

The Society for Judgment and Decision Making first collaborated with Cambridge University Press in 1986, with the publication of *Judgment and Decision Making: An Interdisciplinary Reader,* edited by Hal R. Arkes and Kenneth R. Hammond. As the editors stated in their introduction, "judgment and decision making are of critical importance, and the fact that it is possible to study them in a scientific, empirical manner is a new and exciting event in the recent history of science" (p. 1).

The decade of the 1980s witnessed the flowering of the intellectual seeds planted by theoretical pioneers and seminal researchers in the area of human judgment and decision making. The founding and expansion of the Society was one feature of this growth. At the same time there has been an explosion of research and teaching in departments of psychology, economics, and medicine, with significant practical contributions through applied research and consulting in public and private institutions.

The Arkes and Hammond *Reader* was successful as an outline of the core ideas and approaches of the field and an illustration of the impressive range of useful applications. The Society, with Ken Hammond's encouragement, recognized the potential for a series of books to provide an educational and intellectual focus for the continued growth and dissemination of judgment and decision making research. Ken became the first Chair of the Publications Committee for the Society, devoting enormous amounts of time, creativity, and charm to this new initiative.

The Publications Committee is pleased to have *Inside the Juror* as the inaugural volume in the Society's series, because it exemplifies the fresh ideas, multidisciplinary approaches, attention to theory, empirical research, and application that characterize the field of judgment and decision making. Each subsequent volume in the Series will be devoted to a domain of practical and/or theoretical interest, offering an accessible presentation of the best new ideas and empirical approaches from the field of judgment and decision making.

The Publications Committee
John S. Carroll, Chair
James Shanteau
Don N. Kleinmuntz

Contributors

Kennette M. Benedict   *The John D. and Catherine T. MacArthur Foundation*

Jonathan D. Casper   *Department of Political Science, Northwestern University*

Robyn M. Dawes   *Department of Social and Decision Sciences, Carnegie-Mellon University*

Phoebe C. Ellsworth   *School of Law and Institute for Social Research, University of Michigan*

Reid Hastie   *Department of Psychology, University of Colorado*

Joseph B. Kadane   *Department of Statistics, Carnegie-Mellon University*

Ehud Kalai   *Department of Managerial and Economic Decision Sciences, Northwestern University*

Norbert Kerr   *Department of Psychology, Michigan State University*

Richard O. Lempert   *School of Law, University of Michigan*

Lola Lopes   *Department of Management and Organizations, University of Iowa*

Anne W. Martin   *Decision Science Consortium, Reston, Virginia*

Nancy Pennington   *Department of Psychology, University of Colorado*

David A. Schum   *Department of Operations Research and Applied Statistics, George Mason University*

Sandy Zabell   *Department of Mathematics, Northwestern University*

Editor's preface

Although juror decision making has probably attracted more attention from psychologists, economists, philosophers, mathematicians, and other scholars than any other decision making task, there are only a handful of models that have accrued any empirical support as descriptions of the psychological processes invoked to perform the task. The chapters in this edited book provide a thorough summary of all of the significant models of juror decision making. The chapters in the first half of the volume are descriptions of the models and the research that has been conducted to explicate and evaluate their merits as models of the decision process. The second half of the book is a collection of comments on the models and the enterprise of behavioral science research on juror decision making.

This book, like many other edited collections, is the result of a conference. However, unlike many conference books, it was not written in haste. Rather, the decision to create a book and the writing and revision process was extended over five years. Thanks to the National Science Foundation and Northwestern University, who funded the conference, there was no pressure to produce a report. It was the decision of the conference participants that something useful and possibly enduring could be written on the topic of theories of juror decision making.

Acknowledgments

This volume was initiated by a conference on "Models of Juror Decision Making" held at Northwestern University in 1986 (funds were provided by the National Science Foundation, SES–8600069, and Northwestern University). At the conclusion of the conference it was clear that the major presentations plus the discussion were the ingredients in a comprehensive overview of scientific approaches to juror decision making. Over the next four years, drafts of chapters were generated by the conference participants and, in 1991, final drafts were written. During these years, the editor of the volume (Reid Hastie) was supported at Northwestern University, the Center for Advanced Studies in the Behavioral Sciences (Stanford, California), the American Bar Foundation (Chicago, Illinois), and finally the Center for Research on Judgment and Policy (Boulder, Colorado). Support from these institutions, especially the Center at Stanford and the American Bar Foundation, was generous and essential. The final steps in production, including massive retyping, reference search and verification, and construction of most of the figures was performed by the incomparable Mary Luhring (at the Center for Research on Judgment and Policy). Final revision and editing owes much to the penetrating comments of Ronald J. Allen (Northwestern University Law School), John S. Carroll (Sloan School of Management, MIT), and Robert J. MacCoun (Behavioral Science Department, the RAND Corporation).

Part I

Models of juror decision making

1 Introduction

Reid Hastie

Why do jurors who hear the same evidence frequently disagree on the proper verdict? When and how do preexisting prejudices and attitudes influence jurors' decisions? How do jurors comprehend and apply instructions on the presumption of innocence and the standard of proof? How does a juror resolve conflicts that arise when his or her sense of justice dictates an outcome that conflicts with the appropriate verdict based on the juror's evaluation of the evidence? What types of decisions can we trust jurors to make well and which decisions are beyond the reasoning powers of nonexpert jurors? The authors of the present volume address these questions. But, in contrast to traditional legal scholars and authorities, their approach is scientific. This means that their overarching goal is to create a general, unified, empirically-based theory of the juror's thought processes and behavior.

Each of the major chapters in the present collection proposes a model of juror decision making. Each model is an explicit, precise, internally consistent set of statements about mental representations and processes that would be necessary to predict and explain the decisions made by jurors in realistically complex criminal trials. A basic convention of scientific discourse is that theoretical statements be public. Some of the models are in the form of mathematical equations and assumptions about their application, some in the form of computer programs that perform portions of the juror decision task, and some in the form of verbal statements. The success of these theories of juror decision making is measured by their ability to describe and predict the behavior of jurors in actual trials and in mock jury simulations of trials. And so each chapter also outlines the research by the author and other scientists that is supportive of the model. Perhaps most important, the ultimate goal is to create a unified model that can serve as a coherent summary of the principles that underlie several aspects of the juror's behavior across many variations on the basic decision task. At present, none of the models is preeminently successful; we are at an early stage in the science of juror decision making. But, they are the best candidates for a theory of juror decision making available in any form and in any domain of scholarly inquiry.

What sorts of theories of juror decision making have emerged from the nonscientific traditions of scholarship and practice over the centuries in which the jury trial has been at the center of the Anglo-American justice system? Intuitions (sometimes labeled "fireside inductions") about how jurors will behave have been the primary source of guidance for the formation and application of legal policies. Occasionally, an authority will review the relevant scientific findings (e.g., Wigmore's references to psychological research in his influential volumes on the laws of evidence (1940), Blackmun's lead opinion in *Ballew v. Georgia*, 1978); but authorities usually rely on their personal intuitions for conclusions about jury decision making (cf., opinions in *Apodaca v. Oregon* and *Johnson v. Louisiana*, 1972; *Lockhart v. Mc-Cree*, 1989; and *McClesky v. Kemp*, 1990). The result has been a reactive, fragmented, and sometimes incoherent collection of speculations about juror behavior. We have discovered no unified description of the nature of juror decision processes in the legal literature; certainly none has appeared in the major appellate decisions concerned with the right to trial by jury or in any of the major law reviews during the past fifty years.

The best summary of expert intuitions about juror behavior is probably Kalven and Zeisel's (1966) classic survey of trial judges' opinions about the causes of jury decisions (similar assumptions can be inferred as implicit motivations underlying the Federal Rules of Evidence [1983] and various appellate decisions concerning the right to trial by jury). Essentially, jurors are characterized as rough-and-ready logicians who reason competently about the implications of nontechnical evidence. But, when evidence is technical, sparse, or if the charge involves emotion-provoking events, the juror's sentiments are "liberated" and extralegal considerations (e.g., the race of the defendant or victim, the juror's attitude toward the applicable law, etc.) influence the judgment. Furthermore, a calculus of equities is prominent in juror reasoning; criminal trials are often conceptualized as "quarrels" between the victim and the defendant (much as in civil disputes); and conclusions about guilt are merged with questions about penalty. Although these (largely unconfirmed) intuitions may turn out to be accurate and may be consistent with the scientific theory of juror decision making (when one eventually achieves general acceptance), they fall far short of providing a unified image of the decision process. Even in Kalven and Zeisel (1966) these principles are scattered throughout the text and there is no attempt to present a summary image of the juror.

One development in traditional jurisprudential scholarship is a candidate for the role of a general theory of juror decision making; namely the utilitarian model of rational decision making that has been imported into jurisprudence from economics. Precursors of the "rational model" influenced the earliest American policy makers (e.g., the phrase, "life, liberty, and the pursuit of happiness" in our Declaration of Independence is a reference to Utilitarian philosophers). The model of an optimal rational decision maker has been applied by some jurists to explain criminal behavior, police and attorney behavior, and factfinding by judge or juror (Becker, 1968; Posner, 1985, 1986). This approach is based on a model of an ideally sensitive, perfectly informed, rational decision maker whose decision processes can be summarized by probability theory and a set of mathematical axioms for optimally consistent behavior. (We consider aspects of this approach in the chapters by Hastie, Schum, Schum and Martin, Kalai, and Zabell in this book.)

We do not want to depreciate the value of analyses of juror decision making that are based on the optimistic premise that everyday reasoning is rational. Even if juror decision making is not optimally rational, it is of obvious value to pursue *normative* analyses designed to tell us how we *should* think. But, current empirical research strongly suggests that the strictly rational model is not a valid *description* of individual decision making behavior (Herrnstein, 1990; Kahneman & Tversky, 1979; Lopes, 1987; Mazur, 1991; Payne, 1982; Tversky & Kahneman, 1974). At a minimum, the eventually successful descriptive theory of juror decision making will be a compromise between "top-down" rational rules and "bottom-up" psychological principles (J. R. Anderson, 1990; Arrow, 1982; March, 1978; Simon, 1959, 1978).

It is improbable that behavioral science theories will ever become the primary basis for the design, implementation, and evaluation of legal institutions (cf., Ellsworth, 1988; Faigman, 1991; Tanford, 1990). Nonetheless, we submit that descriptive models of juror decision making have been neglected in the formation of legal policy. References to a shared model of the juror's decision processes or the specification of disagreements in terms of alternate models of juror reasoning would sharpen and advance the analysis in many policy controversies and appellate review of individual cases. The enlightened legal scholar or practitioner should also be interested in scientific findings concerning juror behavior as a check on his or her inductions from personal experience. Furthermore, new empirical studies will also often be the best method to resolve differences of opinion or reduce uncertainty about legal procedures and institutions. At a minimum, the educated attorney, judge, or policy maker should be acquainted with the basics of empirical research methods and findings, because scientific results and arguments are being introduced at trial, appellate, and policy levels with increasing frequency (Ellsworth & Getman, 1987; Rosenblum, Phillips, Phillips, & Merrick, 1978).

The juror's task

The research in the present volume focuses on the manner in which jurors behave before they enter the social context of deliberation in criminal felony cases. Most jurors seem to have reached an initial decision about the appropriate verdict in a typical criminal trial, before entering deliberation (Hastie, Penrod, & Pennington, 1983). And, most theorists agree that the initial distribution of individual jurors' verdict preferences at the start of deliberation is the best predictor of the jury's final verdict (Kalven & Zeisel, 1966). (Research is underway to study jurors' judgments in civil disputes, but this literature is less developed than the empirical analysis of criminal trial decision making; Hensler, 1988; MacCoun, 1987.)

To provide a concrete introduction to the jurors' task, two summaries of typical felony trials are presented as Appendixes to this Introduction (both are based on transcripts of cases that were tried in Massachusetts). One case, *Commonwealth v. Johnson*, has been used extensively in research by Hastie, Penrod, and Pennington (1983) and by Ellsworth (see chapters by Pennington & Hastie and by Ellsworth in this book). In this case, identification of the perpetrator in a murder case is *not* under dispute. However, there is disagreement and conflicting testimony concerning events that occurred before a quarrel that led to the violent death of one man. In this case, the critical issues for jurors' decisions are concerned with the defendant's state of mind and some of his actions preceding and during the quarrel; these events and states of mind must be inferred from complex and conflicting testimony. The second example case, *Commonwealth v. Bryant*, is concerned with the identification of an armed robber. These are typical cases representing serious felonies tried in our courts every day. The two focal issues, state of mind and identification, are typical of the questions that must be decided by jurors in criminal trials.

Figures 1.1 and 1.2 (based on Pennington & Hastie, 1981) outline the events that occur in a typical criminal trial: first, from the perspective of the law, the procedures and the events that are controlled by statutes and tradition; second, from the perspective of a juror. We have made some assumptions about how jurors will conceive of the procedures and events described in Figure 1.1 (the typical events composing a trial according to law) as well as about the order in which some of these events will be addressed when the juror performs the larger task of reaching a predeliberation judgment. Of course, especially for Figure 1.2, there are differences of opinion about how the juror conceives of the larger task and deploys his or her mental resources to perform it; this is what the chapters in the present volume are about. Figure 1.3 provides an example of the categorical structure of the choice set of verdicts that are available to a juror in a typical felony case (cf., judge's instructions for the *Commonwealth v. Johnson* case in Appendix A, following this chapter).

> *Why does the juror's task have such wide appeal to scholars studying decision making?*

The legal judgment task faced by factfinders at trial has received more attention from behavioral scientists and other scholars than any other comparable

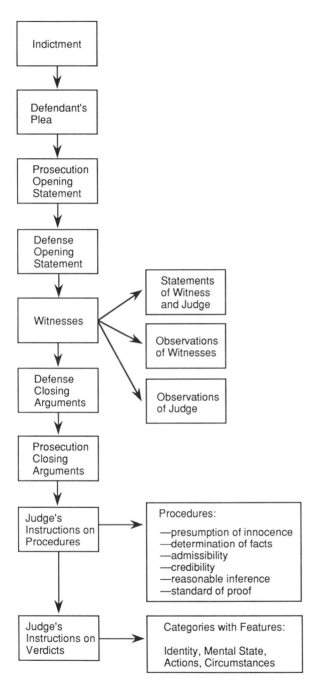

Figure 1.1. The trial events described in terms of the types of information presented to the juror.

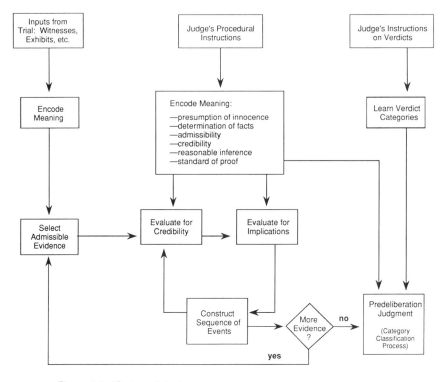

Figure 1.2. The juror's task.

decision task in our society. There are many good reasons for the preeminent role of legal judgment in studies of decision making.

1. It is a well-defined task with explicit rules of procedure, clear methods for recruiting participants, and consistent, stereotyped sequences of events. Although we cannot observe the events in jury deliberation directly, we have a great amount of information about every other aspect of the process. The information and instructions available to the juror are constrained by rules of evidence, statutes, and legal conventions and the jurors' decision task is not defined in an opportunistic or ad hoc manner. Many decisions in everyday life are never recognized as decisions, are deferred, or are selected and defined as decisions in an almost arbitrary manner by the decision maker. But, in the case of juror decisions, there is a definite, socially agreed upon focal event, with well-defined procedures, that is "the decision." There are also thousands of detailed records of trials that can be used to construct experimental simulations of the jurors' task or that can be used as the materials for other types of scholarly analysis.

2. The juror's task is simplified in certain respects: The juror's decision process is insulated from external influences and information in a manner that most other socially important decisions are not; it is also typically performed only once by the juror, thus eliminating many of the complexities

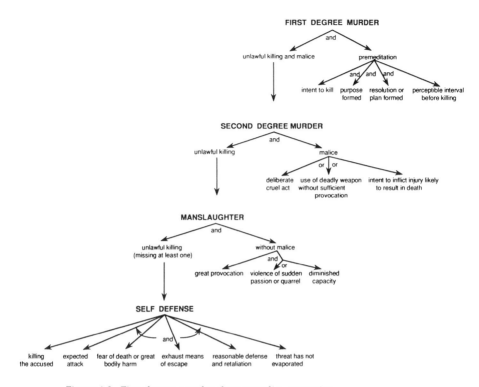

Figure 1.3. First degree murder charge verdict categories.

that occur when the same small group makes a sequence of decisions and individuals involved in the process can "trade votes" with one another.

3. Paradoxically, another motivation for research on juror decision making is that the task is complex and involves almost all higher order thought processes that have been identified by cognitive psychologists. If a researcher wants to study causal reasoning, reasoning under uncertainty, reasoning about the personalities of other people, etc. there are clear examples in almost any legal decision. Furthermore, if the researcher defines the decision task by the nature of the response dimension (choosing an appropriate category classification for an instance, assigning a value on a magnitude or quantitative continuum, making a classification by degree into an ordered category, etc.), again, almost any type of task is available in some legal decision. Perhaps it is best to say that the legal domain provides example judgment problems representing a remarkable range of complexity from narrowly focused judgments, "Did the defendant rob the supermarket?," to the vastly complex, "Did Company V suffer economic damages when firms W, X, and Y conspired to control the price of raw material Z?"

The same point about the rich source of example decision problems available in the record of decided cases can be repeated for non-empirical scholarly analyses. Frequently conceptual points are made in jurisprudential arguments by focusing on extreme cases, distinctive cases, or apparently contradictory cases. Philosophers interested in induction and belief updating have also often referred to legal paradoxes to illustrate intellectual controversies. There seems to be an endless store of paradoxes, enigmas, and intuition-challenging brain-teasers in actual legal cases and in the imaginative hypothetical cases that have been constructed by legal scholars.

4. Juror decisions are a productive task in which to study individual differences. The manner in which jurors are recruited to their service guarantees that there is a wide range of differences on almost any identifiable demographic factor, skill and knowledge, or personality. Any theory that can adequately characterize the decision processes of jurors will be a theory with great generality.

5. Another motivation for empirical research on juror decision making arises because the subject area has become a battleground for competing theories of decision making. For example, a recent volume summarizing a conference at Boston University concerned with the philosophy of science (Green & Tillers, 1986) was characterized as "a battle fought on legal turf among foreign champions" of several competing models for *normative* (optimal) decision making. The legal judgment domain has also been the context for conflict among *descriptive* theories of decision making. The chapters in the present book represent the state of the art in theorizing by behavioral scientists about juror decision making, with at least four competing approaches represented.

6. Juror and jury decisions have also been the focus of psychological research because they have significance outside of their scholarly and scientific appeal. Many researchers study juries because they want to improve legal institutions. For some researchers the motivation acquires a strong moral tone because of the importance, symbolically and in fact, of jury trials to members of our society.

7. Finally, research on jury decisions can be profitable. There are several large consulting firms who sell their services to attorneys or donate their time to causes in which they believe (e.g., the National Jury Project, Litigation Sciences Associates, the Association of Trial Behavior Consultants). Behavioral scientists are employed by these groups to help attorneys prepare cases by conducting surveys to support change of venue motions, design selection strategies for the voir dire, and conduct studies before and during the trial to evaluate jurors' reactions to the evidence (e.g., mock jury pretrial studies and shadow jury studies during the trial). The prospect of $200 an hour consulting fees has considerable drawing power for academic researchers who are lucky to earn $200 a day in university teaching salaries.

Four types of descriptive models

Modern behavioral science has produced four basic models of juror decision making based on probability theory, "cognitive" algebra, stochastic processes, and information processing theory. The major chapters in the present volume provide detailed expositions of each of the approaches, but we will begin with a brief comparative overview.

Probability theory approaches

Logic and probability theory have been the primary sources of "formal" suggestions for the analysis, improvement, and description of legal institutions (see Posner, 1990, for a discussion of the recrudescence of legal "formalism"). The traditional assumption of the formalist approach is that mathematical logic provides a valid description of the underlying structure of legal reasoning and legal argument and perhaps even a description of the reasoning processes of judges and jurors. The enthusiasm for logic as a key to legal doctrine and legal reasoning has waxed and waned, with its high point at the turn of the century and low points from 1930–1950 (during the ascendance of "legal realism," Llewellyn, 1962) and probably today (with the academic popularity of the "critical legal studies" approach, Kelman, 1987). However, "formal" analysis is returning in the form of logic-based expert systems which have already been implemented in highly codified areas of law such as those involving probate and taxes (Ashley, 1990; Association for Computing Machines, 1987; Gardner, 1987; Susskind, 1987) and in the application of probability theory to the factfinding process.

Formal, mathematical probability theory has been applied to elucidate, criticize, and improve legal reasoning (e.g., Lempert has dubbed this approach "the new evidence scholarship," 1986). Like logic, probability theory prescribes "syntactic" rules to guarantee the consistency of inferences. Although alternate formulations of probability theory have been proposed and a variety of interpretations of the term "probability" have been advanced, one approach, now called Bayesian probability theory, has been dominant for centuries (Kaye, 1988). Probability theory can be summarized by a brief list of axiomatic rules that specify permissible operations to be performed on probabilities (numbers in the interval 0 to 1) that will guarantee consistency of reasoning.

Thomas Bayes, a British clergyman concerned with evaluating evidence for the existence of God, proposed an important equation in probability theory that can be derived in three steps from the original probability theory axioms. Bayes' theorem allows the application of probability theory to conditions under which a person wishes to "update" his or her beliefs that certain events will occur on the basis of new evidence concerning the outcomes in a situation. This updating rule appears to be almost ideally suited for the rational adjustment of opinions about hypotheses, such as "the defendant is guilty as charged," in response to evidence in a trial. This has led many legal scholars and probability theorists to propose the application of the theorem as a prescription or description for factfinders' reasoning in legal cases.

An illustration of the interest among scholars in the application of Bayes' theorem to legal reasoning is provided by the papers in a recent issue of *The Boston University Law Review* (Green & Tillers, 1986). A majority of the twenty-two entries in this volume promote the application of Bayes' theorem to elucidate or improve legal reasoning from evidence. The classic example of an application to improve juror factfinding is provided by the prosecution's use of a mathematics instructor as an expert witness to provide the jury with a Bayesian calculation to resolve the question of the identity of a mugger in *People v. Collins* (1968; an insightful exegesis of the *Collins* case is provided in Fairley & Mosteller, 1974). More recently Fienberg and Schervish (1986) have argued for the Bayesian approach to the presentation of evidence to factfinders in legal cases (Fienberg, 1989; Gastwirth, 1992; and Weinstein, 1988, provide reviews of the role of statistics and probability theory in the assessment of evidence by courts; see also Kaplan, 1968; Koehler & Shaviro, 1990; Lempert, 1977).

In the present context, however, we are concerned with the application of Bayes' theorem as a *description* of the manner in which the *factfinder* reasons, rather than as a source of illumination of legal concepts or guidelines for the design of trial procedures. Thus, the primary goal of these applications is to describe the juror's behavior, not to describe the structure of the law or to evaluate and improve jurors' performance.

To clarify what a Bayesian model of the psychological processes engaged in by a juror might be, we will outline the sequence of thought processes that might occur based on the formal mathematical Bayesian analysis. (We emphasize that this conception of a Bayesian process model that could serve as a description of human thought processes is original with us and should not be attributed to other authors concerned with the application of Bayesian theory to the juror judgment task.) A more detailed and definitive exposition of the Bayesian approach is provided by David Schum and Anne Martin's chapters in the present volume (Fischhoff & Beyth-Marom, 1983; Slovic & Lichtenstein, 1971; and von Winterfeldt & Edwards, 1986, especially pp. 163–204, are also useful sources).

The fundamental assumption of the Bayesian approach is that the basic dimension of thought in judgment is the subjective probability. This means that all information relevant to the judgment is conceptualized by the juror on a unitary dimension that represents the strength of belief or subjective probability that an event or condition referenced by the belief has occurred or is true. The notion that we think in terms of subjective probabilities also entails that our reasoning approximates mathematical rules of coherence that give the term probability its meaning. For example, if we are concerned with judging the probability that a conjunction of two events has occurred (e.g., that the defendant had formed a plan to injure the victim and that the defendant had obtained a knife in order to execute this plan), our judgments of closely related propositions should follow certain rules of coherence – namely, that the probability of the conjunction is equal to the probability of

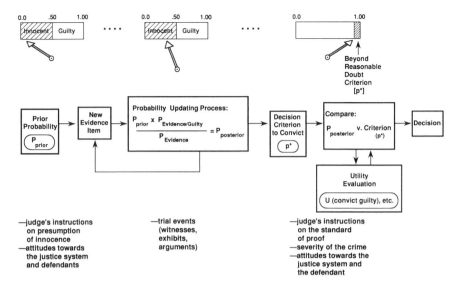

Figure 1.4. Bayesian probability updating model. There are three parts (top to bottom) of this diagram: (a) a hypothetical "probability meter" that indicates the juror's current strength of belief with reference to the hypothesis that the defendant is guilty as charged; (b) a flowchart representation of the events in the judgment process ordered by the time at which they occur; (c) notes on the types of information that are most influential at each stage in the flowchart processing sequence.

our belief that the defendant obtained the knife given he had formed the plan *multiplied by* our probability he had formed the plan under any circumstances. (There are several other generally accepted mathematical rules for calculations with probabilities which taken together provide a standard for "coherent" or rational reasoning.)

If we accept the description of juror judgment as probabilistic inference, six stages are needed to describe the Bayesian process (see Figure 1.4). The Bayesian approach is described as a "single meter model" because all of the results of subprocesses in the judgment sequence are summarized in a single "posterior probability" that represents the juror's current belief about the guiltiness of the defendant (see Lopes, this book, for an introduction to the "meter" image). We might reify this homey metaphor of the juror's belief state by imagining a "mental meter" that is continually adjusted as the juror reasons about the implications of evidence and other information relevant to the judgment.

The Bayesian approach is frequently criticized because it makes the *single* "mental meter" assumption. One objection is that everyday reasoning about uncertainty includes at least two components: a primary evaluation of subjective uncertainty or probability and a secondary evaluation of the unreliability, ambiguity, or weight of the evidence (Cohen, 1977, 1986; Gaerdenfors & Sahlin, 1982). Another objection is based on the fact that most legal decisions are defined by statute to be "multidimensional"; they require the juror to make several component decisions on the elements of crimes or suits, rather than one global judgment. For the moment, suffice it to say that all *descriptive* mathematical models of juror judgment make the assumption of a *single* mental meter to represent the juror's current state of belief regarding the guilt or innocence of the defendant. We will return to this issue in the consideration of each individual model throughout this book.

In the first stage of the judgment process, a juror must create or adopt an initial degree of belief – prior probability – about the conclusions of the judgment to be made in a particular case. We might imagine that the juror entertains a prior probability of .50 that the defendant is guilty as charged before the trial has started; and the "mental meter" is initially set to this value. The Bayesian juror would construct a prior probability by considering the judge's preliminary instructions, his or her beliefs about the conduct of the police, officials, criminals, and attorneys in the relevant jurisdiction, and personal values relevant to the criminal justice system.

After the juror has generated a prior probability, he or she turns to the task of identifying and comprehending units of information that will be processed one-by-one to update the initial belief. The question of what constitutes an item of evidence appropriate to input into the belief updating process lies outside of the scope of Bayesian theory. Presumably, items of information that can be assigned values on the subjective probability dimension could be represented as propositions making assertions with reference to the truth or falsity of conditions in the real world. If the juror behaves as instructed by the judge, most of this information occurs as admissible testimony and exhibits during the trial. (Schum and Martin, this book, provide several examples of the types of evidence items that might enter into a Bayesian analysis in a jury trial.)

Once an item of evidence has been identified, the juror moves to the process described by Bayes' theorem, an equation derived from the axioms of probability theory that prescribes the manner in which the current, prior probability should be combined with a new item of evidence to update belief in the "hypothesis" (e.g., the defendant is guilty) under consideration. This could be conceptualized as setting the "mental meter" to a new value as a result of consideration of each new item of evidence. Note the prior probability that appears in the numerator (and implicitly in the denominator) of the equation in a multiplicative role. This means that if the prior belief takes an extreme probability value like 0 or 1, the equation cannot produce changes in the posterior probability (e.g., multiplying any other term in the numerator of the equation by 0 will yield another numerator of 0 and the entire fraction will evaluate to 0, producing no change). Thus, the mental meter is designed to stop whenever it reaches an extreme value of zero or one.

Once the belief updating process has occurred, the initial prior probability is replaced by the new posterior probability and the cycle of identifying a new evidence item and calculating a new posterior probability occurs again. This cycle of adjustments continues until no new information is available or the juror is asked to render a verdict.

When a categorical verdict decision is required, the next stage in the process constructs a decision criterion or threshold for conviction. Again, Bayesian theory is mute about the factors that will be considered by a juror who constructs a personal decision criterion. It is likely that a juror will consider the judge's instructions concerning the standard of proof (in criminal trials interpreting the phrase "beyond reasonable doubt"), the nature of the charge against the defendant, and his or her personal values concerning the proper functions of the justice system. This decision criterion would be represented on the probability dimension as a number between 0 and 1 and it can be conceptualized as a zone of conviction on the mental meter. Presumably it would be illegitimate for a juror to enter the jury box with a virtually unachievable decision criterion of 1 because this would mean that the decision was preordained in advance of any evidence about the specific case.

The final processing stage for our Bayesian juror involves a comparison of the final posterior probability (reached after the juror has cycled through the evidence processing substages many times) with the threshold probability for conviction. If the belief adjustment process ends with a mental meter reading in this zone, the conclusion is to convict; otherwise, to acquit.

In Figure 1.4 we have indicated that an additional (seventh) stage may occur during this comparison process in which the utilities associated with outcomes of the juror's decision are considered by the juror. The utility evaluation introduces factors beyond the probability that the defendant is guilty into the judgment process. This computation involves a consideration of the costs of losses associated with various actions (verdicts) available to the juror. Although the juror's subjective probability for conviction might exceed the probabilistic threshold to convict, the juror might still acquit because of a further consideration of the perceived high cost or social loss associated with making an erroneous decision (i.e., convicting an innocent defendant). Thus, the comparison stage involves consideration of both probabilities and potential costs associated with errors in judgment (see chapters by Ellsworth, Hastie, and Kerr in this book, for further discussion of this point).

The final decision stage, in which the juror is hypothesized to compare the implications of the evidence with the decision criterion, presents a problem for all current theories of juror decision making. The problem arises because the juror's decision task (in the eyes of the law) is multidimensional, but the psychological models (at least the three meter models we present) assume that juror judgment is on one global dimension of judged culpability or guiltiness. In the trial judge's instructions, the juror is told that he or she must be satisfied beyond a reasonable doubt that *each element* of the charge against the defendant is true (a similar instruction applies the preponderance standard in civil cases). But, there is no additional instruction on how to combine the component decisions; simply decide "no," if any of the elements is not "proved" to a sufficient degree (e.g., "preponderance" or "beyond reasonable doubt").

The Bayesian approach, with its rule that the product of component probabilities is the probability of the conjunction event, runs into the greatest difficulties. Because the Bayesian model assumes a single "belief meter" and because probability theory defines the probability of the global verdict as the product of its element probabilities (see Figure 1.3 for an illustration of the elements associated with some typical criminal verdicts), scholars have posed several "brainteasers" raised by the nature of the ultimate verdict decision. For example, conviction for a four-element crime might have a global probability of less than .75, because each element has been proved at a level of approximately .91; yet, .75 seems a low value for the beyond reasonable doubt standard. Or, we might see a decision for the plaintiff, in a four-element tort suit with each element proved to a level over .60, where the conjunction probability (for the winner) is less than .20 – truly a paradoxical outcome. Or, why should verdicts in cases involving many elements (proven to a certain degree) be acceptable, while a comparable case involving fewer elements (proven to the same degree) seems to require a much higher level of global proof? Or, why should a civil dispute in which the plaintiff establishes two required elements at levels of proof of .4 and .9 be resolved for the defense, when a case with .6 and .6 would be decided for the plaintiff (both global, conjunction probabilities would be .36 in this example)? These examples may be artificial (e.g., they require assumptions of independence among elements that are usually unrealistic), but they are not sophistry. It is unlikely that legislatures and appellate courts have been sensitive to the complexities and possible inequities that are entailed by the multidimensional character of our verdicts, *if* we assume that probability theory describes the best method for evidence combination. These issues were the focus of discussion in the Green and Tillers (1986) conference volume, especially papers by Allen, Cohen, Kaye, and Lempert; we are indebted to Allen (1991) for his insightful discussion of the difficulties for the Bayesian approach raised by Anglo-American principles of judicial proof.

The Bayesian model predicts stringent limits on behavior because of its strong requirements for numerically precise internal consistency among a static system of beliefs and among beliefs before and after adjustment. We have already noted that there is substantial empirical evidence that human behavior does not exactly conform to probability theory principles. However, rough agreement between probability theory and human judgment is still a viable possibility. We have included two chapters by the Bayesian theorist David Schum in this book: a reprint of Schum and Martin's (1982) classic analysis of coherence among componential probability estimates relevant to the guilt or innocence of a defendant, and a second paper in which Schum outlines the recent directions his research has taken (in collaboration with Peter Tillers) concerned with the application of probability theory to the structuring of evidence and information search to provide a full treatment of investigation and inference in legal contexts.

Like other researchers before him, Schum has concluded that Bayesian rules of coherence do not exactly describe human judgment processes; although there are substantial similarities between the implications of the Bayesian model and the manner in which people make inferences in a legal setting (see also Schum & Martin, 1980). Schum develops the hypothesis that humans reason in an essentially Bayesian fashion, but that the Bayesian calculus must be supplemented by principles to describe the manner in which the factfinder selects and structures evidence – that is, which limited subset of the many possible conditional relations between pieces of evidence is considered by a juror?

Algebraic approaches to juror's decision making

Theories of mental processes couched in the form of algebraic equations have been with us since the beginning of scientific psychology. Algebraic models were first used to describe the speed of reactions to a simple stimulus such as a light flash (in studies designed to estimate the speed of nervous transmission) and to summarize the "psychological" relationships between verbal judgments and stimuli that varied in physical intensity – for example, How subjectively bright is a light of a particular physical intensity? The best-known programs of research on algebraic models of judgment processes are associated with Norman Anderson's "Cognitive Algebra" for judgment (N. H. Anderson, 1981), and with Kenneth Hammond's "Lens Model" (Brehmer & Joyce, 1988; Hammond, Stewart, Brehmer, & Steinmann, 1975). Algebraic models also have a long history as mechanisms for the assessment of credibility of religious and philosophical arguments (Burns, 1981; Gigerenzer, Swijtink, Porter, Daston, Beatty, & Krueger, 1989). For example, many efforts to evaluate the credibility of arguments for the existence of a Christian god took the form of algebraic formulae to extract implications from evidence such as miracles. (Obviously, Bayes' theorem fits into this tradition, but it is distinguished by its foundation on a set of axioms that is generally recognized as normatively correct.)

Research on human judgment has converged on the conclusion that one particular algebraic formulation is the most promising as a description of the psychology of inference from evidence. In mathematical terms this equation is called a linear model or a weighted average equation. The averaging process for combining evidence to reach a conclusion has considerable commonsense, intuitive appeal. Passages in such reputable sources as the Bible and the correspondence of Benjamin Franklin reflect the common appeal of a weighted average formulation as a model for practical judgment. Furthermore, although the model is algebraic, the concepts are simple enough that a few minutes of study would allow even a person with only a high school

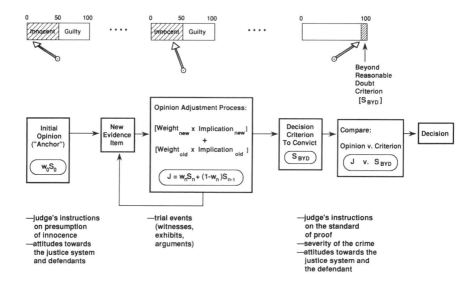

Figure 1.5. Algebraic sequential averaging model. Three parts of the diagram (top to bottom): (a) "opinion meter"; (b) flowchart of processing stages; (c) information relevant at each stage.

education to grasp the basic principle of the model and to understand how predictions are derived from it.

Essentially the weighted average equation prescribes that pieces of evidence can be identified, that a meaning or implication for a judgment can be extracted from each piece of evidence, and that the impact of each piece's implication on the ultimate judgment should be moderated by a weight indicating the importance, relevance, or reliability of the piece of evidence. In a legal judgment, a juror might consider the testimony of an eyewitness to a crime. Suppose this testimony has the clear implication that the defendant was the perpetrator of the crime – "He's the man who robbed my store." But the ultimate impact of the testimony on the juror's eventual judgment will be moderated by the weight placed on the testimony by the juror. A witness who appeared to be unreliable would be accorded a lower weight than a comparable but apparently more reliable witness. Therefore the impact of the testimony will depend on both its meaning and on factors such as the witness's apparent reliability, credibility, and relevance. In the more general formulation of a weighted averaging process, many pieces of evidence are provided to a factfinder, with the model extended to extract implications from each piece of evidence and weight each (relative to other pieces of evidence) in the ultimate judgment.

A flowchart summary of the weighted averaging model as a process model looks similar to the Bayesian probability theory model just outlined (see Figures 1.4 and 1.5). As in the Bayesian model, we are dealing with a single meter in which the results of all the subprocesses are summarized in a current belief and in which the ultimate "categorical" verdict decision is based on the comparison of the final belief meter reading to a threshold to convict. The algebraic model differs from the Bayesian model in at least two key respects: First, in the algebraic model, the fundamental dimension of judgment is not assumed to be a subjective probability, so the rules of coherence among judgments (required by the Bayesian model) are relaxed and extreme judgments (analogous to 0 and 1 probabilities in the Bayesian model) are not final and can still be adjusted when subsequent evidence is received. Second, the details of the belief updating calculation are "additive" (weight each evidence item and *add* the weighted value to the current degree of belief); while the Bayesian model prescribes an intuitively more complicated *multiplication* adjustment calculation.

This type of linear, weighted averaging model is the most popular model in statistical analyses of all types of scientific and actuarial data. Many methods have been developed to "fit" linear regression models of this type to individual judgments to estimate (after the judgments are made) the weights assigned to individual pieces of evidence (Slovic & Lichtenstein, 1971). In the applications reviewed in this book, one of the primary successes of the algebraic approach derives from applying the model to estimate numerical values that can be interpreted as subjects' assessments of the presumption of innocence, the weights accorded to items of evidence (including extralegal, illegitimate sources of information), and the manner in which subjects reason about the standard of proof (e.g., beyond a reasonable doubt).

As with the other single meter models, the weighted average model has been criticized as incomplete or inadequate in application to realistically complicated jurors' tasks (Pennington & Hastie, 1981). But Hastie and Lopes (this book) provide accounts of how the simple weighted average model can be elaborated to apply to more complicated, multidimensional juror judgments. And, as with the Bayesian model, most proponents concede that the model provides only a rough description of *molar* judgment processes. But it is extremely general, and it includes valuable methodological procedures (e.g., methods to rigorously estimate a summary "weight" for each piece of information in the judgment) that are not available in any alternate approach.

Stochastic process models for juror decision making

A third family of mathematical models, stochastic process models, has been applied fruitfully as a description of juror decision making. (Other applications include models of sensation, learning, and choice: Atkinson, Bower, & Crothers, 1965; Estes, 1959; Luce, 1986; Luce & Suppes, 1965.) These models differ from algebraic and probability theory models because they assume that a component of the larger process described by mathematical equations behaves in a random fashion. Unlike the Bayesian model, this probability process is defined in terms of a time parameter and the probabilistic element refers to state transitions over time (measured continuously or in discrete units). This also means that the ultimate "output" of the model, in this case a prediction of juror's judgments, is not a precise estimate of a single point (e.g., the degree of perceived strength of the evidence for guilt in an algebraic model or the posterior probability of guilt in a Bayesian model) but rather a *distribution* of possible values with explicit uncertainty about an individual juror's response to a particular case at a specified point in time.

There are many motivations for including a random process component in a theory of human behavior (Cotton, 1982). Some theorists associate probabilistic components with an attribution of "free will" to the human condition. Others mean that, at least at some sub-behavioral level, the determinants of behavior are truly random and unpredictable; for example, perhaps the behavior of neurons underlying thought is perturbed by unpredictable chemical and atomic events that can only be represented as a stochastic process.

Theoreticians employing stochastic process models of juror decision making do so to indicate that their analysis does not exhaust all determined, predictable components of behavior: at the level of detail at which they study juror decision processes there is considerable unknown (*but still knowable*) causal determination of individual decisions. These theoreticians reason in the same fashion as mathematicians who describe the causally determined (*these mechanical causes are usually unknown, but knowable*) result of a coin toss as the value of a random variable. These researchers would argue that intensive behavioral analyses of individual differences, specific case characteristics, and "microbehaviors" (e.g., vicissitudes of attention) could yield a more complete deterministic account of the juror's performance when judging a single case on a single occasion than they have attempted. However, stochastic theoreticians have deliberately selected a higher level of generality for their analysis and assign many (potentially identifiable) determinants of behavior to a random process. They "pay" for this general level of analysis by deriving predictions only at the level of theoretical *distributions* that can be compared to the distributions of responses that are observed empirically. But, they submit that they have provided a model at the best currently practical level of detail for a useful analysis of juror decision making.

There are also deep questions raised by references to a random process. The definition of a random process is an issue that provokes considerable controversy among the philosophers, mathematicians, and scientists who have considered it (Chaitin, 1975; Kac, 1983; Lopes, 1982). Fortunately, for the purposes of the models introduced in the present volume, a conventional definition in terms of the mathematical properties of "random" variables is available. In the present case (models described by Kerr, this book), a Poisson random process is defined to describe the distribution of "stopping

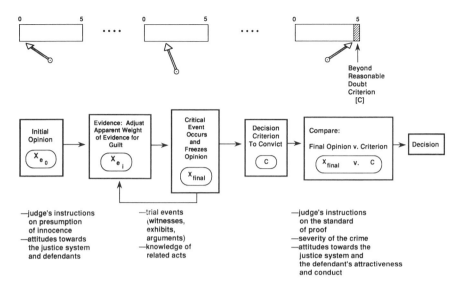

Figure 1.6. Stochastic Poisson process model. Three parts of the diagram (top to bottom): (a) "weight of evidence meter"; (b) flowchart of processing stages; (c) information relevant at each stage.

points" in time at which a juror's thought process terminates to yield a final strength of belief about guilt or innocence of a defendant (e.g., Taylor & Karlin, 1984, p. 175).

Although there is an endless variety of possible stochastic models for judgment, the model that has been developed for juror decision making is of a particularly elegant and general form (Kerr, this book; Thomas & Hogue, 1976). Three general types of subprocesses underlie the global judgment model: (A) an evidence evaluation process, or processes in some versions of the model, in which the implications are extracted in real time as each item of evidence is encountered; (B) a critical event occurrence process in which the evidence evaluation process is "frozen" at its current value; and (C) a comparison process in which the final value of the evidence is compared to a decision criterion to render a "categorical" verdict decision *and* to produce a confidence level associated with the verdict. See Figure 1.6.

The evidence evaluation process has been given a cursory description in stochastic models of juror decision making; evidence for and against guilt is registered by a unitary "apparent weight of evidence" value that could be best described as a binomial random walk through time that moves toward guilty or innocent conclusions in a weaving, haphazard manner (Townsend & Ashby, 1983). We would characterize this as another single meter model in which the current meter setting represents the location of the random walk process between extreme judgments for guilt or innocence. (Interestingly, the stochastic approach was the first to propose multiple meter models, with four meters – monitoring evidence for innocence, evidence for guilt, extraevidentiary information for innocence, and extraevidentiary information for guilt – operating to summarize the implications of the evidence, although this complexity was dropped after an initial consideration. Of course, it was also necessary to postulate an additional stage of processing to combine the final readings of the four meters into a summary value for comparison to the decision threshold.)

The distinctive feature of the stochastic model for juror decision making is the inclusion of a process that operates on the mental meter to "freeze" it into a fixed position. This process has been described as a critical event, perhaps a single piece of evidence that was perceived as decisive by the juror and that disengaged him or her from the consideration of additional evidence. The occurrence of this critical event was represented as a random Poisson process, a relatively rare event that could occur with a fixed probability distributed across time. Once this critical event has occurred, the hypothetical juror has "made up" his or her mind concerning the weight of the evidence and the model proceeds to the last decision stage in which the final mental meter reading is compared to a threshold for conviction. The output of this stage is a verdict and a confidence level, with the confidence directly dependent on the distance between the final evidence value and the threshold value – if the evidence value greatly exceeds (or misses) the threshold, the juror's confidence in the conviction (acquittal) verdict will be high.

As in the case of the other mathematical models, the Poisson process model is not hypothesized to describe the most elementary levels of cognitive processing. Its "description" of the evidence evaluation process is certainly the most abbreviated of all models for juror decision making. But it provides a general characterization of the complete judgment process and it is accompanied by methods for the estimation of parameters that represent the impact of extralegal information (e.g., attractiveness of the victim or defendant), the decision criterion, and the juror's confidence. Perhaps the most important advantage of the Poisson process model is that it includes both the evidence evaluation and comparison to a decision criterion processes within one model. Its applications are the only empirical studies (to our knowledge) in which the joint impact of evidence, instructions, and extralegal factors on both processes have been measured simultaneously.

Cognitive approaches to juror judgment

If the science of psychology has a single, unifying paradigm, it is the image of a symbolic information processing computer. Casper, Ellsworth, and Pennington and Hastie develop versions of a cognitive information processing theory of juror decision making. Pennington and Hastie's explanation-based model provides the most detailed version of this approach; Ellsworth applies a similar cognitive formulation to elucidate individual differences in attitudes and their impact on jurors' decisions; and Casper interprets the "hindsight" effects of testimony about the outcome of a police investigation on jurors' judgments that should, but do not, ignore this outcome in terms of underlying inference and memory processes.

The basic strategy of the cognitive theorists is similar to methods pursued by mathematical modelers. A general framework or theoretical language is developed (analogous to a branch of mathematical theory) and then task-specific process models are "written" in the general language to describe and predict behavior under the conditions being studied empirically. Cognitive theorists defend their efforts to develop an alternative to standard mathematical approaches by pointing out that modern mathematics was developed with the physical sciences as the primary domain of application. It is unlikely that the mathematics developed to describe physical processes will be an ideal medium for theories of behavioral phenomena, especially where the theories depend on complex representations of mental structures and mental processes. Mathematical modelers, of course, note that the cognitive approach is more heterogeneous and less precise than conventional mathematical formulations and therefore the theoretician is constantly faced with the danger of positing incomplete, internally contradictory, or incomprehensible models.

There are formal versions of information processing theories in cognitive psychology (cf. J. R. Anderson, 1976; Atkinson & Shiffrin, 1968) and it is common for well-specified mathematical models to be embedded in a more complicated cognitive framework (e.g., Hastie, 1988; Hastie, Penrod, & Pennington, 1983, chapter 9). J. R. Anderson (1983), Newell and Simon (1972), Newell (1990) and others have developed well-defined, consistent, and general architectures that provide powerful media in which to express theories about cognitive processing. The contrast with mathematical approaches is apparent in our repeated observations that the mathematical models are extremely general, but usually fail to specify details in application such as the representation of individual differences, the effects of subtleties of evidence structure, or the variety of inference forms that are available in human cognitive systems.

Although there is some variation across the "dialects" within the cognitive approach, there are several general concepts that appear in all of the cognitive theories (reviewed by Bower, 1978; Estes, 1989; Hastie, 1986; Posner, 1989; Simon, 1979). The image of a computer and a computer program is often cited to characterize, by analogy, cognitive models. The analogy is apt: Cognitive theories assume there is a fundamental architecture of the mind that has evolved to facilitate the processing of symbols (analogous to the hardware of a computing machine) and that task-specific strategies are developed to cope with problems encountered in everyday life (analogous to computer programs). Thus, cognitive theories come with a series of assumptions about the nature of the cognitive architecture available to execute task-specific strategies; theories take the form of models for the application of the cognitive architecture to solve problems using learned or invented strategies.

1. Cognitive analyses place great emphasis on the description of mental representations: the structure and contents of the information that is processed by the mind. Pennington and Hastie, Ellsworth, and Casper all focus on the mental representation of evidence and decision categories as fundamental to an understanding of jurors' decisions. Pennington and Hastie go the furthest by postulating that a "narrative" structure is imposed on evidence as it is comprehended by a juror who is making a decision in a typical felony case. Pennington and Hastie find that most jurors construct a "story" that can be described by the graph theory structures that psycholinguists have proposed as models for the comprehension of other types of narratives (Mandler, 1984; Trabasso & van den Broek, 1985). Pennington and Hastie's empirical research supports the "psychological validity" of story structures as descriptions of jurors' representations of evidence and demonstrates that the juror's story structure predicts his or her decision and confidence in the decision. Ellsworth and Casper also measure jurors' mental representations of evidence, although they do not commit themselves to the specific story structure format.

Pennington and Hastie note that the decision categories (verdicts) provided by the trial judge need to be characterized as mental representations and they hypothesize that feature lists (Smith & Medin, 1981) from cognitive psychological analyses of noun categories provide a good characterization of the manner in which jurors represent verdict categories after hearing them in the trial judge's instructions.

2. Cognitive theories also include principles for memory activation: How are knowledge structures activated and retrieved from memory? The standard assumption in most cognitive theories is that ideas in memory activate one another by spreading "mental energy" along associative pathways. Thus, if a juror has concluded that testimony about the outcome of a search (drugs were found in the defendant's apartment) is relevant to a police officer's judgment that there was "probable cause" to search the apartment, a juror's thoughts about one of these topics will bring to mind ("activate") thoughts about the other.

3. Cognitive strategies or models of cognitive processes are built out of a collection of elementary information processes that operate to store, retrieve, and transform basic units of information or symbols. Different models employ different lists of elementary information processes; but a typical set was provided by Newell and Simon (1972): discrimination processes; test and comparison processes; symbol creation processes; symbol writing processes; symbol activation or reading processes; etc. Just as in an algebraic model, where more complex processes are built up from the elementary algebraic operators, in a cognitive model complex processes are built up out of the elementary information processes.

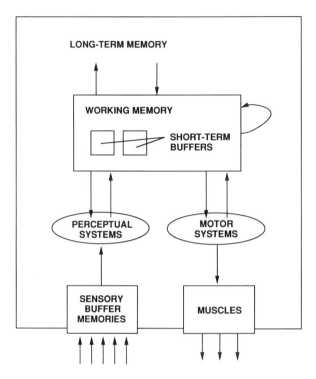

Figure 1.7. Cognitive information processing architecture. A map of the major components of a typical information processing system (arrows indicate flow of information and control).

4. Virtually all cognitive theories include descriptions of an executive monitor that keeps track of the system's goals, current states, and plans to move from current states to desired states. The concept of a well-defined executive processor was probably the key development in cognitive theories that led to their ascendancy over the more "passive," "stimulus-driven" learning theory models that had dominated psychology in the first half of this century (Miller, Galanter, & Pribram, 1960).

5. Finally, we noted that most cognitive theories come with fairly clear commitments to a specific cognitive architecture. The key features of these architectures are alternate memory stores in which mental operations occur and in which information is stored. Usually there are several distinct memories or work spaces with different capacities and different information representation formats (see Figure 1.7). The typical architecture would start with sensory buffer memory stores associated with each of the major senses, with sharply limited capacities and characteristic representational formats that are appropriate to the sensory input channel (auditory, visual, etc.). Second, a central working memory or short-term memory store is typically

postulated and associated with the phenomenological experience of conscious selective attention. Numerous everyday experiences and laboratory demonstrations converge on the conclusion that attention capacities (at least conscious attentional capacities) are limited and provided a "bottleneck" in the information processing system that forces many processes to exhibit a serial, one-stage-at-a-time character. Thus, a juror in a courtroom is limited in the number of sources of information that can be processed simultaneously. If the actions of an attorney, a witness, and the defendant all occur simultaneously, the juror will only perceive, comprehend, and remember information from one of the sources. Finally, most systems assume a virtually unlimited long-term memory store. The limitations on processing information in long-term memory derive from the capacity or time requirements to write a new symbol structure into the long-term store or to find and retrieve a symbol from the store. Usually these limitations are expressed as limits on the capacity to activate symbols in short-term memory (conscious attentional processing).

When all of these components of a cognitive framework are put together – assumptions about information representation, information activation, elementary and complex cognitive processes, control by an executive monitor, and a cognitive architecture prescribing capacity limits – we have a rich and highly constrained language in which to write specific models to predict human behavior in tasks such as juror decision making.

Pennington and Hastie's story model, the most elaborate application of the cognitive approach to juror decision making, identifies three processing substages: evidence evaluation; learning the verdict choice set; and an evidence–verdict match process. During the evidence evaluation stage, the juror encodes evidence items and implications into a network of semantic propositions that eventually resides in long-term memory. An individual juror's network is a selective summary of the evidence that tends to represent an intuitively coherent version of what happened in the events referred to in testimony; coherence is defined with reference to principles of well-formed, plausible narrative structures ("stories") that have been identified in psycholinguistic analyses of text comprehension.

Toward the end of the courtroom proceedings, the judge provides the juror with a choice set of verdict alternatives that the juror learns as best he or she can. Because these verdict options are usually presented only in an oral instruction to the jury, this learning task is a difficult, one-trial event that often produces an incomplete and jumbled long-term memory of the verdicts as lists of features or elements of crimes.

Finally, the juror compares the story representation of the evidence to memories of the verdict category features to find a best match. If a subjectively satisfactory match is found, the juror will conclude with the corresponding verdict and a degree of confidence proportional to the perceived goodness of match, subjective completeness and coherence of the story evidence summary, etc. See Figure 1.8.

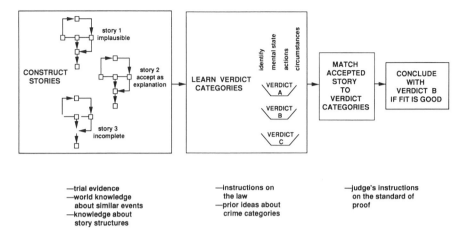

—trial evidence
—world knowledge
about similar events
—knowledge about
story structures

—instructions on
the law
—prior ideas about
crime categories

—judge's instructions
on the standard of
proof

Figure 1.8. Cognitive story model. Major processing stages and notes on the types of information most relevant at each stage.

Note that the image of this cognitive model is very different from the meter model descriptions of the three mathematical formulations. The model provides a finer-grained, molecular description of the evidence evaluation process; but the details of the decision criterion comparison process have not been fully specified. One of the guiding issues in current research on the cognitive model involves the specification of procedures that produce degrees of confidence as natural byproducts of a semantic reasoning process. Several empirical results concerning the "certainty conditions" that lead to high or low confidence in the story–verdict match have been obtained. But a computational model, analogous to the final belief–decision criterion comparison in each of the meter models, has yet to be presented. In the cognitive model, evidence is summarized as a complex semantic graph structure, rather than as a unitary "judgment meter" reading. Note also that considerable simplification is hypothesized to occur in the cognitive model as the semantic structure is constructed from evidence and other relevant information; the motivation for this simplification is the limit on attentional and computational resources imposed by limited capacity of working memory.

Comparative summary

The four major approaches to a theory of juror decision making are difficult to compare directly because each has advantages over the others on different evaluative dimensions. The Bayesian probability theory model is formal, rational, and offers the most convincing prescriptions for improving juror decision processes (see especially recent developments in computer-assisted judgment; Charniak, 1991; Edwards, Schum, & Winkler, 1990; Henrion, Breese, & Horvitz, 1991; and Howard, 1989). However, most empirical research suggests that the Bayesian formulation does not provide a valid description of juror decision processes.

The algebraic weighted average model also has the advantages of a clear formal representation, and it is accompanied by useful scaling procedures that allow the user to quantitatively assess individual juror's values of legally important concepts such as the weight of the evidence, predecision presumptions, and the standard of proof. There is considerably more empirical support for the descriptive validity of the weighted average model, although almost all of this support derives from highly simplified case materials and abbreviated laboratory judgment tasks.

The stochastic Poisson process model is also formal and its special advantage accrues from the inclusion of the evidence evaluation and decision threshold comparison processes into a unitary formulation. This integrated combination provides an object lesson about the manner in which adjustments of one or other process can compensate for each other; the important implication is that models that separate the two processes or ignore one or the other may provide misleading summaries of the complete decision process.

Finally, the cognitive story model is the most comprehensive and detailed of the four theoretical frameworks, and it also is the best-supported in terms of empirical research on realistically complex juror decision tasks. However, it has not reached the state of a fully specified cognitive theory in the form of a computer program simulation model, and some of its substages (e.g., the concluding evidence–verdict match process) are still imprecisely defined.

What is missing from this book?

This book has an "academic" tone; it focuses on the description and evaluation of theories of juror decision making that have been developed and tested in mock-jury and laboratory settings, rather than in actual courtroom trials. However, we believe that these theories will generalize to many aspects of juror behavior in actual trials. All of the research programs presented here have included high-fidelity, realistic mock-jury simulation studies of actual jury decision making. Although there are always limits on generalization from an experimental simulation to another context (real or artificial), there are so many converging results concerning juror behavior from laboratory studies and from surveys of actual jurors that most of the conclusions from the studies reported are surely accurate descriptions of juror behavior in real trials. Nonetheless, one element that is missing from this book is a discussion of the value of these descriptive theories by judges, attorneys, law officers, legislators, and other people actively involved in the formation and implementation of legal policy.

Perhaps the issue of interest to legal professionals that is given the shortest shrift in this book concerns the role of "the juror's sense of justice" in juror decisions (e.g., see the extensive discussion of the juror's values and sense of equity in Kalven & Zeisel, 1966). We should note that one aspect of this issue is addressed by the authors, primarily in their discussions of the juror's applications of a standard of proof in the final stages of the convict–acquit decision. A second comment, based on our own research and on the conclusions of many other empirical studies (e.g., Bridgeman & Marlowe, 1979; Hastie, Penrod, & Pennington, 1983; Pennington & Hastie, 1990; Saks, 1976; Visher, 1987), is that there is little evidence that jurors depart from the factfinding task to follow the dictates of conscience or to apply their sense of fair play when deciding criminal trial verdicts. However, we would hesitate to generalize this conclusion too far; surely there are conditions where jurors' ultimate verdicts are guided by considerations of fairness, equity, and justice that conflict with the "official" legal definition of their task. And it may be that behavioral scientists have been insensitive to the discrepancies between "laws of the officials" and "the laws of the community" (cf., Constable, 1991). Nonetheless, systematic empirical research suggests that jurors' decisions in criminal trials are dominated by the relevant evidence and the "official" factfinding task as defined by the court.

There are also several theoretical points of view that appear in the legal literature on juror decision making and that are not fully represented in this book. These include L. J. Cohen's (1977) Baconian inductive framework, Glen Shafer's (1976) belief functions, Gaerdenfors and Sahlin's (1982) unreliable probabilities, Hallden's Evidentiary Value Model (Gaerdenfors, Hansson, & Sahlin, 1983), Zadeh's Fuzzy Set "Possibility Theory" (1978), and several variants on the Bayesian approach that have considerable merit as philosophical treatises on normative reasoning (e.g., the work of Kyburg, 1983; Levi, 1985; etc. and the compendium by Shafer & Pearl, 1990). We have given these theories short shrift because they are primarily *normative* in intent. There is little empirical research to evaluate their merits as *descriptive* theories, and the few results that have been reported suggest they do not describe everyday reasoning processes.

Although there are the inevitable limits on coverage, this volume is the most comprehensive review of current scientific theories of juror decision making available today. In this introduction we have tabulated the multitude of reasons why scientists, legal authorities, and other scholars should be interested in these theories and the associated research. But the overriding point is that these theories are the best approach available for the prediction, description, and explanation of juror behavior.

Appendix A
Abbreviated version of stimulus trial
Commonwealth v. Johnson

Indictment: The defendant Frank Johnson is charged with killing Alan Caldwell with deliberate premeditation and malice aforethought.

The Defendant's Plea: The defendant, Frank Johnson, pleads *not guilty.*

Officer Richard Harris: On May 21st at about 11:00 P.M. I was on my usual foot patrol when I heard shouts from the direction of Gleason's Bar and Grill and hurried in that direction. From across the street I saw Caldwell (the victim) hit the defendant Johnson in the face. Johnson staggered back against the wall, then came forward and raised a knife above his head with his right hand. I yelled, "Frank, don't do it." But he plunged the knife downward into Caldwell's chest. Caldwell had fallen to the ground by the time I reached the scene. I apprehended Johnson, phoned for a police cruiser and an ambulance.

Cross-examination: I had a clear view of the fight from across the street approximately 75 feet away. I did not see anything in Caldwell's hand although I could not see Caldwell's right hand which was down by the side away from me. Johnson did not resist arrest, but he did say, "Caldwell pulled a razor on me so I stuck him." (This last statement was declared inadmissible by the trial judge.) The knife Harris retrieved from the ground near Caldwell is introduced as evidence. It measures eleven inches from end to end.

State Pathologist, Dr. Robert Katz: I found the following items on the body of Alan Caldwell: a ring, a watch, and small change in the right front pocket, and a straight razor in the left rear pocket. Caldwell was killed by a stab wound to the heart between the third and fourth ribs. I was unable to determine the angle at which the knife entered Caldwell's chest. His blood alcohol level was .032. This is enough alcohol that Caldwell may have been drunk. Caldwell had numerous surgical scars on his body. There were other scars of undetermined origin. The straight razor is introduced as evidence.

Patrick Gleason: I am the owner of Gleason's Bar and Grill. That night I had occasion to run to the window because there were some shouts outside. Actually, I expected it because I had watched Caldwell and Johnson leave the bar together a few minutes before. Through the window I saw Johnson raise his hand up and stab Caldwell. I didn't see anything in Caldwell's hand. Caldwell and Johnson didn't come to the bar together. First, Johnson and his friend Dennis Clemens arrived at about 9:00 P.M. and later Caldwell arrived. Then later, Caldwell and Johnson were talking at the bar and then they walked outside together. On the way out Caldwell put his watch in his pocket. Earlier in the day Johnson and Caldwell had both been in the bar. At that time they were arguing. Caldwell pulled out a razor and threatened to kill Johnson. A couple of patrons said something to Johnson and he left. That was earlier in the afternoon – before this fight in the evening.

Cross-examination: There was a neon light in the window which partially obstructed my view and I could only see Johnson and Caldwell at an angle. Frank Johnson has a reputation for peacefulness and has never caused trouble in the bar. (The judge does not allow Gleason to testify about Alan Caldwell's reputation.)

Dennis Clemens: I stopped at Frank Johnson's home on the evening of May 21st and asked Johnson to join me for a drink at Gleason's, which is where we usually go. Before we went in the bar, we looked around. We didn't see anything. At about 9:30 P.M. Caldwell entered, and after a while motioned Johnson to come and talk. In a few minutes, Johnson and Caldwell left the bar. I could not hear what they said, but went near the front door which was open. I heard a few shouts, saw Caldwell punch Johnson to the ground, and begin to attack him with a razor. Johnson tried to hold Caldwell off but Caldwell attacked, there was a scuffle, Caldwell staggered back, and after about twenty seconds fell to the ground. I didn't go outside to stop the fight because it happened so quickly.

Cross-examination: Johnson and I did not go to Gleason's looking for Caldwell, and Johnson was reluctant to go into Gleason's until we had assured ourselves that Caldwell was not there. I saw the razor clearly in Caldwell's right hand. I didn't see the knife in Johnson's hand because of the angle of the two men.

Janet Stewart: I am a waitress at Gleason's, and on the night of the fight I noticed both Caldwell and Johnson in the grill before the fight. There was shouting outside. When I ran outside I saw Caldwell on the ground. I also noticed Caldwell's car, which I recognized, was parked illegally in front of the grill and would have obstructed a view of the fight from across the street.

Frank Johnson: I was in Gleason's Grill on the afternoon of May 21st. A woman asked me to give her a ride somewhere the next day. Alan Caldwell immediately came over screaming at me and threatening me; he pulled a razor and threatened to kill me. I was quite upset and frightened and I went home and spent the day with my wife and six children until 9:00 P.M. when Dennis Clemens came by and suggested we go out for a drink. When we got to Gleason's Grill, I was afraid to go in but was finally convinced when we could find no evidence that Caldwell was in the grill. Later Caldwell entered and sat at the bar. Twenty minutes later Caldwell motioned me over in a friendly way and suggested we go outside. Caldwell was calm and friendly and I thought he wanted to talk. Once outside though, Caldwell became angry, threatened to kill me, and then hit me in the face with his right fist. The blow knocked me back against the wall and stunned me but I noticed that Caldwell had pulled his razor again. I unthinkingly reached for my fishing knife, pulled it out and held it in front of me to keep Caldwell away. But Caldwell rushed in with his razor and lunged on the fishing knife. The next thing I remember is Officer Harris arriving at the scene. I almost always carry my fishing knife because I am an avid fisherman and my wife does not like the knife to be lying around where the smaller children may pick it up. I couldn't get away from the fight because I was knocked down and cornered against the wall. I reached for the knife instinctively and tried to protect myself. I didn't mean to kill Caldwell.

Cross-examination: I don't think I had my knife with me in the afternoon but I don't really know because I carry it with me a lot.

Judge's Instructions: Now I want to define the elements of the charges against the defendant. These definitions are essential to determining which verdict you should return. The Commonwealth has charged the defendant with murder in the first degree. You actually have four verdict alternatives: murder in the first degree, murder in the second degree, manslaughter, and not guilty by reason of self-defense. Murder in the first degree is a killing committed with deliberately premeditated malice aforethought. Both first and second degree murder require malice aforethought. This includes feelings of hatred or ill will, but is more than that. It means any intentional infliction of an injury where there is a likelihood of causing death. Malice may be inferred from the intentional use of a deadly weapon without just provocation or legal excuse. If you find a killing with malice, then you must return a verdict of at least murder in the second degree. To return a verdict of first degree murder, you must find that the killing was performed with deliberately premeditated malice aforethought. Deliberate premeditation is a sequence of thought processes. You must be convinced that a plan to murder was formed. It is the sequence of thought, not the time taken that determines premeditation; it may take place over weeks, days, hours, or only seconds. First the deliberation and premeditation, then the resolution to kill, then the killing in pursuance of the resolution.

The third verdict alternative is manslaughter. Manslaughter is a killing without malice, a killing resulting from a sudden passion or heat of blood produced by a reasonable provocation or sudden combat. Reasonable provocation requires more than just words or insults or a general dislike or general feeling of anger. Your final verdict alternative is self-defense. If you find that the killing was in self-defense then the defendant is not guilty of a crime and should be found "not guilty." The right to self-defense arises from a threat to one's life but does not come into existence at all until the defendant has exhausted all reasonable means to escape from the confrontation and once the threat is over, the right evaporates. The method one uses to defend oneself can only be reasonable, but this judgment is made with some consideration for the frailties of human impulses in a stress situation. If the defendant does not have a reasonable fear of great bodily harm or has not exhausted all reasonable means of escape or has used more than reasonable force to protect himself, then self-defense does not apply and the defendant is guilty of at least manslaughter. Since the defendant has raised the issue of self-defense, the burden is on the Commonwealth to prove it was not a situation of self-defense. Finally, remember it is your duty to find the defendant guilty of the more serious charge of which he is in fact guilty beyond a reasonable doubt. If the Commonwealth has failed to prove the elements of the charged offenses, it is your duty to find the defendant not guilty.

Appendix B
Abbreviated version of stimulus trial
Commonwealth v. Bryant

Indictment: The defendant Ernest Bryant is charged with the armed robbery of Robert Washburn and his employer, the Topmart Supermarket.

The Defendant's Plea: The defendant, Ernest Bryant, pleads *not guilty.*

Prosecution Opening Statement: My purpose speaking to you now is to outline what the Commonwealth intends to prove in its case. The Commonwealth is going to call three witnesses who will tell you what happened at the Topmart Supermarket on the afternoon of July 5th. Mr. Washburn was a cashier at the market that day and he will tell you how he was confronted by a man who told him he had a gun and ordered him to open the store's safe. He will tell you how the man took money from the safe and left the store. The second witness is Mr. Randall, another employee of the market, who watched the robbery take place. You will also hear from a police officer who will tell you of his investigation of the crime. At the end of the trial I will speak to you again and at that time I will ask you upon the evidence to return a verdict of guilty as charged.

Defense Opening Statement: The Commonwealth has made allegations that it must prove beyond a reasonable doubt in every particular that the law imposes. I ask you to pay careful attention to their witnesses; did they have an opportunity to observe the events they testify about, does what they say sound credible and believable based on your own experience and common sense? Also keep in mind the circumstances under which the witnesses made their observations; was there fear, was there stress, is what they say reliable? We are sure you will be convinced that the Commonwealth has failed to carry the burden imposed on them, namely to prove every element of these crimes beyond a reasonable doubt.

Robert Washburn: On July 5th at about 2:20 I was working as a cashier in the Topmart Supermarket. As I was walking in front of the checkout lanes, a black man stopped me and told me he had a gun. He had his right hand in his pocket at this time. He ordered me to take him to the Courtesy Booth. In the Courtesy Booth he ordered me to open the safe and to turn my back towards him while he filled a canvas bag with money. A few seconds after he left the Courtesy Booth I went to the front of the store and saw him drive by in the passenger's seat of a red car. The defendant is the man who robbed me.

Cross-examination: I was afraid during the robbery. I did not actually see him take the money, but I had a clear view of the robber's face. In my description to the police I said he was wearing a gray t-shirt, sneakers, and a brown leather cap, he was about 6 feet tall. I had conversations with other employees of the supermarket and the police about the crime. I did not identify the robber in police mugshot photographs; but during a subsequent line-up, I did see someone I thought was the robber. Today, I'm sure of the man who committed the robbery.

Edward Randall: On July 5th I was working as a cashier at the Topmart Supermarket. I saw Bob Washburn enter the Courtesy Booth with a stranger and I went over and looked through the window of the booth to see what was going on. I saw the man putting money from the safe into a canvas bag. I watched for a minute and went to the manager's office and told him to call the police. Then I went to the front of the store where I saw the man with the canvas bag leave the store and ride off in a red Ford LTD; I wrote down the license number. The man was black, about 5' 10", medium build, with an Afro haircut, wearing a gray t-shirt, blue jeans, sneakers, and a brown leather cap. Afterwards, I went to the police station and identified the robber in two mugshot photographs. At about 6:00 that evening the police took me to Casey's Bar where I was able to identify the same man. He is the defendant.

Cross-examination: I saw the robber in profile for about a minute, while he was emptying the safe. I was anxious, but I would not say I was scared. After the robbery I talked to Bob Washburn, the clerk, and the manager about what had happened. I looked at photographs in a book that contained blacks, and whites. I don't remember if any other photographs besides the defendant's were repeated in the book. It took me about 5 minutes to find the robber in the group of patrons at Casey's Bar. The police also showed me more photographs a few days after the crime. There were 2 pictures of the defendant in that set of about 6 photographs and I picked him out as the robber, again. Then at the probable cause hearing the police showed me 2 more photographs of the defendant, this time wearing a cap, and I identified him again.

Officer William Stone: At about 2:30 on July 5th I received a radio call reporting a robbery at the Topmart Supermarket. At the market I interviewed the witnesses and got a description and license number of a car (which had been stolen) and of a person who robbed the store of almost $10,000. The description was of a black male, 25–35 years of age, Afro hair cut. I took the witnesses, Washburn and Randall, to the police station and showed them a book of mugshots. Randall identified 2 photographs of the defendant. I took the two witnesses to Casey's Bar where Randall picked the defendant out of a crowd of about 20 patrons, saying, "That looks like the man." Five days later I returned to the Topmart Supermarket and showed Randall and Washburn a set of 10 photographs. Randall positively identified the defendant, Ernest Bryant; Washburn was very unsure of an identification.

Cross-examination: When I obtained the original description from the witness, only Randall gave me a description; both witnesses were together. I am not sure exactly how many photographs were in the mugshot book at the police station, or how many of the photographs in the book were of black males. I took them to Casey's because the defendant is known to frequent that bar. There were 10 photographs (not 6 as Washburn said) of black males in the second photograph spread that was shown to the witnesses. There were 2 photographs of the defendant in this set and one of those photographs was masked with tape to make a better representation of the defendant's hair style. No one else in the set was represented in 2 photographs or masked with tape; this may possibly have "emphasized" the defendant.

Re-direct Examination: Exhibit #1 is a brown leather cap that I found in the defendant, Bryant's, pocket when I arrested him. The first identification made of the defendant was by Randall of photographs in the mugshot book at the police station immediately after the events in the supermarket.

Cross-examination: We never found the money stolen in the robbery or the stolen car used as a getaway vehicle.

The defense did not present any witnesses in this case.

Defense Closing Statement: This case is one you will have to resolve based on a conviction that the person sitting in the prisoner's dock was the same person who went into the Topmart Supermarket back in July and robbed the place of ten thousand dollars. I want to urge you to consider the frame of mind of the people you have heard today. Somebody comes in and says he has a gun and he's about to rob this place. The witness testified he was in fear. It must have been a terribly stressful situation, not knowing whether or not someone is about to end your life in a matter of seconds. That's the frame of mind of the first witness and more or less of the second witness. The description you hear could fit any one of thousands of black men in this city, and that's all you get. Now why is that? The explanation is simple; no one really saw the robber.

Then what happens? We go into a procedure handled by the police that at best was sloppy. People are very subject to suggestion and that's what happened here. The witnesses are given a chance to talk to each other, to influence each other, and then they're shown photographs. Nobody could tell how many photographs or what kind. There was some kind of identification by one of the witnesses and then they're taken to Casey's Bar, everyone goes down all together. There was no line-up, no controlled procedure, where you could fairly try to make an identification. After about five minutes, no one was exactly sure how long, Randall decides he sees a person he can identify, and suddenly Washburn is now making recognitions he couldn't before. That's the power of suggestion taking its toll.

Now we have another procedure with Randall shown six or ten photographs, we'll never know how many for sure as they were not preserved to show you. Out of that six or ten there are two of this defendant, but no repeat photographs of anyone else. Look at the suggestability of that procedure. Finally we have another procedure and now it's down to only two photographs and they are both of the defendant. This is a relentless, suggestive procedure that pointed inevitably to a situation where the witnesses were forced to pick the defendant's picture.

I want to leave you with one thought: the annals of criminal justice are rife with cases of mistaken identity. This isn't just my opinion, it's the opinion of the great Supreme Court justice Felix Frankfurter. I suggest to you that the Commonwealth has failed to prove every single element of this crime beyond a reasonable doubt.

Prosecution Closing Statement: Now, what have the Commonwealth's witnesses told you? You have the police officer, and I would agree with the defense attorney that his procedures were not the best. He didn't have a line-up and he admits it's possible that the two witnesses influenced each other. But consider his honesty; he could have tried to pad his story, but he tells you about his procedures and doesn't try to make excuses. You hear from two witnesses who identify the defendant as the robber. One witness is not so confident, but the other gets to look at the robber through the window of the Courtesy Booth for a minute; he also gets to watch him walk out of the supermarket, get into a car and drive right by him. He has a long time to observe and he's not scared. These witnesses saw a man come in and rob the store and they have a memory in their mind's eye of what that man looked like. They were looking in the photographs for the man from the store and it's the man they identified in the photographs, in the bar, at the probable cause hearing, and again today.

When you go into deliberation I hope you will remember that our law is very protective of the defendant's rights, but that the Commonwealth has rights too. When the Commonwealth has proved its case beyond a reasonable doubt, as it has today, then it is entitled to your verdict of guilty.

Judge's Instructions: You, the jury, must decide what the facts are in this case. It is for you to determine, based on your experience, background, and observations, what you believe and how much weight to give to each of the witnesses. In addition to the testimony and exhibits, you may use reasonable inferences to help you determine the facts in this case. You must, however, be careful not to speculate or guess. There are many things which must not be used in determining the facts: (A) You must not draw any inference from the fact that the defendant was indicted. (B) The background or race of the defendant or anyone else involved in this trial should not be used to draw inferences or to determine the credibility of a witness. (C) You should not decide anything based on the number of witnesses who testified for one side or the other. (D) The fact that mugshots of the defendant exist and were used by the police should not prejudice you against the defendant. (E) Statements by the attorneys or the judge are not evidence.

Now let me define the charges against the defendant.

Robbery is the taking, by force or threat of violence or by putting one in fear, the property belonging to another, with the intent to permanently deprive him of that property. In this case there is little question that a robbery did occur.

Armed Robbery is an aggravated form of robbery in which a dangerous weapon is used. A dangerous weapon is any instrumentality capable of inflcting serious injury or death. If you find a gun was used in this case, as a matter of law a gun is a dangerous weapon. It may be that there never was a dangerous weapon. However, if you find that the person being robbed could reasonably be put in fear or had a reasonable belief that a dangerous weapon was being used, that is enough to constitute a dangerous weapon. So, for example, if someone put his hand in his pocket as if there were a gun in the pocket, and the victim could reasonably believe that it was a gun, then that is enough to find that a dangerous weapon was used even if it turned out to be his fingers or a toy weapon.

Thus you must find whether or not a robbery occurred, whether or not an armed robbery occurred, and if it did occur, whether or not it was the defendant who committed the robbery or armed robbery.

Now I will instruct you on some of the procedures to follow in making your decisions.

The burden of proof is on the prosecution; because of the presumption of innocence and the burden of proof, the defendant has no responsibility to prove he is innocent. He does not have to take the witness stand, nor provide any witnesses. You should not make any inferences from the fact he did not take the stand or offer witnesses.

The Commonwealth is required to prove beyond a reasonable doubt that the defendant is guilty. Beyond a reasonable doubt means you must be satisfied to a moral certitude, to a reasonable certainty, that the defendant is guilty. Beyond a reasonable doubt does not mean an absolute certainty. If the Commonwealth has not proved its case beyond a reasonable doubt, you must find the defendant not guilty.

Having these instructions in mind, you will now deliberate to a unanimous verdict. If the verdict is guilty, each of you must agree that the defendant is guilty; if the verdict is not guilty, each of you must agree that he is not guilty.

References

Allen, R. J. (1991). *The nature of juridical proof.* Unpublished manuscript, Northwestern University Law School, Chicago, IL.

Anderson, J. R. (1976). *Language, memory, and thought.* Hillsdale, NJ: Erlbaum.
  (1983). *The architecture of cognition.* Cambridge, MA: Harvard University Press.
  (1990). *The adaptive character of thought.* Hillsdale, NJ: Erlbaum.

Anderson, N. H. (1981). *Foundations of information integration theory.* New York: Academic Press.

Apodaca, Cooper, and Madden v. Oregon, 406 U.S. 404 (1972).

Arrow, K. J. (1982). Risk perception in psychology and economics. *Economic Inquiry, 20*, 1–9.

Ashley, K. D. (1990). *Modeling legal argument: Reasoning with cases and hypotheticals.* Cambridge, MA: MIT Press.

Association for Computing Machines. (1987). *Proceedings of the first International Conference on Artificial Intelligence and the Law.* New York: ACM Press.

Atkinson, R. C., Bower, G. H., & Crothers, E. J. (1965). *An introduction to mathematical learning theory.* New York: Wiley.

Atkinson, R. C., & Schiffrin, R. M. (1968). Human memory: A proposed system and its control processes. In K. W. Spence & J. T. Spence (Eds.), *The psychology of learning and motivation: Vol. 2. Advances in research and theory* (pp. 89–195). New York: Academic Press.

Ballew v. Georgia, 435 U.S. 223 (1978).

Becker, G. S. (1968). Crime and punishment: An economic approach. *Journal of Political Economy, 76,* 169–217.

Bower, G. H. (1978). Experiments on story comprehension and recall. *Discourse Processes, 1,* 211–232.

Brehmer, B., & Joyce, C. R. B. (1988). *Human judgment: The SJT view.* Amsterdam: North-Holland.

Bridgeman, D. L., & Marlowe, D. (1979). Jury decision making: An empirical study based on actual felony trials. *Journal of Applied Psychology, 64,* 91–98.

Burns, R. M. (1981). *The great debate on miracles: From Joseph Glanvill to David Hume.* Lewisburg, PA: Bucknell University Press.

Chaitin, G. J. (1975). Randomness and mathematical proof. *Scientific American, 232*(5), 47–52.

Charniak, E. (1991). Bayesian networks without tears. *AI Magazine, 12*(4), 50–63.

Cohen, L. J. (1977). *The probable and the provable.* New York: Oxford University Press.
    (1986). The role of evidential weight in criminal proof. *Boston University Law Review, 66,* 635–649.

Constable, M. (1991). What books about juries reveal about social science and law. *Law and Social Inquiry, 16,* 353–372.

Cotton, J. W. (1982). Where is the randomness for the human computer. *Behavioral Research Methods and Instrumentation, 14,* 59–70.

Edwards, W., Schum, D. A., & Winkler, R. L. (1990). Murder and/of the likelihood principle: A trialogue. *Journal of Behavioral Decision Making, 3,* 75–89.

Ellsworth, P. C. (1988). Unpleasant facts: The Supreme Court's response to empirical research on capital punishment. In K. C. Haas & J. A. Inciardi (Eds.), *Challenging capital punishment: Legal and social science approaches* (pp. 177–211). Newbury Park, CA: Sage.

Ellsworth, P. C., & Getman, J. G. (1987). Social science in legal decision-making. In L. Lipson & S. Wheeler (Eds.), *Law and the social sciences* (pp. 581–636). New York: Russell Sage.

Estes, W. K. (1959). The statistical approach to learning theory. In S. Koch (Ed.), *Psychology: A study of a science: Vol. 2. General systematic formulations, learning and special processes* (pp. 380–491). New York: McGraw-Hill.
    (1978). The information processing approach to cognition: A confluence of metaphors and methods. In W. K. Estes (Ed.), *Handbook of learning and cognitive processes: Vol. 5. Human information processing* (pp. 1–18). Hillsdale, NJ: Erlbaum.

Faigman, D. L. (1991). "Normative constitutional fact-finding": Exploring the empirical component of constitutional interpretation. *University of Pennsylvania Law Review, 139,* 541–613.

Fairley, W. B., & Mosteller, F. (1974). A conversation about Collins. *University of Chicago Law Review, 41,* 242–253.

Federal Rules of Evidence for United States Courts and Magistrates. (1983). St. Paul, MN: West.

Fienberg, S. E. (Ed.). (1989). *The evolving role of statistical assessments as evidence in the courts.* New York: Springer-Verlag.

Fienberg, S. E., & Schervish, M. J. (1986). The relevance of Bayesian inference for the presentation of statistical evidence and for legal decisionmaking. *Boston University Law Review, 66,* 771–798.

Fischhoff, B., & Beyth-Marom, R. (1983). Hypothesis evaluation from a Bayesian perspective. *Psychological Review, 90,* 239–260.

Gaerdenfors, P., Hansson, B., & Sahlin, N.-E. (Eds.). (1983). *Evidentiary value: Philosophical, judicial, and psychological aspects of a theory.* Lund, Norway: Gleerups.

Gaerdenfors, P., & Sahlin, N. (1982). Unreliable probabilities, risk taking, and decision making. *Synthese, 53,* 361–386.

Gardner, A. v. d. L. (1987). *An artificial intelligence approach to legal reasoning.* Cambridge, MA: MIT Press.

Gastwirth, J. L. (1992). Statistical reasoning in the legal setting. *American Statistician, 46,* 55–69.

Gigerenzer, G., Switjtink, Z., Porter, T., Daston, L., Beatty, J., & Krueger, L. (1989). *The empire of chance: How probability changed science and everyday life.* New York: Cambridge University Press.

Green, E. D., & Tillers, P. (Eds.). (1986). [The Boston] symposium [Special issue]. *Boston University Law Review, 66,* 377–952.

Hammond, K. R., Stewart, T. R., Brehmer, B., & Steinmann, D. O. (1975). Social judgment theory. In M. F. Kaplan & S. Schwartz (Eds.), *Human judgment and decision processes* (pp. 271–312). New York: Academic Press.

Hastie, R. (1986). A primer of information-processing theory for the political scientist. In R. R. Lau & D. O. Sears (Eds.), *Political cognition* (pp. 11–39). Hillsdale, NJ: Erlbaum.

(1988). A computer simulation model of person memory. *Journal of Experimental Social Psychology, 24,* 423–447.

Hastie, R., Penrod, S. D., & Pennington, N. (1983). *Inside the jury.* Cambridge, MA: Harvard University Press.

Henrion, M., Breese, J. S., & Horvitz, E. J. (1991). Decision analysis and expert systems. *AI Magazine, 12*(4), 64–91.

Hensler, D. R. (1988). Researching civil justice: Problems and pitfalls. *Law and Contemporary Problems, 51,* 55–65.

Herrnstein, R. J. (1990). Rational choice theory: Necessary but not sufficient. *American Psychologist, 45,* 356–367.

Howard, R. A. (1989). Knowledge maps. *Management Science, 35,* 903–922.

Johnson v. Louisiana, 406 U.S. 356 (1972).

Kac, M. (1983). Marginalia: What is random? *American Scientist, 71,* 405–406.

Kahneman, D., & Tversky, A. (1979). Prospect theory: An analysis of decision under risk. *Econometrica, 47,* 263–291.

Kalven, H. K., Jr., & Zeisel, H. (1966). *The American jury.* Boston: Little, Brown.

Kaplan, J. (1968). Decision theory and the factfinding process. *Stanford University Law Review, 20,* 1065–1092.

Kaye, D. H. (1988). What is Bayesianism? A guide for the perplexed. *Jurimetrics Journal, 28,* 161–177.

Kelman, M. (1987). *A guide to critical legal studies.* Cambridge, MA: Harvard University Press.

Koehler, J. J., & Shaviro, D. N. (1990). Veridical verdicts: Increasing verdict accuracy through the use of overtly probabilistic evidence and methods. *Cornell Law Review, 75,* 247–279.

Kyburg, H. E. (1983). Rational belief. *Behavioral and Brain Sciences, 6,* 231–273.

Lempert, R. O. (1977). Modeling relevance. *Michigan Law Review, 75,* 1021–1057.

(1986). The new evidence scholarship: Analyzing the process of proof. *Boston University Law Review, 66,* 439–477.

Levi, I. (1985). Impression and indeterminacy in probability judgment. *Philosophy of Science, 52,* 390–409.

Llewellyn, K. N. (1962). *Jurisprudence: Realism in theory and practice.* Chicago: University of Chicago Press.

Lockhart v. McCree, 106 S. Ct. 1758 (1986).

Lopes, L. L. (1982). Doing the impossible: A note on induction and the experience of randomness. *Journal of Experimental Psychology: Learning, Memory, and Cognition, 8,* 626–636.

(1987). Procedural debiasing. *Acta Psychologica, 64,* 167–185.

Luce, R. D. (1986). *Response times: Their role in inferring elementary mental organization.* New York: Oxford University Press.

Luce, R. D., & Suppes, P. (1965). Preference, utility, and subjective probability. In R. D. Luce, R. R. Bush, & E. Galanter (Eds.), *Handbook of mathematical psychology,* (Vol. 3, pp. 249–410). New York: Wiley.

MacCoun, R. J. (1987). *Getting inside the black box: Toward a better understanding of civil jury behavior* (Technical Rep. N-2671-ICJ). Santa Monica, CA: The RAND Corporation.

Mandler, J. M. (1984). *Stories, scripts, and scenes: Aspects of schema theory.* Hillsdale, NJ: Erlbaum.

March, J. G. (1978). Bounded rationality, ambiguity, and the engineering of choice. *Bell Journal of Economics, 9,* 587–608.

Mazur, J. E. (1991). Straining the word "optimal." *Behavioral and Brain Sciences, 14,* 227.

McClesky v. Kemp, 107 S. Ct. 1756 (1987).

Miller, G. A., Galanter, E., & Pribram, K. (1960). *Plans and the structure of behavior.* New York: Holt, Rinehart, & Winston.

Newell, A. (1990). *Unified theories of cognition.* Cambridge, MA: Harvard University Press.

Newell, A., & Simon, H. A. (1972). *Human problem solving.* Englewood Cliffs, NJ: Prentice-Hall.

Payne, J. W. (1982). Contingent decision behavior. *Psychological Bulletin, 92,* 382–402.

Pennington, N., & Hastie, R. (1981). Juror decision making models: The generalization gap. *Psychological Bulletin, 89,* 246–287.

People v. Collins. (1968). *California Reporter, 66,* 497–507.

Posner, M. I. (Ed.). (1989). *Foundations of cognitive science.* Cambridge, MA: MIT Press.

Posner, R. A. (1985). An economic theory of the criminal law. *Columbia Law Review, 85,* 1193–1231.

(1986). *Economic analysis of law* (3rd ed.). Boston: Little, Brown.

(1990). *The problems of jurisprudence.* Cambridge, MA: Harvard University Press.

Rosenblum, V. G., Phillips, C., Phillips, S. H., & Merrick, H. (1978). *The uses of social science in judicial decision making.* Report to the National Science Foundation, Washington, DC.

Saks, M. J. (1976). The limits of scientific jury selection: Ethical and empirical. *Jurimetrics, 17*, 3–22.

Schum, D. A., & Martin, A. W. (1980). *Probabilistic opinion revision on the basis of evidence at trial: A Baconian or a Pascallian process?* (Research Rep. 80-02). Houston, TX: Rice University, Department of Psychology.

(1982). Formal and empirical research on cascaded inference in jurisprudence. *Law and Society Review, 17*, 105–151.

Shafer, G. (1976). *A mathematical theory of evidence.* Princeton, NJ: Princeton University Press.

Shafer, G., & Pearl, J. (Eds.). (1990). *Readings in uncertain reasoning.* San Mateo, CA: Morgan Kaufmann.

Simon, H. A. (1959). Theories of decision-making in economics and behavioral science. *American Economic Review, 49*(3), 253–283.

(1978). Rationality as process and as product of thought. *American Economic Review, 68*(2), 1–16.

(1979). Information processing models of cognition. *Annual Review of Psychology, 30*, 363–396.

Slovic, P., & Lichtenstein, S. (1971). Comparison of Bayesian and regression approaches to the study of information processing in judgment. *Organizational Behavioral and Human Performance, 6*, 649–744.

Smith, E. E., & Medin, D. L. (1981). *Categories and concepts.* Cambridge, MA: Harvard University Press.

Susskind, R. (1987). *Expert systems for legal decision making.* New York: Oxford University Press.

Tanford, J. A. (1990). The limits of a scientific jurisprudence: The Supreme Court and psychology. *Indiana Law Journal, 66*, 137–173.

Taylor, H. M., & Karlin, S. (1984). *An introduction to stochastic modeling.* Orlando, FL: Academic Press.

Thomas, E. A. C., & Hogue, A. (1976). Apparent weight of evidence, decision criteria, and confidence ratings in juror decision making. *Psychological Review, 83*, 442–465.

Townsend, J. T., & Ashby, F. G. (1983). *Stochastic modeling of elementary psychological processes.* New York: Cambridge University Press.

Trabasso, T., & van den Broek, P. (1985). Causal thinking and the representation of narrative events. *Journal of Memory and Language, 24*, 612–630.

Tversky, A., & Kahneman, D. (1974). Decision making under uncertainty: Heuristics and biases. *Science, 185*, 1124–1131.

Twining, W. L. (1985). *Theories of evidence: Bentham and Wigmore.* London: Weidenfeld & Nicholson.

Visher, C. (1987). Juror decision making: The importance of the evidence. *Law and Human Behavior, 11*, 1–17.

von Winterfeldt, D., & Edwards, W. (1986). *Decision analysis and behavioral research.* New York: Cambridge University Press.

Weinstein, J. B. (1988). Litigation and statistics. *Statistical Science, 3*, 286–297.

Wigmore, J. H. (1940). *A treatise on the Anglo-American system of evidence in trials as common law* (3rd ed.). Boston: Little, Brown.

Zadeh, L. (1978). Fuzzy sets as a basis for a theory of possibility. *Fuzzy Sets and Systems, 1*, 3–28.

2   Some steps between attitudes and verdicts

Phoebe C. Ellsworth

The paradox of individual differences

Most research that has attempted to predict verdict preferences on the basis of stable juror characteristics, such as attitudes and personality traits, has found that individual differences among jurors are not very useful predictors, accounting for only a small proportion of the variance in verdict choices. Some commentators have therefore concluded that verdicts are overwhelmingly accounted for by "the weight of the evidence," and that differences among jurors have negligible effects. But there is a paradox here: In most cases the weight of the evidence is insufficient to produce first-ballot unanimity in the jury (Hans & Vidmar, 1986; Hastie, Penrod, & Pennington, 1983; Kalven & Zeisel, 1966). Different jurors draw different conclusions about the right verdict on the basis of exactly the same evidence. That these differences are consequential is indicated by the frequently replicated finding that first ballot splits are the best-known predictor of the final jury verdict. In most laboratory studies of jury decisions, there are some *juries*, as well as jurors, that reach nonmodal verdicts. The inescapable conclusion is that individual differences among jurors make a difference.

Of course these influential individual differences need not be differences in character or philosophy of life. The process by which a juror comes to a decision about the right verdict may resemble Brownian motion more than it does the Galilean laws of cause and effect. First, many trials are long and any given juror's level of attention is likely to vary considerably. Different jurors will be especially attentive or especially inattentive to different bits of the testimony, and thus their final impressions of what was said will differ. Some of the factors that affect level of attention may be systematic and predictable. As an academic, for example, I will probably be especially attentive to the testimony of experts, particularly other psychologists, while the attention of my fellow jurors may wander. When it comes to testimony about the identity and trajectory of a bullet, a hunter may be a more attentive witness than I.

Other attentional differences may be more haphazard. For example, one juror may have a sleepless night and attend poorly to witnesses on the afternoon of the following day while another witness is well rested and alert. Or, one juror may be inattentive while she daydreams or worries about whether her business is running smoothly in her absence, whereas another juror focuses intently on the witness at the the front of the courtroom.

Second, haphazard, unpredictable events that occur outside the courtroom may influence jurors' judgments. For example, a juror may read a relevant newspaper article, have a relevant conversation, or observe a relevant incident on an evening between trial days, and see things differently the next day. The event could be as obviously pertinent as a conversation with a spouse or a friend about the proper verdict in the case, or it might be an apparently irrelevant event such as a chance encounter with a person who resembles a witness or defendant. These outside events will vary unsystematically among jurors, and thus may be responsible for unpredictable individual differences in judgments that cannot be discovered at voir dire.

But of course most lawyers and most researchers are interested in individual differences that can be identified before trial: clearly recognizable characteristics of the juror that make a difference in his or her propensity to favor one side. This class of factors comprises systematic background characteristics of the juror that he or she brings into the jury box at the start of the case. This class of factors can be broken down into subsets such as individual differences in beliefs and knowledge about how the world works or should work; enduring personality traits, preferences, and attitudes; mental capacities; past experience; and a hodgepodge of biological, social, and economic factors that are often labeled "demographic background." Individual differences such as these have received the most attention from researchers, scholars, and legal professionals who want to predict, understand, and steer the outcomes of jury trials. There are probably several reasons for the high level of interest in predicting predeliberation verdict preferences from individual differences in attitudes, personality, and demographic characteristics.

First, in our culture there is an almost irresistible compulsion to attribute differences in behavior to differences in a person's personality, attitudes, or background. This tendency to see causes of behavior in the person rather than the situation has been labeled a "fundamental error of social perception" (Ross, 1977), and it is a bias that affects professional students of behavior as well as the person in the street. Indeed, some personality researchers have accused other researchers of being blind to the truth about the actual variability of personality because of our cultural habit of attributing individual differences in behavior to stable properties of the individual (Mischel, 1968). A glance at a sample of modern trial tactics handbooks reveals that attorneys, like almost everyone else in our culture, incessantly generate hypotheses – some common, some bizarre – about the ways that personality, gender, ethnicity, and occupation affect jurors' decisions (see Hastie, Penrod, & Pennington, 1983: chapter 6 for examples; Appleman, 1968; Bodin, 1954; Rothblatt, 1966).

Second, the practice of selecting jurors by exercising peremptory challenges in a voir dire proceeding has channeled a great deal of energy into discovering ways to discriminate between prosecution (or plaintiff) and defense jurors on the panel of prospective jurors (cf. discussion in Hastie, Penrod, & Pennington, 1983, chapter 6). Indeed a small industry of jury selection experts has evolved that provides advice to attorneys about what to ask during voir dire (Bonora & Kraus, 1979; Schulman, Shaver, Colman, Emrich, & Christie, 1973). Most of these experts are social scientists who rely on survey methods and clinical intuition to pick jurors with the right personalities, attitudes, or prejudices to assist the side that has employed them in winning at trial.

Third, the "classic" study in the field of research on jury decision making concluded that the distribution of jurors' individual verdict preferences before deliberation predicted the verdict at the end of deliberation in "nine out of ten juries" (Kalven & Zeisel, 1966: p. 488). The implication was that an account of the manner in which predeliberation verdicts arose, with a focus on the reasons for differences among jurors who heard the same case, would provide us with the answer to the question of the final verdict.

But, alas, when an intelligent person is faced with the task of choosing among many candidates for a small number of positions, there is a pervasive tendency to see evidence for individual differences where little or none exists. What is called "personality" is a complex product of current situation and personal history that is rarely manifested in a simple, enduring, cross-situational behavioral propensity. Furthermore, the scanty scientific evidence concerning the utility of systematic jury selection techniques does not suggest that these methods provide much leverage to control the verdict by the side that employs them. Kalven and Zeisel's "nine out of ten" rule is an exaggeration of the strength of the relationship between initial verdict preferences and the jury's verdict, especially so when the jury is faced with several verdict choices, or several counts, or any task more complex than a simple guilty–innocent choice. Nonetheless, some stable individual differences apparently do matter and this chapter is a review of the research on an attitudinal individual difference that does predict jurors' verdicts. Discovering and analyzing an individual difference that *does* have some predictive value allows us to study the *mechanisms* by which the internal propensity affects the judgment of a legal case, and thus may guide our search for other meaningful individual difference variables in a manner that goes beyond the usual low-level stereotyping social scientists and lawyers have employed.

Systematic scientific research on the relationships between individual differences in juror background and verdicts has taken three forms: analyses of national surveys relating aggregate trends in jury verdicts to aggregate trends in public attitudes (e.g., Levine, 1983); studies of the correlations between jurors' characteristics and the actual trial verdicts they retrospectively report (Costantini & King, 1980; Moran & Comfort, 1986); and studies of the correlations between juror background factors and juror verdicts in controlled mock-jury tasks. In a pure form this research seeks stable characteristics of the individual juror that predict his or her tendency to favor one verdict or another at different points in time and even in different cases (although we usually expect to find a tendency that is exhibited for very similar cases, e.g., violent crimes against a person).

The search for individual differences that predict verdict preferences or behavior in deliberation might set out inductively by first trying to identify individuals who have a stable tendency to convict or to acquit and then, after "convictors" and "acquitors" have been identified, to search for characteristics of the jurors that discriminate between the two groups. Rarely, however, do we have a sufficient string of decisions by the same juror, except in the most abstract and cursory of case presentations, to use this method. In practice, research has usually proceeded in the reverse direction – starting with a hypothesis about a characteristic of the juror that will predict verdicts and then working "forward" to see if the predictor discriminates between jurors who favor different verdicts. In fact, because research in this area is so nascent, the typical study begins with a guess about an individual difference (or differences) and looks for correlations with juror verdicts in a single case (cf. Hastie, Penrod, & Pennington, 1983, for a review and an example).

Early studies seeking individual differences that would predict verdict choices sometimes adopted a global hypothesis that there were some people who would be conviction prone for virtually any criminal case and others who would be acquittal prone for virtually any case, something akin to "hardliners" and "bleeding hearts." For the most part research has not found simple individual differences in juror decisions (Saks, 1976; Saks & Hastie, 1978; Suggs & Sales, 1978). However, a more sophisticated "interactionist" perspective now guides most research and the usual expectation is that there will be "case X individual interactions" so that one individual may exhibit a tendency to convict in certain types of (similar) cases, but not all cases. This shift from a search for "global conviction proneness" to selective conviction proneness follows a similar development of research sophistication in the area of personality and individual differences where there has been a shift from the search for global cross-situational individual differences to a search for "person X situation interactions" (Bem & Allen, 1974).

In our own research we have focused on jurors' attitudes toward capital punishment. Individual differences in specific attitudes about legal institutions seem to be one of the only clear exceptions to our general conclusion that there are no simple individual difference effects in legal judgments. (Another is the tendency for females to give harsher verdicts in rape cases, cf. Hans, 1982). There is a well-established relationship between a juror's attitude toward capital punishment and the tendency to vote for conviction or acquittal. Jurors who favor the death penalty tend to favor conviction more than jurors who oppose the death penalty. The relationship is modest in strength; for example, when indexed by an r^2 statistic between a scaled measure of attitude intensity and conviction proneness the typical value would be $+.04$, not much better than the predictive value of a major league baseball player's batting average on the likelihood that he will get a hit at a particular "at bat" (Abelson, 1985). But the relationship keeps showing up, appearing in a great variety of research designs across a range of real and artificial criminal case decisions. However, there do seem to be some instances in which the relationship is attenuated or even reversed. For example, there is some evidence that jurors who favor capital punishment tend to be conviction prone for major felonies but tend to be acquittal prone in comparison to jurors who oppose capital punishment when deciding driving-while-intoxicated cases.

Our initial goal was to find out whether attitudes toward the death penalty did in fact predict other proprosecution attitudes and verdict preferences in actual cases. Once the basic relationship had been established, we went on to explore some possible mechanisms by which general attitudes might affect verdicts in particular cases.

A generic model for jury decision making

A review of the literature on individual juror decision making suggests a variety of subprocesses that contribute to the final decision (see the other chapters in this book). Seven conceptually distinct components that constitute a modal model for performance of the decision task have been singled out by Pennington and Hastie (1981). These are listed below, with no implication that the order presented here is necessary or even typical.

1. The juror takes in information from trial events. Probably most of this information is legally relevant evidence, but extralegal information ranging from nonverbal cues provided by a witness's behavior to off-the-record statements made by an attorney or witness would also be included in the category. Understanding individual variability in outcomes at this stage of the judgment process requires an effective theory of the factors that influence selective attention.

2. The juror constructs a causal–sequential representation of the facts in the case. In Pennington's terms, the juror is attempting to construct a valid story of the events that occurred relevant to the criminal charges (see Pennington, this book). According to Pennington and Hastie (1986) there is a definite relationship between the outcome of this stage of the judgment process and the ultimate verdict. However, as yet no one has been able to predict the form of evidence representation from information available about a juror's background or anything else.

3. In the meantime, the juror attempts to evaluate the credibility of the information conveyed by the witnesses. This includes evaluations of the individual witness's demeanor, character, and motivations as well as judgments of the plausibility of statements made by witnesses with reference to the juror's knowledge of how the world works. Undoubtedly, the factors that affect perceptions of credibility in other contexts apply to the courtroom as well, factors such as perceived power, competence, trustworthiness, and similarly to the juror (Zimbardo, Ebbesen, & Maslach, 1977), along with other more case-specific characteristics such as the "fit" of the witnesses's appearance and demeanor to his or her role in the story the juror is constructing.

4. The juror is supposed to separate admissible from inadmissible evidence in order to ignore inappropriate information when deciding on a verdict. Advice on the performance of this task is provided in the judge's instructions during the trial and in the final instructions concerning admissibility. We know of no research on individual differences in performance of this subtask. The ways in which inadmissible or extralegal evidence may influence a juror can range from blatant intentional disregard of the judges' instructions to subtle alterations in the construal of the rest of the evidence in jurors who make a sincere effort to ignore the inadmissible evidence and believe that they have succeeded (Gerbasi, Zuckerman, & Reis, 1977; Ross, 1987).

5. The juror learns the legal categories relevant to the verdict. In criminal cases the verdict definitions are provided in the judge's instructions on the law. There is considerable variability across jurors in their performance of this subtask, but no simple, direct relationship has emerged between success in learning the verdict definitions and a bias to favor the prosecution or defense (Hastie, Penrod, & Pennington, 1983).

6. The juror attempts to relate the evidence to the legal categories in order to select the appropriate or best-supported verdict.

7. The juror compares his or her strength of belief in the verdict to a legal standard of proof, usually the beyond reasonable doubt instruction in a criminal case. Kerr (this book), Thomas and Hogue (1976) and others have shown that variations in subjective threshold to convict are predictive of verdicts. But, we do not know of a useful a priori predictor of variations in the threshold.

Our research on individual juror decision making suggests that jurors do not perform these seven component tasks in a fixed temporal sequence, do not necessarily perform all of the tasks before deliberation begins, and do not perform all of the tasks with a high degree of competence. Our observations suggest that jurors concentrate on comprehending trial events, constructing a fact sequence, evaluating credibility, and relating the evidence to a legal category. However, they do not seem to spend a great deal of time trying to define the legal categories, evaluating the admissibility of evidence they are using, or testing their final conclusion against a standard of proof. In fact, many jurors simply appear to select a sketchy stereotyped theme to summarize what happened (e.g., "cold-hearted killer plots revenge," "nice guy panics and overreacts") and then choose a verdict on the basis of the severity of the crime as they perceive it.

Research on the relationship between attitudes toward capital punishment and juror decision making

We chose to study attitudes toward capital punishment in part because they are generally strongly held and closely related to other attitudes about the criminal justice system (Ellsworth & Ross, 1983) and in part because they are legally consequential. In a trial in which the defendant faces possible execution, citizens who strongly oppose the death penalty are not allowed to serve as jurors. They are excluded from service both at the ultimate stage of the trial concerned with the penalty and at the earlier stage in which the jury decides whether or not the defendant is guilty. The empirical relationship between death penalty attitudes and verdicts is legally significant because several defendants have appealed their convictions on the grounds that a "death-qualified jury" is more likely to convict than a standard jury with no one excluded on the basis of their anticapital punishment attitude (the most important cases include *Hovey v. Superior Court,* 1980; *Lockhart v. McCree,* 1986; *Witherspoon v. Illinois,* 1968). These defendants claim that the jury decision process is biased against them if there is a correlation between death penalty attitudes and verdicts *and* potential jurors are excluded from service on the basis of their attitudes.

Another good reason to study individual differences in attitudes toward the death penalty is that there was already good evidence for the relation between these attitudes and verdicts. During the past thirty years social scientists have conducted more than a dozen studies using survey methods, posttrial interviews with actual jurors, and mock-jury simulation experiments to study the attidue–verdict relationship. Every study found that jurors who did not oppose the death penalty were more likely to convict than jurors who opposed the penalty. In our view, the answer to the basic "prediction question" is firmly established; attitude toward the death penalty, a fairly stable individual difference, does predict jurors' verdicts in a wide range of criminal cases. Having replicated this relationship in our own research (Cowan, Thompson, & Ellsworth, 1984), we turned to the "mediation question" where we have tried to determine which components of the global juror decision process are influenced by the attitude.

Attitudes as individual differences

Psychologists have developed the concept of attitude to represent an internal mental state that indicates a propensity or predisposition to respond in one manner or another (Campbell, 1963; McGuire, 1969, 1983). Attitudes can be thought of as beliefs that have three properties; they refer to a condition, object, or event in the real world; they include a prescription of evaluation, goodness, or preference; and they provide implications for behavior. Attitudes rarely exist in isolation. Rather they come as bundles or constellations of related beliefs, and a scientifically ineffable but intuitively sensible consistency seems to apply *locally* to constellations of closely related attitudes. However, global and strict logical consistency do not seem to apply (Abelson, Aronson, McGuire, Newcomb, Rosenberg, & Tannenbaum, 1968). In the case of attitudes toward the death penalty, the subject of the attitude statement is the legal institution of punishing criminals by execution. The evaluative component of the attitude is usually measured as a preference: Is the person whose attitude is measured in favor of or opposed to the existence of the legal institution of capital punishment? The implications for action include social endorsement ("Would you vote for new legislation that would establish/repeal capital punishment?") and, most important in the context of juror decision making, ramifications of the belief for related behaviors ("As a juror, would you refuse to impose the death penalty on a convicted defendant in any case, no matter what the evidence was?").

In legal contexts the most significant implication for behavior associated with attitudes toward the death penalty is concerned with the possibility that the attitude will influence jurors' decisions in a criminal trial. The most direct implication is that during the penalty phase of the trial a juror who strongly opposed the death penalty will be unable to follow a trial judge's instructions to consider imposing a death penalty. The reverse extreme is also legally significant, and a juror who is so enthusiastic about the capital punishment that he or she would automatically vote for the death penalty whenever it is available would also be excluded from impanelment. The attitude might also influence a juror's behavior at the guilt–innocence phase of the trial. Of special legal significance is the possibility that a juror who strongly opposes the death penalty cannot be impartial when deciding on a verdict in a capital case. Even knowing that execution is only a possibility might incline the juror to acquit, or convict of a lesser charge. The covariation of people's attitudes toward capital punishment with other attitudes in conformity with some rule of psychological consistency has also been investigated. There is a degree of local consistency among beliefs related to the criminal justice system such that a person's attitude toward the death penalty is correlated with a constellation of other attitudes (Boehm, 1968; Jurow, 1971). Specifically, a person who opposes the death penalty is likely to exhibit other attitudes that are associated with an emphasis on due process guarantees in the criminal justice system. For example, in comparison to people who oppose the death penalty, people who favor capital punishment tend to be more concerned about high levels of violent crime, to exhibit less sympathy for criminal defendants, to be more suspicious of defense attorneys, and to exhibit more favorable attitudes toward prosecuting attorneys and the police (Bronson, 1970; Fitzgerald & Ellsworth, 1984; Tyler & Weber, 1982; Vidmar & Ellsworth, 1974). It has been argued (Ellsworth & Ross, 1983; Tyler & Weber, 1982) that attitudes toward the death penalty are an especially pure example of "symbolic attitudes" (Sears & Kinder, 1971), emotionally based attitudes that serve to express a person's ideological self-image – as a practical person who takes a no-nonsense approach to crime or as a champion of the individual against the mistakes and prejudices of the state.

We view this constellation of attitudes as analogous to a set of premises in a logical argument that serve as the bases for inferences that are generated when a juror is asked to make a decision in a specific criminal trial. We believe that a juror's attitude toward the death penalty predicts his or her verdict because it is embedded in this constellation of relevant beliefs about the justice system. For example, if we consider a juror who strongly favors capital punishment, several beliefs in the constellation will operate to produce a guilty verdict. His positive attitude toward the prosecution side of the case will lead him to attend to the prosecuting attorney and to see the prosecution story as more plausible; similarly for police officers called as witnesses. His suspicion of defense attorneys will cause him to discount the testimony of defense witnesses, and render the defense less persuasive. His lack of sympathy for the defendant and his worries about the high levels of crime he perceives in his society will lead him to be relatively unconcerned about the possibility of a mistaken conviction, and may even lower his personal standard of proof to convict for any charge. Just the reverse pattern of biases would be expected to apply to a juror who was strongly opposed to capital punishment. The point is that because attitudes toward the criminal justice system come in a "bundle," they will operate concomitantly to influence several aspects of a complex decision process to produce a bias toward one outcome.

The distributed character of the influence of the constellation of attitudes on the verdict decision will render it virtually undetectable to a subjective introspection. Legal decisions by their very nature require the decision maker to resolve a host of ambiguities and incompletenesses in the patchwork of evidence presented at trial. The ultimate decision also requires the application of presumption of innocence and standard of proof instructions that are demonstrably imprecise and subject to large differences of interpretation (cf. Fletcher, 1968; Shapiro, 1986; Simon & Mahan, 1971). It is not surprising that individual jurors may feel that they have performed in a rigorous and rational manner, yet reach sharply divergent conclusions. In fact, one of the most surprising experiences for jurors in many cases is to discover, at the start of deliberation, that other jurors could disagree with them on a verdict that seems patently obvious (Ellsworth, 1989).

We have examined three ways in which an attitude might affect a verdict. First, we thought that a juror's attitude might influence his or her evaluation of witness credibility. Social psychologists have established that an audience is more persuaded by a communicator toward whom they have a favorable attitude than by one they dislike or oppose (Hovland, Janis, & Kelley, 1953). Our specific hypothesis is that jurors who favor the death penalty will find police witnesses and prosecutors more credible and persuasive than will jurors who oppose the death penalty. On the other hand, jurors who oppose the death penalty should find defense attorneys and witnesses relatively more persuasive.

Second, inferences partially based on attitudes about the criminal justice system should affect the juror's construction of a fact sequence or story to summarize the evidence that he or she accepts as credible. Many statements by witnesses are ambiguous in their implications or may be fitted into an overall fact sequence in several places. There is evidence from research by cognitive and social psychologists that attitudes influence the perception of a complex event by influencing gap-filling inferences and the resolution of ambiguities in the interpretation of stimulus information. As a general principle ambiguous or incomplete information will tend to be interpreted in a fashion that is consistent with a person's initial attitudes and that confirms their expectations (Chapman & Chapman, 1967; Ross, Lepper, & Hubbard, 1975; Snyder, Tanke, & Berscheid, 1977; Vallone, Ross, & Lepper, 1985). Death penalty attitudes may also be correlated with the relative availability of various crime "scripts." Insofar as a juror's own script matches the story presented in the prosecution case, the prosecution story will seem "natural," plausible, and familiar. In effect, one's attitudes affect one's Bayesian prior probability estimates of the truth of any particular story presented in court. In the context of a criminal trial our hypothesis is that jurors who favor the death penalty, and also favor the prosecution side of the case, will tend to interpret ambiguous and incomplete evidence in a manner consistent with the prosecution theory of the case, while jurors who oppose the death penalty will resolve perceptual questions to fit the defense theory.

Third, we thought that the ultimate step in the juror's decision, the application of the judge's instructions on the reasonable doubt standard of proof, might be influenced by the juror's attitudes toward the death penalty. The beyond-reasonable-doubt standard creates a decision threshold that varies across individuals (Simon & Mahan, 1971; *U.S. v. Fatico*, 1978). Thus, just as an attitude might influence a juror's perceptions of ambiguous information about an objective event, an attitude might influence a juror's interpretation of the subjective degree of confidence associated with the term "beyond reasonable doubt." The specific hypothesis we entertain is that those favoring the death penalty would have a lower threshold for conviction than those opposed to the death penalty.

We assessed our subjects' attitudes toward the death penalty in two ways. First, we asked them to complete a set of questionnaire items designed to assess their attitudes on a five-point scale with endpoints labeled "strongly opposed" and "strongly in favor" (Capital Punishment Attitude

Questionnaire – Form A; Jurow, 1971). Second, the subjects answered several questions designed to determine their eligibility for inclusion on a death-qualified jury based on legal precedents established by the Supreme Court (*Witherspoon v. Illinois*, 1968).

Is your attitude towards the death penalty such that as a juror you would never be willing to impose it in any case, no matter what the evidence was, or would you consider voting to impose it in some cases? (A) I would be unwilling to vote to impose it in any case. (B) I would consider voting to impose it in some cases.

A response of (A) meant the subject was a "Witherspoon Excludable" juror.

Now suppose that you were a juror in the first part of the trial, just to decide whether the accused person is guilty or not guilty of the crime. The judge instructs you that in reaching your verdict you are only allowed to consider evidence presented in court, and must follow the law as he will state it to you. If the accused is found guilty, there will be a separate trial to decide whether or not he or she will get the death penalty. Which of the following expresses what you would do if you were a juror for the first part of the trial? (A) I would follow the judge's instructions and decide the question of guilt or innocence in a fair and impartial manner based on the evidence and the law. (B) I would not be fair and impartial in deciding the question of guilt or innocence knowing that if the person was convicted he or she might get the death penalty.

Any subjects who answered (B) to this item were eliminated from service in the research because jurors who say they cannot judge guilt fairly are excluded from service at trials. Because of the legal significance of the distinction between death-qualified jurors and excludable jurors, in most analyses we separated our subjects into two groups according to their classification as death-qualified or excludable.

Empirical research on the impact of attitudes on juror decisions

The method we used to test our first two hypotheses concerned with credibility evaluation and evidence interpretation was a simulated juror decision making task. We showed jury-eligible California residents a videotaped fragment of the criminal trial (Thompson, Cowan, Ellsworth, & Harrington, 1984). The tape depicted the testimony of a police officer who had been on crowd control duty at a rock music concert. The officer testified that the defendant refused to follow his instructions and then assaulted him. The defendant's testimony was also presented. He claimed that he did not resist the officer, that he was behaving in an orderly manner, and that the officer abused him verbally with racial slurs.

Subjects, instructed in the role of jurors, viewed the videotape and then answered questions designed to assess their evaluations of witness credibility and to capture some of the inferences they made from the testimony on the tape.

As we had predicted, jurors who were in favor of the death penalty (death-qualified) evaluated the evidence in a manner more favorable to the

Table 2.1. *Mean evaluations of evidence by death-qualified and excludable subjects: Study 1*[a]

| Question | Group[b] | | |
	Death-qualified	Excludable	*t*-value
Credibility of witnesses			
1. Officer's truthfulness	4.55	3.44	3.42[c]
2. Defendant's truthfulness	3.69	3.05	1.76
3. Relative accuracy of witnesses	4.35	3.25	2.49[d]
Plausibility of facts			
4. Defendant threatened to punch officer	4.15	2.87	2.49[d]
5. Defendant struck officer	4.45	2.37	4.25[c]
6. Officer was cut by bottle	2.81	1.85	1.78
7. Defendant was limping	3.68	3.45	0.48
8. Officer used racial slurs	4.44	3.65	1.68
9. Defendant was derogatory to officer	5.00	4.31	1.65
Inferences from facts			
10. Who initiated the struggle?	4.06	2.35	3.36[c]
11. Was the officer too rough?	4.18	3.10	2.05[d]
12. Defendant's breaking police line justified?	4.00	1.95	4.09[c]
13. Officer antagonistic to defendant?	4.37	3.05	2.70[d]
Attributions about the witnesses			
14. Defendant had previous trouble with police	4.80	3.50	2.76[d]
15. Officer had racial bias	3.12	2.60	1.38
16. Defendant unduly hostile to police	4.45	3.50	2.69[d]

[a] The scale ranged from 1 to 6; higher numbers indicate evaluations more favorable to the prosecution.
[b] Death-qualified n = 19; excludable n = 16.
[c] $p < .05$.
[d] $p < .01$.

prosecution than did jurors who were opposed to the death penalty (excludables). We assessed our subjects' judgments of credibility by asking direct questions about the truthfulness of each witness and indirect questions about the plausibility or accuracy of six assertions taken directly from the witness's testimony. Mean responses of the death-qualified and excludable subjects are presented in the top panel of Table 2.1. On the average, death-qualified subjects responded more favorably to the prosecution than did excludable subjects on every one of the nine items; for four of the nine items this difference was statistically significant. These results strongly support our hypothesis that death penalty attitudes influence evaluation of credibility. Although the result is essentially correlational, there is no doubt that the attitudes (both the specific penalty attitudes and the related criminal justice attitudes) existed before subjects saw our tape of the policeman and the defendant, implying that the attitudes caused the judgments.

Seven additional questionnaire items, presented at the bottom of Table 2.1, capture some of the subjects' inferences from the testimony. Again we present average ratings for the death-qualified subjects and the excludable subjects for each item. The direction of each inference is consistent with our hypothesis that death-qualified jurors will be more favorable to the prosecution side of the case; five of the seven differences were statistically significant. The inference questions ask for subjects' judgments about issues that are relevant to their decisions but were not addressed directly in testimony. For example, there were no references in testimony to the defendant's prior experience with the police, but death-qualified subjects were more likely than excludable subjects to infer that the defendant had had prior trouble with the law. Again we found that attitude toward the death penalty predicted decision-relevant reasoning.[1]

We also examined the relationship between the subjects' global index of attitudes toward capital punishment on Jurow's scale and a summary index of their responses on all sixteen of the questionnaire items (credibility and inference items). The correlation between the Jurow scale value and the evidence evaluation index was $+.60$ (statistically significant at the $p < .01$), a remarkably high coefficient in the context of the small or nonexistent correlations between general attitudes and interpretation of specific situations obtained in most research.

Because of the correlational nature of the analysis, and because a person's attitude toward the death penalty is correlated with a constellation of other attitudes relevant to the criminal justice system, it is not clear exactly which attitudes may have served as "premises" for our subjects' inferences about credibility and evidence implications. For example, the willingness to make inferences from assertions in the testimony may have been conditioned simply on their liking and trust for one witness over the other. Perhaps an application of a method such as those proposed by Schum and Martin (1982), involving multiple ratings of subelements of the evidence and the contingencies among them, or the method proposed by Pennington and Hastie (1985), in which subjects "think aloud" as they listen to the trial information, might elucidate some of these fine-grained questions.

The findings of this first experiment were corroborated in a second mockjury experiment in which subjects rated the credibility of six witnesses who

---

[1] A reviewer suggests that perhaps subjects, anticipating that they would later vote for death, reinterpreted the story in order to justify their penalty decision. Thus the inferences subjects draw from the facts are not based on the mechanisms we propose, but on subjects' need to create consistency with their own expected sentencing behavior in this case. This is a plausible psychological mechanism in the abstract, but not in this particular case, as the death penalty would never be an option in a simple assault and battery case involving only minor injuries. In addition, the subjects' death penalty attitudes had been assessed two to six weeks earlier, along with a number of other variables, and so were unlikely to be salient to the subjects at the time they participated in the study.

presented evidence in a two and a half hour reenactment of a murder trial (Cowan et al., 1984). Again we divided subjects into two groups, excludables (opposed to the death penalty or neutral) versus death-qualified (in favor of the death penalty). After viewing the trial and deliberating in twelve-person mock juries for an hour, these subjects rated the "believability" and "helpfulness" of each witness. The mock-jurors' attitudes predicted the average differences in ratings of all witnesses and these effects were significant for each of the prosecution witnesses considered individually. Replicating the results from our first study, excludable mock jurors rated the prosecution witnesses less believable and less helpful than did death-qualified mock jurors.

Our third hypothesis concerned the relationship between attitudes toward capital punishment and a juror's personal threshold for conviction associated with the beyond-reasonable-doubt standard of proof. The simplest research method would be to ask subjects to assign a numerical value (i.e., a probability estimate) corresponding to the degree of certainty that they would have to have to convict a defendant under the beyond-reasonable-doubt standard. For example, Simon and Mahan (1971) asked various groups of potential jurors what subjective probability of guilt they would require before voting to convict a criminal defendant. They found that the mean probability stated by jury-eligible citizens was .79. Proceeding with the direct approach we would then look for a relationship between an individual's rated subjective probabiloity for the threshold and their attitudes toward capital punishment.

We did not pursue the direct approach. First, we doubt that untrained subjects can accurately express their decision thresholds as numerical probabilities (cf. Behn & Vaupel, 1982). Second, the standard-of-proof instruction as presented in many legal trials seems to include more than the meaning expressed in a single numerical probability. Efforts to better define the standard of proof with alternate expressions such as "to a moral certainty" and historical analyses of the vicissitudes in definitions popular in various courts imply that the concept is richer than a single number (e.g., Fletcher, 1968; Shapiro, 1986). Finally, we already had evidence that jurors' attitudes toward capital punishment did not predict their global estimates of the level of certainty necessary to justify a verdict of guilty. Estimates were highly variable, and both death-qualified and excludable subjects gave mean probability estimates of about 86 percent (Cowan et al., 1984). Obviously, if there are differences, a better method was needed to detect them.

We started with a consideration of the two possible errors that can be made when a juror renders a verdict in a criminal case: The juror can acquit a defendant who should have been convicted or the juror can convict a defendant who should have been acquitted. We assume that jurors associate a degree of regret or "disutility" with each of these errors. Furthermore, we assume that the juror's threshold for conviction is related to the relative regret associated with each type of error. Specifically, we assume that the greater the regret the juror feels for a mistaken conviction relative to a mistaken acquittal, the higher will be his or her threshold of conviction. We do not assume that our subjects are perfect normative utility maximizers, but we assume that the difference in felt regret from erroneous convictions and acquittals does correspond to some degree to the threshold for conviction.

Based on the assumption of a relationship between regret and decision criterion, we designed a method to assess the regret associated with the two types of errors in a series of hypothetical cases. We used the difference between the degrees of regret associated with a lenient error (false acquittal) and harsh error (false conviction) to calculate an index to reflect each subject's threshold of conviction. Our prediction was that jurors who favor capital punishment would show less regret for wrongful convictions than for wrongful acquittals, compared to jurors opposed to capital punishment.

Experimental subjects were asked to consider sixteen hypothetical situations and to express the degree of regret they felt in each situation as a number ranging between 0 and 100. Zero indicated that they felt no regret and one hundred indicated that they felt the most regret they could possibly feel. The sixteen situations were defined with reference to possible outcomes of a murder trial. The subjects were asked to imagine that they had served on a jury that reached one of four possible verdicts: guilty of first degree murder, guilty of second degree murder, guilty of manslaughter, or not guilty. Furthermore, they were to imagine that after the trial, evidence was uncovered that demonstrated conclusively that the defendant was actually guilty of one of the three crimes or innocent. The sixteen hypothetical case situations were composed by combining each of the four jury verdicts with each of the four posttrial evidence outcomes. Thus, four of the situations represented correct jury verdicts and twelve represented errors.

For the analysis we separated subjects (jury-eligible California residents) into two groups, death-qualified and excludables, with reference to the Witherspoon question (see above). A refined statement of our hypothesis would be that when a juror made an error in a harsh direction, by convicting an innocent defendant or convicting a defendant of a crime more severe than the crime actually committed, death-qualified subjects would show less regret than excludable subjects. In contrast, when the jury's error was in the lenient direction, acquitting a guilty defendant or convicting a guilty defendant of a crime less severe than that actually committed, the death-qualified jurors would express more regret than the excludable jurors. This is the pattern that we observed (see Table 2.2); the difference in regret expressed by death-qualified and excludable subjects was statistically significant.

Death-qualified subjects expressed nearly equal regret for harsh and lenient errors, while the excludables expressed more regret than the death-qualified subjects for harsh errors and less for lenient errors. As we noted above, this result is consistent with the constellation of attitudes that are associated with a procapital punishment position; namely a concern for crime control and a sympathy for the prosecution side of legal cases. Conversely,

Table 2.2. *Mean regret expressed by death-qualified and excludable subjects: Study 2*[a]

| | Crime defendant actually committed | | | |
| | 1st degree murder | 2nd degree murder | Manslaughter murder | Not guilty |
Verdict of jury				
1st degree murder				
d.q.[b]	0.67	43.2	54.33	68.86
Exc.[c]	7.50	66.07	70.71	90.71
2nd degree murder				
d.q.	45.00	0.33	49.13	68.20
Exc.	27.14	7.14	53.12	85.71
Manslaughter				
d.q.	54.00	46.33	0.0	69.20
Exc.	49.28	44.64	8.2	73.57
Not guilty				
d.q.	73.73	70.53	60.20	0.0
Exc.	71.78	61.07	58.21	6.43

[a] Higher numbers indicate greater regret. Death-qualified n = 15; excludable n = 14.
[b] d.q. = death-qualified.
[c] Exc. = excludable.

the constellation of attitudes associated with opposition to the death penalty fits the pattern of regrets expressed by excludable subjects; namely, these subjects will have more sympathy for the defendant and more concern for due process considerations in the operation of the criminal justice system. We believe that our measures of degree of regret have direct implications for a juror's decision threshold to convict in criminal cases. However, we must emphasize that the step from regret ratings to a conclusion about subjective standards of proof is based on the assumption that the juror's reasoning bears some resemblance to the popular subjective expected utility model for decision making (Edwards, 1954). This assumption is common in the legal literature (Blackstone, 1769/1962) and it is also compelling intuitively. Some researchers (e.g., Nagel, 1979) have been willing to accept this assumption in its strongest form and calculate absolute numerical values for the probability threshold to convict based on jurors' rated "disutilities." We believe that our data shows that death-qualified jurors and excludables differ in the relative level of their thresholds for conviction, but we stop short of an exact numerical derivation.

Summary of research on juror's predeliberation decisions

The three studies we have summarized help us understand links in the chain of mediating factors that connect the constellation of attitudes associated with a person's attitude toward the death penalty and the decision concerning guilt or innocence in a criminal trial. Essentially, we have supported our hypotheses that the jurors' attitudes influence three components of the larger decision process: evaluation of witness credibility, inferences that go beyond the given evidence, and the value of the juror's personal standard-of-proof threshold for conviction. This research illustrates a productive approach to the study of individual differences in juror decision making. We started with the finding that there was a consistent and pervasive relationship between jurors' attitudes toward the death penalty and their propensities to acquit or convict in criminal trials. Second, following Pennington and Hastie (1981), we abstracted seven components of a generic model of the juror decision process that we felt were likely to mediate the attitude–decision relationship: evaluation of witness credibility, inferences from the evidence, and setting a subjective standard of proof. We then conducted a series of experiments to evaluate the impact, or correlation, of attitudes toward the death penalty on verdict decisions. The key to our approach is the intermediate step in which we attempted to spell out how global attitudes might affect verdicts in particular cases.

Individual differences in juror behavior in deliberation

As we noted above, we disagree with Kalven and Zeisel's generalization that in nine out of ten juries the verdict is determined by the distribution of initial verdict preferences at the start of deliberation (Kalven & Zeisel, 1966: p. 488). One reason we believe this generalization may be an exaggeration stems from the findings of other mock-jury research. Hastie, Penrod, and Pennington (1983) found that in more than 25 percent of their mock juries a faction that was initially in the minority at the start of deliberation prevailed. Although we know very little about the method Kalven and Zeisel used to collect the data on which their conclusion is based (the study is referenced in a footnote and no further reports of its methods or results are available), it may be that the simple two-choice guilty-or-innocent verdict allows for less movement, e.g., through compromise. Also it is likely that a juror's postdeliberation recollections would be biased to suggest that the juror subscribed to the jury's final verdict all along. Similar effects have been reported in research on voters' retrospective reports of voting in political elections, where voters report that they voted for the winner more often than they actually did, and in other studies of "hindsight phenomena" (Fischhoff, 1975; Hawkins & Hastie, 1990). Furthermore, even if most final verdicts can be predicted as simple functions of the initial distribution of the verdict preferences, it still is an important scientific problem to understand the social mechanisms that translate initial preferences into the ultimate verdict. And finally, there are still significant legal questions which derive from guarantees of due process. Surely a convicted defendant would feel cheated if he or she knew that the guarantee of an impartial, thorough, deliberation process was cut short after the first jury ballot.

What sort of behaviors in deliberation would be of significant interest in an analysis of individual differences, specifically individual differences in juror attitudes? First, and most obviously, we would like to predict what contributions are made by jurors to the discussion and deliberation. Attitudes should give us some leverage in predicting what prodeath and antideath penalty jurors will say. For example, the constellation of due process attitudes associated with the antideath penalty stance implies that these jurors would be more likely to speak for the defense side of the case, more likely to cite the presumption of innocence and standard-of-proof instructions, and more critical in their evaluations of credibility of testimony from the prosecution side of the case. In contrast, the constellation of attitudes associated with the prodeath stance leads us to expect that these jurors would make more remarks in favor of the prosecution side of the case; should evaluate the credibility and implications of testimony from prosecution witnesses as more important and more substantial than statements by defense witnesses; and should emphasize crime control factors over due process factors, for example by citing the danger of allowing the defendant to return to the streets unpunished. These predictions are relatively uncontroversial and follow directly from the concepts associated with the attitude difference we have studied.

There are other individual differences in behavior which might be associated with the attitude individual difference, but which are not associated with differences in jurors' backgrounds in a direct fashion. For example, there are substantial differences in the amounts of talking done by different jurors on the same jury. Typically four jurors out of twelve consume more than half of the talking time. Three variables are known to predict the amount of talking. One variable, labeled "worldly success" by Hastie, Penrod, and Pennington (1983), comprises social status and education; more "successful" jurors talk more than less successful ones. Second, juror gender matters; men talk more than women. It is interesting to note that the one-and-one-half to one differential in speaking rates has not changed since the 1950s when Kalven and Zeisel conducted their original mock-jury experiments (Strodtbeck & Lipinski, 1988), despite apparent shifts in the conceptions of male and female social roles. Third, occupancy of the foreman's role is associated with higher amounts of talking; the foreman talked about twice as much as any other juror. We would also like to be able to predict which jurors will be most susceptible to persuasive influence from other jurors; who is likely to have a change of mind on the jury? However, the search for predictors of the "wavering" and the "stubborn" juror has been inconclusive.

As we anticipated, the primary effects of the death penalty attitude variable on behavior during deliberation appear in our analyses of the content of statements made by jurors. Our conclusions are based on a mock-jury

Table 2.3. *Each mock juror classified by attitude toward the death penalty and the side of the case favored by a preponderance of the juror's statements in deliberation* [a]

Juror type	Statement type			Total
	Unclear [b]	Proprosecution	Prodefense	
Excludable	4	8	18	30
Death-qualified	11	91	84	186
Total	15	99	102	216

[a] $X^2(2) = 6.05$, $p < .05$.
[b] "Unclear" means juror made an equal number of proprosecution and prodefense statements, or made no statements in deliberation.

study in which California residents qualified to serve as jurors watched the reenactment of a murder trial used in our previous research and then deliberated for a minimum of an hour in an attempt to reach a verdict. None of the mock juries reached a verdict within the first hour of deliberation, but the contents of this deliberation provide an indication of what would occur in the first stages of a deliberation that ran to a conclusion. Again, we divided our subjects into excludable and death-qualified jurors and we tabulated the remarks they made during deliberation. First we classified the overall set of statements made by each juror by counting the number of proprosecution and prodefense statements made by each juror. If a majority of the statements were proprosecution we classified the juror in the proprosecution column of Table 2.3; conversely, if the majority of the statements were prodefense we classified the juror in the prodefense column; and if the corpus of statements made by a juror did not clearly support either side of the case we listed them in the "unclear" column. Two hundred sixteen mock jurors were crossclassified by their status on the attitude variable (excludable versus death-qualified) and by the balance of statements during deliberation (proprosecution, prodefense, unclear). A significant association was observed between these two variables, indicating that excludable jurors tended to favor the defense side of the case in discussion to a greater extent than did death-qualified jurors.

We also reviewed the corpus of statements made by each juror with reference to the number of remarks they made in favor of a guilty verdict versus a not guilty verdict, and again produced a two-way table with juror attitudes (excludable versus death-qualified) and verdict favored (guilty, not guilty, unclear) as the two factors defining the table. Again, a significant relationship was observed between the two variables such that excludable jurors were more likely to speak for a not guilty verdict than were death-qualified jurors.

Conclusion

Most of the published writing on the effects of individual differences on juror's verdicts consists either of overoptimistic claims that various personality or background variables are reliable indicators of a proprosecution or prodefense juror, or of gloomy criticisms of these claims, typically ending with the equally simplistic claim that the evidence determines the verdict and that individual differences do not. A review of the relevant research indicates that the usual hoary or trendy stereotypes are not very useful (race, class, gender, occupation, and nationality on the hoary side; power speech, color preferences, locus of control, and dress on the trendy side; authoritarianism somewhere between). But we also know that juries are rarely unanimous on the first ballot, and thus, because the evidence presented is the same for all the jurors, individual differences must make a difference. The evidence presented is the same, but the evidence perceived by the jurors is not.

Some of these influential individual differences may be accidental, as when a juror suddenly remembers that she forgot to pay the mortgage bill and misses a few minutes of crucial testimony. This sort of error may often be corrected in deliberation. Others may be understandable in retrospect, but unforeseeable in advance, as when the victim turns out to be the spitting image of the juror's deceitful Uncle Louie. Many may be attitudes that only become influential in relation to very specific case facts, but may be potentially discoverable through an extensive voir dire.

Death penalty attitudes are more general, yet they still provide some predictive power. Thus they allowed us a laboratory to explore how a general attitude might affect a person's interpretation of a body of evidence, and his or her response to it. We have argued that the process may involve an accumulation of many slight differences – in perceptions of the plausibility of witnesses, in the availability of different scripts or stories for the crime, in the unarticulated sense of how much doubt is reasonable doubt. Sometimes the accumulation of these tendencies will be sufficient to move a juror across the line from one verdict to another, sometimes not. There are undoubtedly other ways in which general attitudes can affect jurors' decisions about evidence, and there are probably other attitudes that predict verdicts in certain domains of cases. The kitchen-sink approach of tacking a sheaf of questionnaire measures onto a jury study in case something turns out significant is likely to continue to produce discouraging results. More carefully crafted studies of specific intermediate processes may prove more fruitful, both for understanding verdicts and for understanding attitudes.

References

Abelson, R. P. (1985). A variance explanation paradox: When a little is a lot. *Psychological Bulletin, 97,* 129–133.

Abelson, R. P., Aronson, E., McGuire, W. J., Newcomb, T. M., Rosenberg, M. J., & Tannenbaum, P. H. (1968). *Theories of cognitive consistency: A sourcebook.* Chicago: Rand-McNally.

Appleman, J. A. (1968). Selection of the jury. *Trial Lawyer's Guide, 12,* 207–239.

Behn, R. D., & Vaupel, J. W. (1982). *Quick analysis for busy decision makers.* New York: Basic Books.

Bem, D. J., & Allen, A. (1974). On predicting some of the people some of the time. *Psychological Review, 81,* 506–520.

Blackstone, W. (1962). *Commentaries on the laws of England of public wrongs.* Boston: Beacon. (Original work published 1769)

Bodin, H. S. (1954). *Selecting a jury.* New York: Practicing Law Institute.

Boehm, V. R. (1968). Mr. Prejudice, Miss Sympathy and the authoritarian personality: An application of psychological measuring techniques to the problem of jury bias. *Wisconsin Law Review, 1968,* 734–750.

Bonora, B., & Krauss, E. (Eds.). (1979). *Jurywork, systematic techniques: A manual for lawyers, legal workers and social scientists.* Berkeley, CA: National Jury Project.

Bronson, E. J. (1970). On the conviction proneness and representativeness of the death-qualified jury: An empirical study of Colorado veniremen. *University of Colorado Law Review, 42,* 1–32.

Campbell, D. T. (1963). Social attitudes and other acquired behavioral dispositions. In S. Koch (Ed.), *Psychology: A study of a science* (Vol. 6, pp. 94–172). New York: McGraw-Hill.

Chapman, L. J., & Chapman, J. P. (1967). Genesis of popular but erroneous psychodiagnostic observations. *Journal of Abnormal Psychology, 72,* 193–204.

Costantini, E., & King, J. (1980). The partial juror: Correlates and causes of prejudgment. *Law and Society Review, 15,* 9–40.

Cowan, C. L., Thompson, W. C., & Ellsworth, P. C. (1984). The effects of death qualification on jurors' predisposition to convict and on the quality of deliberation. *Law and Human Behavior, 8,* 53–79.

Edwards, W. (1954). The theory of decision making. *Psychological Bulletin, 51,* 380–417.

Ellsworth, P. C. (1989). Are twelve heads better than one? *Law and Contemporary Problems, 52,* 205–224.

Ellsworth, P. C., & Ross, L. (1983). Public opinion and capital punishment: A close examination of the views of abolitionists and retentionists. *Crime and Delinquency, 29,* 116–169.

Fischhoff, B. (1975). Hindsight ≠ foresight: The effect of outcome knowledge on judgment under uncertainty. *Journal of Experimental Psychology: Human Perception and Performance, 1,* 288–299.

Fitzgerald, R., & Ellsworth, P. C. (1984). Due process vs. crime control: Death qualification and jury attitudes. *Law and Human Behavior, 8,* 31–51.

Fletcher, G. P. (1968). Two kinds of legal rules: A comparative study of burden-of-persuasion practices in criminal cases. *Yale Law Journal, 77,* 880–935.

Gerbasi, K. C., Zuckerman, M., & Reis, H. T. (1977). Justice needs a new blindfold: A review of mock jury research. *Psychological Bulletin, 84,* 323–345.

Hans, V. (1982, June). *Gentlewomen of the jury.* Paper presented at the annual meeting of the Law and Society Association, Toronto, Ontario, Canada.

Hans, V. P., & Vidmar, N. (1986). *Judging the jury.* New York: Plenum.

Hastie, R., Penrod, S. D., & Pennington, N. (1983). *Inside the jury.* Cambridge, MA: Harvard University Press.

Hawkins, S. A., & Hastie, R. (1990). Hindsight: Biased judgments of past events after the outcomes are known. *Psychological Bulletin, 107,* 311–327.

Hovey v. Superior Court, 28 Cal. 3d 1 (1980).

Hovland, C. I., Janis, I. L., & Kelley, H. H. (1953). *Communication and persuasion: Psychological studies of opinion change.* New Haven, CT: Yale University Press.

Jurow, G. (1971). New data on the effect of a "death qualified" jury on the guilt determination process. *Harvard Law Review, 84,* 567–611.

Kalven, H. K., Jr., & Zeisel, H. (1966). *The American jury.* Boston: Little, Brown.

Levine, J. P. (1983). Jury toughness: The impact of conservatism on criminal court verdicts. *Crime & Delinquency, 29,* 71–87.

Lockhart v. McCree, 106 S. Ct. 1758 (1986).

McGuire, W. J. (1969). The nature of attitudes and attitude change. In G. Lindzey & E. Aronson (Eds.), *The handbook of social psychology* (2nd ed.): *Vol. 3. The individual in a social context* (pp. 136–314). Reading, MA: Addison-Wesley.

McGuire, W. J. (1983). A contextualist theory of knowledge: Its implications for innovation and reform in psychological research. In L. Berkowitz (Ed.), *Advances in experimental social psychology* (Vol. 16, pp. 1–47). Orlando: Academic Press.

Mischel, W. (1968). *Personality and assessment.* New York: Wiley.

Moran, G., & Comfort, J. C. (1986). Neither "tentative" nor "fragmentary": Verdict performance of impaneled felony jurors as a function of attitude toward capital punishment. *Journal of Applied Psychology, 71,* 146–155.

Nagel, S. (1979). Bringing the values of jurors in line with the law. *Judicature, 63,* 189–195.

Pennington, N., & Hastie, R. (1981). Juror decision-making models: The generalization gap. *Psychological Bulletin, 89,* 246–287.

(1985). *Causal reasoning in decision making.* Unpublished manuscript, University of Chicago.

(1986). Evidence evaluation in complex decision making. *Journal of Personality and Social Psychology, 51,* 242–258.

Ross, L. (1977). The intuitive psychologist and his shortcomings: Distortions in the attribution process. In L. Berkowitz (Ed.), *Advances in experimental social psychology* (Vol. 10, pp. 173–220). New York: Academic Press.

(1987). The problem of construal in social inference and social psychology. In N. Grunberg, R. E. Nisbett, & J. Singer (Eds.), *A distinctive approach to psychological research: The influence of Stanley Schachter.* Hillsdale, NJ: Erlbaum.

Ross, L., Lepper, M. R., & Hubbard, M. (1975). Perseverance in self-perception: Biased attributional processes in the debriefing paradigm. *Journal of Personality and Social Psychology, 32,* 880–892.

Rothblatt, H. B. (1966). Techniques for jury selection. *Criminal Law Bulletin, 2*(4), 14–29.

Saks, M. J. (1976). The limits of scientific jury selection: Ethical and empirical. *Jurimetrics Journal, 17,* 3–22.

Saks, M. J., & Hastie, R. (1978). *Social psychology in court.* New York: Van Nostrand Reinhold.

Schulman, J., Shaver, P., Colman, R., Emrich, B., & Christie, R. (1973, May). Recipe for a jury. *Psychology Today*, pp. 37–44; 77–84.

Schum, D. A., & Martin, A. W. (1982). Formal and empirical research on cascaded inference in jurisprudence. *Law and Society Review, 17,* 150–151.

Sears, D. O., & Kinder, D. R. (1971). Racial tensions and voting in Los Angeles. In W. Z. Hersch (Ed.), *Los Angeles: Viability and prospects for metropolitan leadership* (pp. 51–88). New York: Praeger.

Shapiro, B. J. (1986). "To a moral certainty": Theories of knowledge and Anglo-American juries 1600–1850. *The Hastings Law Journal, 38,* 153–193.

Simon, R. J., & Mahan, L. (1971). Quantifying burdens of proof: A view from the bench, the jury, and the classroom. *Law and Society Review, 5,* 319–330.

Snyder, M., Tanke, E. D., & Berscheid, E. (1977). Social perception and interpersonal behavior: On the self-fulfilling nature of social stereotypes. *Journal of Personality and Social Psychology, 35,* 656–666.

Strodtbeck, F. L., & Lipinski, R. M. (1988). *Women jurors, then and now.* Unpublished manuscript, University of Chicago, Social Psychology Laboratory.

Suggs, D., & Sales, B. D. (1978). The art and science of conducting the voir dire. *Professional Psychology, 9,* 367–368.

Thomas, E. A. C., & Hogue, A. (1976). Apparent weight of evidence, decision criteria, and confidence ratings in juror decision making. *Psychological Review, 83,* 442–465.

Thompson, W. C., Cowan, C. L., Ellsworth, P. C., & Harrington, J. C. (1984). Death penalty attitudes and conviction proneness: The translation of attitudes into verdicts. *Law and Human Behavior, 8,* 95–113.

Tyler, T. R., & Weber, R. (1982). Support for the death penalty: Instrumental response to crime or symbolic attitude. *Law and Society Review, 17,* 21–45.

U.S. v. Fatico, 458 F. Supp. 388–413 (1978).

Vallone, R. P., Ross, L., & Lepper, M. R. (1985). The hostile media phenomenon: Biased perception and perceptions of media bias in coverage of the Beirut massacre. *Journal of Personality and Social Psychology, 49,* 577–585.

Vidmar, N., & Ellsworth, P. C. (1974). Public opinion and the death penalty. *Stanford Law Review, 26,* 1245–1270.

Witherspoon v. Illinois, 391 U.S. 510 (1968).

Zimbardo, P. G., Ebbesen, E. B., & Maslach, C. (1977). *Influencing attitudes and changing behavior: An introduction to method, theory, and applications of social control and personal power* (2nd ed.). Reading, MA: Addison-Wesley.

3   The influence of outcome information and attitudes on juror decision making in search and seizure cases

Jonathan D. Casper and Kennette M. Benedict

A juror's decision is the product of a complex set of factors including, at a minimum, the juror's personal history, character, and social background; attitudes, ideologies, and values; limits and proclivities of his or her cognitive processes; the nature of the evidence presented at trial; and legal rules that are supposed to govern the ways in which the evidence is interpreted, weighted, and applied to the decision. We start with the assumption that no single current scientific approach will be adequate, by itself, to provide an account of even the most common phenomena of juror decision behavior. However, building blocks for a useful hybrid theory are available in several cognate disciplines comprising elements from sociological and psychological theories of personality and social structure, political science concepts of ideologies and legitimating values, cognitive information processing theories of problem solving and judgment, and jurisprudential analyses of rules of evidence and institutions of trial procedure. The present program of research is an attempt to develop the type of eclectic theoretical framework that we think is necessary for an adequate scientific analysis of legal decision making. We use path analysis statistical models in the research because they provide a method of data analysis appropriate to capture the complex causality manifested in legal decision phenomena.

Our program of research focuses on the relationship between the attitudes that jurors bring into the jury box and the manner in which they respond to certain judicial instructions. The instructions on which we focus represent a common procedure at trial; instructions to the jurors to ignore evidence they have heard or seen, to strike information from memory and consideration when deciding the case.

To anticipate our conclusions, we will argue that jurors are not successful at ignoring information that they have been given, even when instructed to do so by the trial judge. We also find that a jurors' attitudes toward the police and the criminal justice system moderate the influence of the "stricken evidence" on their decisions. Finally, applying data analysis methods that are relatively novel to cognitive psychology, we conclude that the impact of attitudes and extralegal information is mediated primarily by the jurors' cognitive interpretation and representation of the trial evidence.

A legal dilemma

In many jury trials a special problem arises when jurors are exposed to evidence or information that they should not consider when reaching a legally proper decision. The most common remedy at trial is for the judge to instruct the jurors to ignore the evidence at the time it is first heard and then to repeat the instruction in the final charge to the jury before deliberation begins. The problem of striking evidence from the jury's consideration arises in many legal contexts. For example, in civil cases jurors occasionally overhear information about insurance, and they are routinely instructed to ignore it. On the criminal side, they sometimes hear information about a defendant's prior record of convictions or arrests and are instructed to ignore such information in considering the issue of guilt or innocence. Sometimes, in highly publicized cases, the judge will explicitly instruct the jury that they are to disregard any information they obtain from the news media concerning the case. These situations are a legal dilemma because intuitions and the results of scientific research suggest that judge's instructions are ineffective in blocking the influence of the extralegal information on a juror's decisions (e.g., Doob & Kirshenbaum, 1972; Hans & Doob, 1975; Padawer-Singer & Barton, 1975; Sue, Smith, & Caldwell, 1973; Wissler & Saks, 1985; see review in Hawkins & Hastie, 1990).

Civil suits to deter illegal searches

In our own research we have focused on a particular case of the potentially biasing effects of extralegal information. In colloquial terms we are interested in the biasing effects of "knowing the end of a story on judgments that are supposed to be based on the story, without knowledge of its ending." Two examples of this special form of potential bias arise in legal proceedings. In many medical malpractice and product liability suits, the judgment of whether to award damages to a plaintiff depends, at least in part, upon a judgment about the defendant's behavior (e.g., Was it negligent?). But the judgment is not supposed to depend on the outcome that occurred after the behavior. The relevant legal standard is based upon what the defendant knew or ought to have known prior to the "end of the story." Of course, in all these cases some bad outcome has occurred that led to the law suit, and jurors are fully aware of this outcome when they make their decisions.

A second example of a situation in which the "end of the story" may bias judgments that are to be based only on the circumstances preceding the outcome occurs in cases that arise when a citizen is the subject of a police search, and the citizen claims that the search was illegal. In this situation a federal law (Section 1983 of 42 U.S. Code) provides a remedy to citizens who feel they have been mistreated by the police. The citizen has the right to bring a civil damage suit against the officers who conducted the allegedly illegal search to seek a monetary award to compensate the citizen (plaintiff) for harm done and to punish and deter illegal conduct by the offending officers. In such a case the juror's decision depends upon whether the search was lawful, which in turn is supposed to depend on a consideration of information available to the police before they initiated the search. The juror is instructed to ignore information about the outcome of the search. Furthermore, in these cases, unlike medical malpractice and product liability cases, the outcome of the search is not obvious to the juror from the mere existence of the law suit. A citizen may bring such a suit whether or not the search uncovered evidence of illegal conduct. Nonetheless, if evidence of illegality was obtained, this result is typically brought to the juror's attention by defense attorneys representing the police. Of course, as in the examples above, the judge instructs the jury to ignore information about the outcome when reaching a decision about the legality of the police officer's conduct. But, as we have suggested, this instruction is unlikely to have the legally required effects.

Let us take a more detailed look at the decision required from the jurors. The key issue to decide whether or not the police acted illegally in conducting their search usually revolves around whether or not the officers had *probable cause* to believe the plaintiff was guilty of the crime *before* they initiated their search. The existence of probable cause is the condition that makes the police search lawful. The presentation to the jury of information showing that the outcome of the search revealed that the citizen whose person or premises were searched was guilty of a crime has an obvious potentially biasing effect on judgments of whether or not probable cause had been satisfied. Intuitively the inference that the police had cause seems to follow almost irresistibly from the citizen's criminal behavior. Thus, we hypothesize that if a juror is informed that the outcome of the search revealed that the citizen was guilty of a crime, in hindsight the juror will be likelier to believe that the police officer's motives were reasonable and that the probable cause requirement had been satisfied before the search was initiated. We also hypothesize that an instruction from the judge to ignore the outcome of the search in deciding the issue of probable cause is an ineffective procedure to eliminate the influence of the outcome information.

Hindsight phenomena in legal decision making

Before we turn to our own research on the effects of the outcome information on judgments of the police officers' conduct in such situations, we will briefly review the literature on the psychology of judgment concerned with hindsight effects. Psychologists have observed a number of phenomena in laboratory settings that are pertinent to the admonition-to-ignore remedy usually employed to eliminate the potential bias introduced by exposing jurors to extralegal information. All of this research leads us to doubt the effectiveness of the exclusionary instruction. For example, there are many studies of peoples' ability to follow "directed forgetting" instructions in memory tasks. In these experiments subjects are instructed to erase or un-learn information that has been previously stored in memory (Bjork, 1972). Subjects cannot erase previously learned information. Another example is provided by decision researchers' efforts to design "debiasing" procedures that will allow decision makers in nonlegal tasks to divert their attention from inferior evidence that may produce biases in their ultimate judgments. Again, effective debiasing procedures are difficult to construct. Further-more, direct instructions to ignore the potentially biasing information rarely work. Another closely related class of phenomena involves subjects' ability to reconsider a judgment when instructed that the evidence on which it was originally based is invalid. Subjects' inability to rejudge a situation or to reverse the influence of the invalid information is so extreme that the phenomena has been labeled "the perseverance effect" (Ross, Lepper, & Hubbard, 1975).

Research by Fischhoff (1975) is directly pertinent to the type of case with which we are concerned in which information about an *outcome* biases judg-ments of the previous events in a narrative. Fischhoff had people read de-scriptions of historical events and psychiatric clinical cases and then he varied the outcome of the event reported to different groups of subjects (e.g., the British forces *or* the Gurka forces were victorious in a war in India). Subjects who had been given an outcome were asked to discount the outcome information and to make a judgment of the probability they *would have assigned to the outcome without knowledge of the outcome*. This judg-ment is exactly parallel to the judgment required of jurors in the civil suits against police officers alleged to have conducted an illegal search. Fisch-hoff compared these "ignore the evidence" hindsightful judgments against judgments made by subjects who did not receive information about an out-come. He found that the experimental subjects (told the outcome) consis-tently overestimated the probability that they would have assigned to the outcome they had been given. These results have been replicated in other settings and in tasks with control conditions that demonstrate that the hind-sight effect is robust and is not an artifact of the experimental method.

A related series of studies by Dellarosa and Bourne (1984) showed that presenting the outcome of an event affected subjects' ability to recall evi-dence relevant to the prediction of the outcome. The materials used in their experiments included judgments of a stock market price, medical diagno-sis, and a criminal trial. The evidence relevant to the decision in each of these contexts included information that would support a positive or nega-tive outcome. Once subjects were told the "true outcome," their memories of the evidence were biased to favor recall of evidence consistent with the outcome they had been given. One implication is that outcome-based recall would reinforce the hindsight effect observed by Fischhoff.

A common theme underlies Fischhoff's interpretation of the hindsight effect, Dellarosa and Bourne's interpretation of the outcome-biased memory effect, and our hypothesis about the effects of an exclusionary instruction on juror decision making. This theme is reflected in several other chapters in the present book (e.g., Pennington and Ellsworth, both this book) and it involves the assumption that a juror creates a summary mental representation of decision-relevant events and that this mental representation is the basis for the juror's ultimate decision. Our hypothesis is that outcome information and information about events prior to the outcome interact with one another to produce a unitary mental representation in the juror's memory. Thus, the police officer's testimony about a furtive movement, a partially glimpsed object, or the reliability of an informant will be interpreted differently and incorporated in a different form in the juror's mental representation of what happened, if the juror knows that the officer actually found evidence of a crime committed by the citizen who is now suing the officer. Fischhoff called this synergistic effect of evidence and outcome information "creeping determinism" because he felt that the outcome influenced the memory representation of the evidence in a subtle manner that was virtually impossible for the decision maker to detect. Furthermore, as the research by Fischoff, Dellarosa and Bourne, and others demonstrates, it is virtually impossible for the decision maker to "undo" the effects of the outcome information (see review by Hawkins & Hastie, 1990).

The impact of outcome information on judgments

The primary hypothesis motivating our research is that information about the outcome of the search will affect jurors' judgments of the liability of police officers alleged to have conducted an illegal search. We want to emphasize that our hypothesis is that the effects of outcome information will be indirect, mediated by its effects on inferences made when jurors construct a mental representation of the evidence. Like several other contributors to the present book, we believe that the juror's global decision process is distributed over several stages or subtasks of processing. One early subtask attempted by the juror is to evaluate the evidence to produce a mental conceptualization of its key features. This intermediate mental representation is then the basis for subsequent decisions concerning responsibility, liability, and awards.

In his discussion of decisions of judges on motions to exclude evidence in criminal cases on the grounds the evidence was the product of an illegal search, Skolnick (1967) appears to concur with our suggestion that information about the outcome of a search may have *indirect* effects on the legal decision maker instructed to disregard the information:

If something is found, the moral burden immediately shifts to the suspect. The illegality of a search is likely to be tempered – even in the eyes of the judiciary – by the discovery of incriminating evidence on the suspect. For example, when a suspect turns out actually to possess narcotics, the perception of surrounding facts and circumstances about the reasonableness of the arrest can shift in only one direction – against the defendant and in the favor of the propriety of the search – even if the facts might have appeared differently had no incriminating evidence been discovered. (p. 221)

An alternate hypothesis would be that outcome information has a direct effect on the later decision stages. For example, information that the plaintiff was himself guilty of the crime that prompted the police search might directly affect judgments about an appropriate award, without influencing the juror's interpretation of the evidence concerning the police and citizen's actions. This alternative interpretation, of a direct effect on the final decision stage, would be consistent with other research showing that information about a trial participant's character affects a juror's threshold to decide for one side or the other (see Kerr, this book). Or, if one did not want to invoke a hypothetical subjective threshold for the decision, one could simply postulate that information implying that the plaintiff is guilty of a crime reinforces the juror's natural resistance to say that a police officer has performed an illegal act. In a moment, we will outline a research method that allows us to discriminate between the distinct or joint indirect and direct effects of outcome information on the judgment with empirical data.

The role of attitudes in juror decision making

We have focused on the interaction between case-specific evidence information and case-specific outcome information. But we believe that another kind of information, generic beliefs and attitudes about the world and the criminal justice system, also influences the final decision. Our concept of attitudes derives from the broad notions of systems of attitudes or ideologies provided by philosophers, sociologists, and political scientists, rather than from the more restricted concept of an attitude as a molecular "predisposition to act" current in the psychological literature. A useful definition of ideology in the sociological tradition is provided by Bell: "an interpretative system of political ideas embodying and concretizing the more abstract values of a polity (or social movement) which, because of its claim to justification by some transcendant morality (for example, history), demands a legitimacy for its belief system and a commitment to action in the effort to realize those beliefs" (1967, p. 595, note 6).

For our purposes the key points in this definition comprise the emphasis on a *system* of beliefs: the link between the beliefs and justifications in terms of *moral values* or other motivations; the attribution to the belief system of a *political legitimacy*; and the accompanying commitment to *action* to realize the beliefs.

In the context of the criminal justice system in America, scholars have identified two contrasting ideologies that are associated with different segments of the population. Packer (1968) has noted that there is a tension in our society between a view of the criminal justice process as a mechanism for crime control and the contrasting view of the same process as a mechanism to preserve individual privacy and to avoid errors when applying sanctions to punish illegal behavior. The crime control ideology comprises a set of beliefs and values that prescribe extensive discretion for the police in the conduct of their duties, promoting speed and efficiency in the apprehension, conviction, and punishment of those who violate the law. The due process view stresses the citizen's right to privacy and the minimization of prosecution of innocent citizens, yielding an ideal criminal investigation process that is constrained by rules and procedures that make it difficult for the police to interfere in the lives of citizens.

In examining the role of values in juror decision making, we have focused on two different ideological domains. In our first study we assessed the role of general political ideologies on decisions about damage awards. We viewed ideology as a large, organized system of beliefs, linked to fundamental values with implications for behavior. We hypothesized that for such a general ideology to have a substantial effect on a juror's decision, the juror must possess a *consistent system* of attitudes. Evidence from research on political attitudes has suggested that many individuals subscribe to heterogeneous collections of attitudes that are not apparently consistent with any systematic orientation (what Converse, 1964, calls belief systems not characterized by "constraint"), and that such attitude structures are less strongly related to political activity. Thus we hypothesized, in the first study, that damage awards by jurors with consistent political attitude structures would be influenced by their general ideologies, but such effects would not be observed among jurors with less constrained political belief structures.

In the second study, we focused upon attitude structures more directly related to the issue domain of the legal case. We examined the relationship of juror attitudes toward the importance of crime control and due process concerns in the administration of justice to their damage awards. With the greater verisimilitude of the second study and the introduction of detailed judicial instructions, we expected that the more diffuse political attitudes would not be significantly related to damage awards. We hypothesized that jurors more attached to a crime control ideology would be less inclined to punish police activity, regardless of other considerations, e.g., the outcome of the search itself. In contrast, persons more attached to a due process ideology would, we believed, be more likely to side with citizens who complain about police intrusions into their private lives. Essentially, our hypothesis is that ideology will act to influence the knowledge representation produced by the juror as an intermediate step on the way to his or her ultimate decision. Our empirical methods were designed to identify both indirect (mediated by the knowledge structure) and direct effects of juror attitudes on their verdicts, if either or both are present.

Our hypothesis that the juror's ideology will work its effects indirectly by guiding the formation of a knowledge structure can be further refined by considering the process by which attitudes might be linked to evidence knowledge structures. The influence of attitude on the intermediate knowledge structure might be in the form of an uncoordinated collection of gap-filling, disambiguating inferences. Under this mechanism, the attitudes would be applied to the evidence comprehension task as a set of relatively disparate premises that can be activated independently to make appropriate, local inferences necessary to comprehend any description of a sequence of events such as those that might be testified about in a trial.

Under this view, differences in verdicts might be accounted for by postulating different assumptions about various aspects of the world relevant to the crime events held by jurors who reach different decisions. For example, we might imagine a conservative, crime control adherent who believed that "most drug sales are transacted by blacks"; "police officers tell the truth"; and "sellers of drugs behave in suspicious and furtive ways." In contrast, a liberal, due process oriented person might believe that "large drug sales are usually transacted by professional criminals"; "police officers often lie to convict a defendant"; and "major drug dealers are careful, confident, normal-appearing people." The beliefs held by each person would not necessarily be stored in close association in long-term memory, but would all be activated at some point in the course of rendering a verdict in a drug search case like ours. Furthermore, different collections of beliefs would lead to different inferences concerning the likelihood of guilt of a defendant charged with the crime.

The impact of the seriousness of the crime on verdict judgments

Our primary focus in the present research is on the interactive influence of attitudes, extralegal outcome information, and case-specific evidence on the verdict decision. However, our intuitions suggested that another factor, the seriousness of the criminal activity involved in the police search, might also play a role. When the crime involved in the search for evidence is serious, the tension between crime control and due process interests is heightened and juror attitudes were expected to play a more significant role in the damage award process. In the same way, the role of outcome knowledge – particularly the information that the suspect was indeed guilty of a serious crime – would be expected to have a stronger effect. When the crime involved is trivial, both these variables were expected to play less significant roles, for the crime control interests in such cases would be less salient and thus attitudes and outcome information would be less important to the award decision. More specifically, we anticipated that with serious crimes the awards would be on average smaller and correlated with attitudes and outcome information. With a relatively trivial crime, awards would be larger and attitudes and outcome would play a smaller role in the process.

One interpretation of the moderating effects of the seriousness of the crime involved would predict a direct effect of crime seriousness on the juror's verdicts. For example, jurors may be struggling with a tension between charges against police officers implying that they acted illegally and should be punished and their natural inclination to support the police. Under this interpretation, when the citizen who is suing the police is clearly guilty of a serious crime, the juror would be less willing to resolve the tension in favor of the plaintiff citizen.

A second interpretation also predicting a direct effect of crime seriousness on verdicts is inspired by the work by Gleason and Harris (1976), who found that judgments about leniency of punishment were affected by whether or not the decision maker believed there was a likelihood that he or she could be in a similar situation. In the present context, the notion is that a juror could more easily imagine himself or herself committing a minor crime than a major crime. Thus, their sympathies would be more with the plaintiff-citizen, *with whom they could identify,* for a minor crime offense; in contrast, the balance of sympathies would favor the police side of the case when the plaintiff citizen was guilty of a major offense (reducing the chance that the juror would identify with the plaintiff).

Empirical research

We have conducted two mock-juror experiments in which subjects made decisions in a civil suit brought against police officers by a citizen who claimed his apartment was searched illegally. In both experiments we manipulated information about the outcome of the search (whether or not incriminating evidence was found in the citizen's apartment) and, in the second experiment, we varied the nature of the crime of which the citizen may or may not have been guilty when the police searched the apartment. We also measured each subject's general attitudes relevant to the due process–crime control ideology dimension, the subject's liberal–conservative political dimension, the subject's interpretation and recall of evidence information from the case materials, the subject's judgment of liability, and the amounts of the awards levied against the police officers, if a plaintiff's verdict was returned.

In a departure from the analysis of most psychology experiments, we attempted to develop a statistical model of the direct and interactive effects of the major variables that might influence the ultimate decision. The type of model we used, called "path analysis," is designed to summarize the mutual influence among members of a set of causally related variables. The hypotheses we stated at the beginning of this chapter are concerned with direct or indirect influence of attitudes, outcome information, and the nature of the crime attributed to the plaintiff. Path analysis provides an effective statistical methodology to assess these alternate hypotheses stated in terms of direct versus indirect influences of several variables upon one another.

In our first experiment, college students read a summary of the events surrounding the search of the plaintiff's apartment, summaries of the plaintiff's and defense's arguments, and judge's instructions on how to decide liability and set a damage award. Then they indicated the dollar amount of damages they would award within a range from zero dollars to $50,000.

The essential facts of the case concerned two police officers, assigned to the narcotics squad, who received a tip from an informant that a drug sale would take place in a certain apartment building. The officers went to the apartment building and knocked on the first door next to the entrance. The knock was answered by a man (now the plaintiff) who approximately, but not exactly, fit the informant's description of the drug dealer. The man asked the police to leave him alone and tried to shut the door. The officers pushed into the apartment, knocked the man to the floor, and then handcuffed him. Then they searched the apartment. Three experimental conditions were created at this point in the case summary by providing different outcomes of the police search of the apartment. In the guilty version, the police discovered a substantial cache of heroin in the apartment. In the neutral version, there was no reference to the outcome of the search. And, in the innocent version, the police found no evidence of drugs in the apartment. Our sample of subjects was divided into thirds, with each group receiving one version of the case materials.

We followed the presentation of the evidence and the reported outcome of the search with a series of questions designed to measure the knowledge structure the subject had created from this information. These "memory reconstruction" items included a subset of questions that dealt with factual information directly presented in the written materials (e.g., "What did the officers find in their search of the apartment?"); and questions about items that were ambiguous in the written materials (e.g., "How experienced were the police officers in narcotics work?"). Several of the reconstruction questions probed to discover inferences subjects had made about the state of the police officers' knowledge prior to the search: "Prior to the informant's call, how certain were the police that (the plaintiff) had been dealing in drugs?"; "Based on everything they knew up to the time they entered the apartment, how sure do you think the police were that the man that answered the door was a drug dealer?"; and "How closely did the man who answered the door fit the description of the drug dealer that the officers had been given?"

Following the reconstruction items, subjects read summaries of the arguments presented by both sides of the case, and instructions on how to set a damage award. The instructions stressed the issue of whether the citizen's rights had been violated. If they thought the officers did not violate the plaintiff's civil rights then the plaintiff should receive nothing. If they thought that the plaintiff's rights were violated, then in order to compensate the plaintiff and to punish the officers to deter them from future violations, an award of up to $50,000 could be given.

Table 3.1. *Damage awards as a function of*
the three outcome treatments in Experiment 1

Treatment	Mean award[a]	Median award
Guilty	$16,090 (s.d. = 15,437)	$10,000
Neutral	$22,748 (s.d. = 16,030)	$20,000
Not guilty	$24,834 (s.d. = 17,868)	$20,023

[a] $F(2,373) = 9.1$, $p < .001$.

The final questionnaire items assessed the subject's attitudes toward the police (e.g., "In general how do you feel about police officers?"), attitudes toward the criminal justice system (e.g., "Tapping telephones of people suspected of planning crimes is necessary to reduce crimes?"), and questions about government and politics including public policy preferences, rated personal level of interest in politics, and rated political activity levels.

The mean damage awards are presented in Table 3.1 (first column) for each of the three outcome conditions. It is obvious that outcome information did have an effect on the damage award. The awards assigned by subjects provided with information implying the plaintiff was guilty of drug dealing were lower (more favorable to the defense side of the case, the police officers) than awards in the neutral and innocent outcome versions. Thus, we obtained the basic hindsight effect that was the primary motivation for the research. Awards for the neutral and innocent outcome versions seemed to be about the same. The most plausible explanation of this lack of a difference is that subjects assume innocence of the suspect in the neutral outcome version of the materials, essentially equating it with the innocent version. The similarities between the neutral and innocent conditions occurred in both studies and may be the products of several processes (see Casper, Benedict, & Kelly, 1988; Casper, Benedict, & Perry, 1989, for further discussions).

We attempted to go beyond simple tests for effects of the manipulated independent variables by fitting a path analysis model to summarize the causal influence relations among independent variables, measures of subject's attitudes, the subject's knowledge structure constructed from the evidence and outcome information, and the subject's damage award.

The first step in fitting this model was to create variables for each of the candidate sources of causal influence. The manipulated independent variable in the experiment, outcome of the search, was entered on an ordinal scale ranging from 1 (guilty version) to 3 (innocent version). (A path analysis using dummy-coded variables for the guilty and innocent versions, with the neutral condition serving as the reference category, yielded substantially the same results as those we report here.) We formed a unitary scale (reconstruction index) from our memory reconstruction questionnaire items to index the extent to which each subject recalled or interpreted events to be favorable or unfavorable to the police officer defendants in the suit (scale values ranged from 0 indicating totally in favor of the police defendants to 7 indicating totally in favor of the citizen plaintiff). Our hypotheses concerning the effects of ideology and its component attitudes required two indices of slightly different aspects of each subject's belief system. First, we used responses to the five political attitude issue items (i.e., attitudes about military defense spending, inflation and unemployment, government assistance to minorities, etc.) to construct an index of ideological consistency. Subjects whose responses to the items showed a consistent liberal or a consistent conservative pattern were classified as high in ideological consistency; other subjects, whose responses showed a mix of conservative and liberal attitudes, were classified as low in ideological consistency. Second, we used a standard 7-point liberal–conservative scale, developed for use in voting research, as our measure of political liberalism. This unitary measure of liberalism was chosen because it taps the respondent's basic self-perception of ideology rather than a sample of particular issue-specific attitudes. It seemed appropriate to examine this general level of value orientation in the first experiment where the stimulus materials lacked detailed judicial instructions about the criteria for damages and, thus, the award decision might be influenced by general policy positions.

Our first analysis of the correlational structure of the data focused on the basic hindsight mechanism hypothesis that we presented to account for the impact of outcome information on subjects' awards. We predicted the effect of outcome information would be mediated by the subject's interpretation and memory of the evidence; thus the effect of outcome knowledge will *not* be directly on the award, but will be indirect, mediated by evidence interpretation. This model is diagramed in the top panel of Figure 3.1 and, as predicted, the path coefficients show only an indirect influence of the outcome, mediated by evidence interpretation, on the award. Thus, our hypothesis underlying the hindsight effect is supported.

In addition to our basic hypothesis of indirect outcome version effects, we predicted that the consistency of a mock-juror's ideology would moderate the effects of his or her attitude orientation on the award. To evaluate this prediction we separated our sample of subjects into two subgroups: one subgroup comprising subjects who exhibited a consistent ideology (either consistently conservative or consistently liberal) and the other subgroup of subjects exhibiting inconsistent ideologies. Recall, we had hypothesized that a mock-juror's attitude orientation would have an impact on his or her award only if he or she exhibited a consistent ideology. The path analysis models for each subgroup fitted separately are diagramed in the

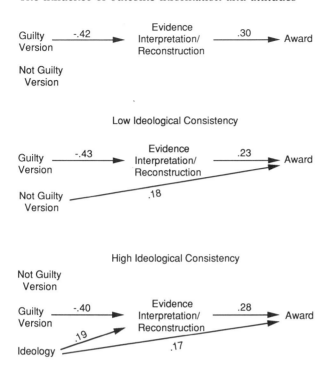

Figure 3.1. Causal model showing the relationship between outcome version, evidence interpretation, and award in Experiment 1.

lower panels in Figure 3.1. It is apparent that for the low consistency group, attitude orientation (on the liberal–conservative dimension) was not related to awards either directly or indirectly. However, for the high consistency mock jurors, attitude orientation showed both direct and indirect influences on the award.

In summary, we have demonstrated the hindsight effect of outcome information on awards that we hypothesized might occur in Section 1983 civil suits brought against police officers alleged to have conducted an illegal search. We have made a strong case, using path analysis models, that the effect represents the type of hindsight bias identified by Fischhoff (1975): The impact of the outcome information was mediated by its influence on subjects' construction of a knowledge structure to interpret and summarize the evidence describing the behavior of the citizen and the police in the disputed events. Attitudes also influenced awards, but consistency of subjects' political ideology exercised a moderating influence on the impact of attitudes. Attitudes were related to the final award only for mock jurors who possessed a consistent belief system. The attitudes of mock jurors who lacked a consistent ideology were not related, directly or indirectly, to their awards.

Table 3.2. *Proportion of mock jurors making any damage award (in %)*

	Type of case			
Outcome information	Murder	Sale of heroin	Possession of marijuana	All cases
A. Compensatory damages[a]				
Guilty	.84	.73	.91	.83 (174)
Neutral	.89	.93	.93	.92 (179)
Innocent	.90	.93	.92	.92 (183)
All versions	.88 (174)	.87 (182)	.92 (180)	.89 (536)
B. Punitive damages[b]				
Guilty	.47	.38	.70	.52 (174)
Neutral	.63	.62	.69	.65 (179)
Innocent	.70	.61	.74	.68 (183)
All versions	.60 (174)	.54 (182)	.71 (180)	.62 (536)

[a] Case $F = 1.56$ (n.s.); Version $F = 5.17$ ($p = .01$).
[b] Case $F = 5.84$ ($p = .01$); Version $F = 5.79$ ($p = .01$).

A second experiment was conducted using a more realistic simulation method and a slightly more elaborate experimental design, in which we added a manipulation of the seriousness of the crime attributed to the plaintiff citizen by the police. We also compared the responses of subjects from two populations, adults called for jury service in the Cook County circuit court of Illinois and college students. In fact, we noticed no substantial differences in the patterns of awards from the two groups of subjects. In the present report, we will combine the data from the two samples, but we would like to note that the similarity in responses of members of the two groups gives us increased confidence that findings from a sample of college students will generalize to the behavior of typical citizens eligible for jury duty.

The procedures and case materials in Experiment 2 were based on those used in Experiment 1. However, we increased the fidelity of the simulation by videotaping the closing statements of the two attorneys and the judge's instructions in the realistic courtroom setting. We also included a second independent variable, manipulating the nature of the crime that motivated the police officers' search. The judge's instructions concerning the criteria to be applied in deciding whether the search was lawful and the manner in which an award should be decided were much more extensive than in Experiment 1. We presented the full legal pattern instruction provided for such cases, including an explicit judicial admonition to disregard the outcome of the search in deciding upon damage awards. Finally, we expanded

Table 3.3. *Average damage awards (in U.S. $)*

Outcome information	Type of case			
	Murder	Sale of heroin	Possession of marijuana	All cases
A. Compensatory damages[a]				
Guilty	1,263	1,083	1,426	1,254 (174)
Neutral	1,428	1,470	1,411	1,437 (179)
Innocent	1,455	1,550	1,494	1,500 (183)
All versions	1,383 (174)	1,369 (182)	1,444 (180)	1,399 (536)
B. Punitive damages[b]				
Guilty	10,360	7,359	21,684	13,035 (174)
Neutral	17,716	15,902	19,439	17,685 (179)
Innocent	21,228	17,098	23,585	21,650 (183)
All versions	16,517 (174)	13,487 (182)	21,578 (180)	17,188 (536)

[a] Case $F=0.75$ (n.s.); Version $F=7.25$ ($p=.001$).
[b] Case $F=7.61$ ($p=.01$); Version $F=7.41$ ($p=.001$).

the questionnaire measures at the end of the experiment providing measures of both compensatory and punitive damage awards, and additional measures of each subject's attitudes toward the police and the criminal justice system.

The experimental independent variable design comprised two factors. Three outcome versions were defined by information provided to mock jurors about the citizen plaintiff's culpability for the crime that motivated the search: guilty, neutral, and innocent. The second factor was a manipulation of the seriousness of the crime that motivated the police search: investigation of a murder, investigation of substantial sale of heroin, or the relatively minor offense of possession of a small quantity of marijuana. In addition to the experimental design, we created measures of the subjects' attitudes on the due process versus crime control dimension, attitudes toward the police, and a variable indexing the type of subject (jury-eligible citizen versus college student). We constructed an eleven-item measure of the extent to which the knowledge structure created by subjects as a summary of the evidence tended to include interpretations that favored the plaintiff or the defendants. Recall that we expected indirect effects of our independent variables on the award to be mediated by their effect on the knowledge structure described by this reconstruction index.

Subject's average dollar awards for compensatory and punitive damages are presented in Tables 3.2 and 3.3. A large majority of the subjects (approximately nine out of ten) found for the plaintiff in the case and most of these subjects awarded the maximum compensatory damage value of

$1,800. The stimulus materials had been purposefully prepared such that most subjects would make compensatory damage awards, for the legal rules require that jurors make such awards prior to considering punitive damages, and the latter are at the heart of the tort remedy. Thus, we obtained a "ceiling effect" on the compensatory damage measure, making it less sensitive to our manipulated variables. Nonetheless, there was a main effect of outcome information (guilty versus neutral versus innocent), but the seriousness of the crime that motivated the search did not reliably affect compensatory awards. Punitive damages, which could range from zero dollars to $50,000, were affected by both outcome version and seriousness of the crime. Essentially we can summarize these results by noting there are two groups of responses: awards under conditions where the plaintiff is not definitely guilty of any serious illegality versus conditions in which the plaintiff is almost certainly guilty of a serious crime (the two conditions in which the police search uncovered evidence that the plaintiff was guilty of a murder or of heroin sales). In these latter two conditions, where the plaintiff appears to be a serious criminal, there is a definite shift in verdicts to be more favorable to the police officers. Only in these conditions does the probability of a plaintiff's award drop significantly and only in these conditions do the average amounts of compensatory and punitive damages drop dramatically.

In Experiment 2, we examined not only the general political liberalism item, but also attitude items dealing with criminal justice policy (e.g., police rights to incarcerate a suspect without trial, the discretion police ought to have when questioning suspects, the privilege against self-incrimination, police options to tap telephones, and so forth), including an item to measure general attitudes toward police officers. The greater realism and the inclusion of detailed judicial instructions may have resulted in a stronger sense of the role constraint, because the general liberal–conservative scale was not related to awards or interpretations of testimony. The attitude scales dealing with criminal justice policies and police behavior were, however, related to both dependent variables.

To review our basic hypotheses, our expectation was that information about the outcome of the search, attitudes toward due process, and attitudes toward the police would have indirect effects on the ultimate damage awards through their effects on the intervening knowledge structure indexed by our measure of memory reconstruction. We hypothesized that crime seriousness would have similar indirect effects as well as influencing damage awards directly. Finally, we did not present definite hypotheses about the effects of membership in the two subsamples of subjects (college student versus jury-eligible citizen), as this factor could have either direct or indirect effects on the award. However, we used the path analysis modeling approach to assess the extent and form of subject subsample differences.

Figure 3.2 presents path diagrams depicting the best fitting causal models for compensatory (upper panel) and punitive damage (lower panel) awards. The general pattern of mediation observed in Experiment 1 is replicated for

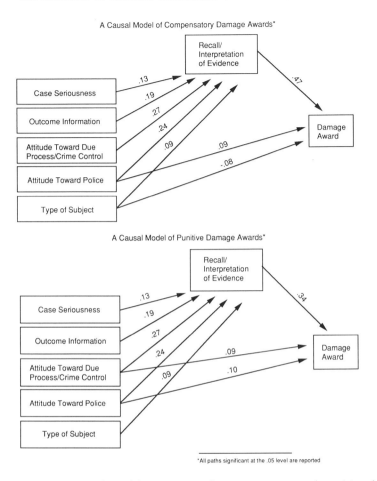

Figure 3.2. Causal models to account for compensatory and punitive damage awards for high and low attitudinal consistency subjects in Experiment 2.

most of the causal relationships in each diagram. The knowledge structure measures, our eleven-item scale of interpretation of the testimony, acts as mediator for almost all of the causal paths from measured and manipulated causes to awards. Attitudes toward the police also exhibit a direct effect on the damage award decision, as do due process attitudes on punitive damages. We view these findings as suggesting that both outcome knowledge and domain-specific attitudes influence juror awards in these cases and that their effects are, in important ways, attributable to their impact on jurors' interpretation of evidence presented during the trial.

Conclusions

Results of our research are consistent with the operation of a hindsight bias mechanism in legal judgments. Juror decisions were influenced by outcome information, information about crime seriousness, and the juror's personal attitudes about the criminal justice system even when jurors are directly instructed to disregard these factors. Furthermore, the causal influence of these factors is mediated by subjects' intermediate knowledge structures, constructed to aid them in their decisions. We have studied these phenomena in the context of a particular type of legal decision, Section 1983 civil suits brought against police officers charged with conducting an illegal search, but we believe there are a variety of other legal circumstances in which hindsight biases affect jurors' judgments. There are many procedures at trial whereby jurors are instructed to ignore information but in which they apparently do not. These include admonitions to disregard trial testimony, instructions to use evidence for one limited purpose (e.g., to evaluate witness credibility but not defendant guilt), instructions to disregard information obtained from pretrial publicity, the occurrence of injury in judgments about liability in medical malpractice and product liability cases, and judicial decisions in criminal cases concerned with the admissibility of evidence seized by the police. We believe that the method of data analysis we have used, fitting a causal model to summarize the simultaneous and sequential causal influences of all of the important variables, is a fruitful tactic to pursue in research on juror decision making. None of the other traditional approaches (for example, those represented in this book) have this integrative, coherent, systematic character.

References

Bell, D. (1967). *The end of ideology: On the exhaustion of political ideas in the fifties* (rev. ed.). New York: Free Press.

Bjork, R. A. (1972). Theoretical implications of directed forgetting. In A. W. Melton & E. Martin (Eds.), *Coding processes in human memory* (pp. 217–235). Washington, DC: Winston.

Casper, J. D., Benedict, K., & Kelly, J. R. (1988). Cognitions, attitudes and decision-making in search and seizure cases. *Journal of Applied Social Psychology, 18,* 93–113.

Casper, J. D., Benedict, K., & Perry, J. L. (1989). Juror decision making, attitudes, and the hindsight bias. *Law and Human Behavior, 13,* 291–310.

Converse, P. E. (1964). The nature of belief systems in mass publics. In D. E. Apter (Ed.), *Ideology and discontent* (pp. 206–261). New York: Free Press.

Dellarosa, D., & Bourne, L. E., Jr. (1984). Decisions and memory: Differential retrievability of consistent and contradictory evidence. *Journal of Verbal Learning and Verbal Behavior, 23,* 669–682.

Doob, A. N., & Kirshenbaum, H. M. (1972). Some empirical evidence on the effect of s. 12 of the Canada Evidence Act upon an accused. *Criminal Law Quarterly, 15,* 88–96.

Fischhoff, B. (1975). Hindsight ≠ foresight: The effect of outcome knowledge on judgment under uncertainty. *Journal of Experimental Psychology: Human Perception and Performance, 1,* 288–299.

Gleason, J. M., & Harris, V. A. (1976). Group discussion and the defendant's socioeconomic status as determinants of judgments by simulated jurors. *Journal of Applied Social Psychology, 6,* 186–191.

Hans, V. P., & Doob, A. N. (1975). Section 12 of the Canada Evidence Act and the deliberations of simulated juries. *Criminal Law Quarterly, 18,* 235–253.

Hawkins, S. A., & Hastie, R. (1990). Hindsight: Biased judgments of past events after the outcomes are known. *Psychological Bulletin, 107,* 311–327.

Packer, H. L. (1968). *The limits of the criminal sanction.* Stanford, CA: Stanford University Press.

Padawer-Singer, A. M., & Barton, A. H. (1975). The impact of pretrial publicity on jurors' verdicts. In R. J. Simon (Ed.), *The jury system in America: A critical overview* (pp. 123–139). Newbury Park, CA: Sage.

Ross, L., Lepper, M. R., & Hubbard, M. (1975). Perseverance in self-perception: Biased attributional processes in the debriefing paradigm. *Journal of Personality and Social Psychology, 32,* 880–892.

Skolnick, J. H. (1967). *Justice without trial: Law enforcement in a democratic society.* New York: Wiley.

Sue, S., Smith, R. E., & Caldwell, C. (1973). Effects of inadmissible evidence on the decisions of simulated jurors: A moral dilemma. *Journal of Applied Social Psychology, 3,* 345–353.

Wissler, R. L., & Saks, M. J. (1985). On the inefficacy of limiting instructions: When jurors use prior conviction evidence to decide on guilt. *Law and Human Behavior, 9,* 37–48.

4 Algebraic models of juror decision processes

Reid Hastie

The use of algebraic equations to describe mental processes has been common in psychology since the field became an empirical science. The earliest experimental psychologists utilized algebraic equations to describe the translation of physical stimulation into subjective experience (e.g., Fechner, 1860/1966). Today psychologists use equations to describe many aspects of thought and behavior, ranging from the most peripheral sensory processes of "early vision" to elaborate cognitive processes in problem solving and decision making.

The basic image of the decision maker according to the algebraic modeling approach is a "judgmental accountant" who converts all information relevant to a judgment into numbers representing the implications of each piece of evidence and the importance that should be accorded to each of them and then calculates a weighted sum to provide a "bottom line" evaluation. Benjamin Franklin advised his friends to make decisions using a "prudential algebra" and described it as an accountant tabulating credits and debits to determine the ultimate value of a course of action or choice alternative (in Bigelow, 1887, p. 522). Another image of this process is a physical device that determines the center of gravity of a balance beam from which hang weights (weight represents the implication or "scale value" of an item of evidence) that pull the beam down on the left or right (direction represents guilt or innocence) according to their location on the beam (distance from the fulcrum represents credibility, relevance, or importance of the evidence).

In the application to juror decisions, for example, if an eyewitness should identify the defendant as a person who was seen in the vicinity of a robbery, the juror would infer the implications of "presence at the scene" for guilt and then weight that implication by the apparent reliability of the witness. Or, a juror who hears testimony from a police officer that he observed a fight in which the defendant raised his arm over his head to stab down into the victim's chest would evaluate this assertion for its implications concerning the defendant's claim of self-defense and weight its implications by the credibility of the police officer (examples in this chapter refer to materials in the *Commonwealth v. Johnson* and *Commonwealth v. Bryant* cases summarized in the Appendix to Chapter 1 of this book). These algebraic models suppose that items of evidence which might come in any of several forms (e.g., the testimony of a witness, an exhibit, a demonstration, or even in a "nonevidentiary" argument from an attorney) are all converted into a common numerical metric representing their meanings on a single innocent–guilty continuum.

It is important to recognize the significance of the acceptance of a quantitative representation of the "meaning" of information such as the evidence presented at trial. Once we shift to numbers, we have implicitly conceded that operations on numbers are admissible models of mental processes. Historically, many early psychologists drew the line at the initial step to quantification of perceptions or judgments. For example, William James resisted the "quantification error" in research on perception and sensation: "our feeling of pink is surely not a portion of our feeling of scarlet; nor does the light of an electric arc seem to contain that of a tallow-candle in itself" (1890/1950, Volume 1, p. 546, see also Boring, 1963).

After the information has been converted into numbers, usually ranging from 0 (implies innocent) to 100 (implies guilty), the decision maker's thinking process is represented by algebraic calculations. On the surface these numbers may look like probabilities (researchers applying probabilistic models require responses on 0.0–1.0 or odds ratio scales, rather than 0–100 percentage scales), but the equation used to combine the values is not consistent with standard probability theories. Rather, each number representing a piece of information is weighted according to its perceived importance and relevance to the ultimate judgment and then all the weighted numbers are summed to yield a global average evidence value.

Actually two general types of algebraic information combination processes have been proposed in applications to jurors' decision making. The first represents the process by which the evidence is combined as a one-step calculation in which all of the sources of evidence are evaluated (on the innocent–guilty continuum) and then one global weighting and adding calculation is performed.

The second "sequential" algebraic model also supposes that the basic judgment process is a matter of weighting and adding the values of pieces of evidence. However, the sequential model assumes that the process operates repeatedly, calculating a current average value by weighting the past opinion (based on evidence received up to that point in time) and calculates a new opinion according to the perceived strength of implication of the most recent piece of evidence and the importance (weight) of the new information. The basic image of the sequential decision process is of movement of a frequently updated current opinion along a unitary innocent–guilty belief continuum.

The most comprehensive algebraic approaches to perception and judgment are associated with Information Integration Theory (Anderson, 1981, 1983) and with Social Judgment Theory founded on Brunswik's "probabilistic functionalism" and exemplified in the algebraic "Lens model" (Brehmer & Joyce, 1988; Brunswik, 1943; Hammond, 1966). Information Integration Theory and the Lens model are similar conceptually, although they differ on some principles of methodology, but they both conclude that a weighted average provides a valid description of human judgment in a variety of tasks. Some of Anderson's seminal developments of Information Theory described jurors' reasoning as a weighted averaging process (Anderson, 1959). Following Anderson's lead other researchers have used algebraic models to study juror decision making (e.g., Kaplan & Kemmerick, 1974; Kaplan & Miller, 1978; Ostrom, Werner, & Saks, 1978) and other aspects of legal judgment such as sentencing, bail-setting, and appellate review (e.g., Ebbesen & Konečni, 1975; McFatter, 1978; Nagel, 1962; Ulmer, 1963).

The basic weighted average model

Theorists applying the algebraic modeling approach conceptualize the task of the juror as involving the integration of conflicting information from several sources into a decision to convict or acquit the defendant in a criminal trial. The juror arrives at a degree of belief that the defendant is guilty based on the implications of relevant information and this belief is then compared with a decision criterion value representing an interpretation of the standard of proof (usually "beyond reasonable doubt"). If the strength of belief in the defendant's guilt is greater than the criterion, then the decision is to convict.

Several sources of information influence the juror's decision: testimony, observations of the defendant, preexisting biases, and other information at trial such as the judge's instructions, and attorneys' arguments. These sources of information are used to make inferences about the defendant's ability to commit the crime, his or her motivation, opportunity, character, and so on. These intermediate beliefs are then combined into a single judgment of strength of belief in the defendant's guilt. The basic combination rule applied to integrate the information is a weighted average of an initial opinion and information from the several sources identified above. For example, Ostrom, Werner, and Saks (1978; see also Kaplan & Kemmerick, 1974; Kaplan & Miller, 1978) expressed the weighted average using the following equation.

$$J = \frac{w_0 s_0 + \sum_{i=1}^{k} s_i w_i}{w_0 + \sum_{i=1}^{k} w_i} \tag{1}$$

In this equation J is the strength of belief in the defendant's guilt on the judgment dimension. J (in the Ostrom et al. formulation) is limited to values between 0 and 100, where 0 indicates strongest belief in innocence and 100 indicates strongest belief in guilt. The scale values of the initial disposition (s_0) and each information item (s_i) represent the positions of the items on the judgment dimension (ranging from 0 to 100) indicating each item's implications for guilt or innocence. In the typical application of this model, the value for each information item is assumed to be independent of other information item values even when combined. The weights (w's) are assigned to the initial disposition (w_0) and to each information item (w_i). In the context of a juror's judgment the initial disposition (s_0) and its weight (w_0) are interpreted as a numerical summary of the juror's initial presumption or beliefs concerning guilt or innocence prior to hearing any evidence. The initial weight (w_0) can be interpreted as representing the juror's degree of resistance to evidence at trial and his or her tendency to be rigid or unresponsive to evidence (i.e., if w_0 is large, the juror's prior beliefs, independent of the evidence, will exert a dominant influence on the juror's ultimate decision).

The w_i represent the importance of each information item for the required judgment, with k the number of information items considered by the juror. Note that the numerator of the equation is the weighted sum of the evidence item values and the denominator is the sum of the weights. The "absolute" weights (w_0 and w_i) are not constrained to values in the 0 to 1 interval, but the "relative" or "effective" weights (w_i/Sw_i) which determine the ultimate, measurable impact of each evidence item are constrained to the 0 to 1 interval and they will sum to one – this makes the final judgment a weighted *average* of the initial attitude (s_0) and the evidence item (s_i) values.

The standard assumption in applications of the weighted average model to juror judgment is that the absolute weight for a specific piece of evidence will be constant across different sets of evidence. However, the relative weight can vary as a function of other items of evidence in the set. Thus, for example, the witness who testifies about the defendant's presence in the neighborhood of a robbery will always receive a particular constant absolute weight (probably determined primarily by the witness credibility), but the relative weight might be very high (near one) if little other testimony was presented to the juror or very low (near zero) if much other important testimony (e.g., physical evidence linking the defendant to the crime) was also presented. This assumption of constant absolute weights and interdependent relative weights means that the model will predict realistic "configural" effects: The ultimate impact of any piece of evidence will vary depending on the context of other relevant evidence that is available. A medium important piece of evidence will have a dominant effect on the final decision when other evidence is unimportant, but it may have a minor effect when the other evidence is highly important. Such a principle can explain why a moderately strong prosecution case could dominate the final decision in the context of a weak defense case, but the same prosecution would be overwhelmed in the context of a strong defense.

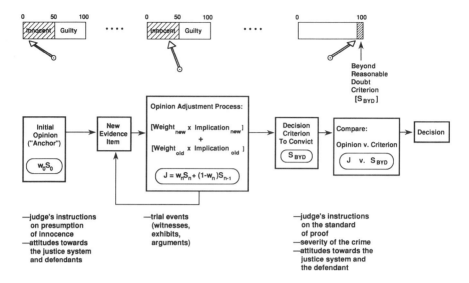

Figure 4.1. Algebraic weighted average model. The top panel of the diagram summarizes the operations of the model in terms of the mental opinion meter that indicates the juror's strength of belief in the defendant's guilt; the middle panel depicts the processing stages of the averaging model in terms of a flowchart diagram; and the bottom panel summarizes some of the types of information that are hypothesized to affect processing in each sub-stage of the model.

The Information Integration Theory framework separates the processing of evidence into two basic stages: valuation of evidence and then integration of evidence. Valuation involves the translation of semantic or physical information into a mental scale value (s_i) for each identifiable information item. Once the information item has been evaluated, s_i may be thought of as its psychological representation (Anderson, 1980). Integration is the subsequent process whereby the psychological representations (s_i) are combined to yield an overall response. The integration operation, for an averaging model, involves weighting each s_i according to its relevance to the judgment and then adding the weighted scale values (since the weights are required to sum to 1, the result is an average of the evidence item values). We would add a third process to the standard Information Integration model that involves the comparison of the ultimate belief to a decision criterion that is determined by the juror's individual views of the trial process and the judge's instructions on the standard of proof (usually "beyond reasonable doubt").

Figure 4.1 represents the Information Integration Theory, averaging rule, as a process (Anderson, 1980). The evaluation operation is represented by the function $V(e_i)$, and the integration operation is represented by the function $I(w(s_i))$ or the expanded weighted average equation for the term J (see Equation 1 on p. 86).

Research on input and valuation processes

An information item can be a single piece of evidence expressed in a sentence (Ostrom et al., 1978); a larger set of statements that are evidential contrasted with a set of statements that are nonevidential (Kaplan & Kemmerick, 1974); a set of statements relating to a molar conceptual component of the case (e.g., all statements with implications for the defendant's opportunity to commit the crime; Kaplan, 1977); or the conclusion of an inference formed earlier in the integration process (e.g., an attribution of responsibility based on information about the foreseeability of an outcome; Kaplan, 1975). Each information item is evaluated for its implication on the dimension of judgment, in this case, a unidimensional judgment scale ranging from 0 (certain innocence) to 100 (certain guilt). The output of the evaluation operation is a single value attached to each evidence item, which could be called its "probative value" (Kaplan, 1975; Ostrom et al., 1978; Wigmore, 1937).

Most of the tests of algebraic models in juror decision making tasks have been conducted using the Functional Measurement methods associated with the Information Integration tradition (Anderson, 1981). A factorial analysis of variance experimental design is used to plan the experimental conditions. In a typical design, stimulus cases are constructed in which evidence items are the independent variables with their values manipulated to vary the psychological scale values of each designated component of the evidence. For example, a generic evidence item associated with opportunity to commit a crime (e.g., a witness testifies that the defendant was seen in the neighborhood in which a burglary occurred), might be varied experimentally so that its value would be high (close to 100, implicating guilt) or low (close to 0, implicating innocence). The outcome dependent variable measure would be the juror's rated strength of belief in guilt or a judgment of strength of evidence in favor of guilt (on a 0 to 100 scale).

Several experiments have studied the effects of varying the values of information items within and across case types. For example, items were constructed to imply high versus low incrimination value by the information presented (Kaplan, 1977; Kaplan & Kemmerick, 1974; Ostrom et al., 1978) and positive versus negative descriptions of the defendant's character (Kaplan & Kemmerick, 1974). The averaging model predicts that the scale values of evidence items will combine linearly under the assumption that weights are constant over stimulus manipulations; that is, the scale values for information items are independent and should show no interaction in different combinations. This prediction has been supported by one study in which two information sets were varied simultaneously (Kaplan & Kemmerick, 1974). In this study the change in the increment in the judgment of guilt due to a change in the incriminating value of evidential information was the same for persons described by desirable or undesirable characteristics.

To our knowledge, only one experiment has rigorously attempted to estimate scale values and evidence item weights. Ostrom et al. (1978) constructed stimulus sets that varied in set size (containing 1, 3, or 6 items) and were composed of items at two levels of incrimination value. Assumptions about the constancy of weights across incrimination value and set size allowed parameters s_0, s_h (high scale value items), s_l (low scale values), w_0 and w_h/w_l to be estimated from the subjects' judgments. As predicted, the estimated incrimination values for the high incrimination sets of evidence items were greater than those for the low incrimination sets, although both were unexpectedly high. Ostrom et al. also concluded that differences between cases (rape, murder, and theft) could be effectively summarized by differences in the scale value and weight parameters.

One perennial problem for the application of algebraic process models to a naturally occurring event such as a trial is the specification of information items. Typically this problem has been solved in laboratory paradigms (like the Kaplan and Ostrom et al. experiments) by constructing abbreviated legal cases in which it makes intuitive sense to consider sentences or sets of sentences as items. But the claim that the meaning of any item of information (its scale value) will be the same no matter what other pieces of evidence are presented seems untenable if we think about evidence in a realistic trial situation. For example, testimony about a defendant's cautious behavior before entering a bar implies one conclusion in the context of evidence that he is afraid to encounter a patron of the bar who previously had threatened him and another conclusion given evidence that he and a companion had been searching for the other patron earlier in the day. Or, evidence about possession of a concealed deadly weapon implies one conclusion if we know the defendant is a fisherman who usually carries a knife and another conclusion if we know that he rarely carries a knife (see the *Commonwealth v. Johnson* case summary in the Appendix to Chapter 1 of this book).

A proponent of the weighted averaging, cognitive algebra approach would argue that the general form of the model is not expected to account for fine-grained semantic effects (as in the "cautious behavior before entering the bar" example). But, care needs to be exercised in any application of the model to choose the appropriate breakdown of a realistically complicated corpus of evidence into pieces that preserve the model's assumption of independence of meaning.

Another limit on current algebraic applications is the assumption that the valuation dimension can be represented by a single, interval scale labeled degree of guiltiness, probability of guilt, or strength of evidence for guilt. This simplification of the judgment task is unrealistic when we attempt to apply the model to the juror's task in real courtroom trials. For example, typically, there are at least four attributes or dimensions that must be specified to define any criminal behavior: identity, actions, attendant circumstances, and mental state (J. Kaplan, 1978). The separability of these dimensions is illustrated by the fact that in many real cases there is complete agreement among jurors about one or more of the dimensions, but disagreement on others. For example, the jurors may agree that the defendant was the robber (identity), but disagree about whether or not it was legally an armed robbery (actions).

Proponents of the algebraic approach would postulate that the single ultimate dimension representing global guiltiness is itself inferred as the result of an averaging process performed on the individual component judgments each inferred by a sub- (averaging) process. A multistage integration process of this type has been developed by Anderson and Farkas (1975) in research on attributions of responsibility and Lopes (this book) outlines an application to juror decision making. Furthermore, Oden (1977, 1979) has provided examples of how the cognitive algebra approach can be combined with fuzzy set theory to model human classification judgments with multiattribute categories. Thus, although the multidimensional representation of evidence implications and a multiattribute category classification model have not yet been applied to juror decision tasks, appropriate process models are already available in the algebraic modeling approach.

Evidence integration processes

In the weighted averaging model the integration process consists of two stages. First, each evaluated item (received from the preceding evaluation process) is assigned a weight according to its importance relative to other evidence items. The importance weight has been interpreted as reflecting the perceived credibility of a witness, the admissibility or relevance of evidence as indicated by the trial judge, the persuasiveness of the witness, etc. (Himmelfarb, 1975; Kaplan, 1977; Kaplan & Kemmerick, 1974). Thus, the weighting stage subprocess can be further divided into its ingredient components including sub-subprocesses such as the selection of evidence for admissibility and evaluation for credibility.

Some trial procedures would be expected to influence the weight assigned to an information item leaving the evaluation of the information for its implications concerning guilt or innocence unaffected. For example, when the judge instructs a juror on how to use trial evidence (e.g., only to assess credibility) or to disregard evidence (give it a weight of zero) these instructions would not be expected to affect the implications of the evidence for incrimination, but should affect the jurors' weighting of particular evidence items.

All applications of the averaging model predict that an increase or decrease in the influence of any item or set of information should be interpreted as a change of its weight. Kaplan and Kemmerick (1974) varied instructions to jurors about how to use information about the character of the defendant. Kaplan (1977) varied information provided to jurors about the reliability of pieces of evidence. However, neither study obtained results that could be unequivocally interpreted as weighting process effects.

In the Ostrom et al. (1978) study, the weighting parameters for initial disposition (w_0) and evidence items (w_i) were empirically estimated. Ostrom et al. assumed that weights were constant for high and low incrimination evidence sets and that a weight assigned to a single evidence item alone was equivalent to the weight assigned to that item within a larger set. Empirical support was obtained for the first assumption (constant weights), thus lending indirect support to the psychological interpretation of the subprocesses involved in valuation and weighting stages. However, this conclusion must be qualified by noting that evidence items were carefully chosen (by the experimenters) to maintain their incriminating, probative impact independent of set size or the content of other evidence items in the set.

The second subprocess in the integration stage is the actual combination of the weighted scale values of evidence items. In the averaging model the scale values are multiplied by their respective weights, summed, and then divided by the total weight (the sum of the weights for all of the individual items). The result is a single value representing the subjective degree of guilt or probability of guilt. The integration operation can introduce a confusion between two types of weights: The raw absolute weights represented directly in the model as w's and the effective relative weights which, for each item, depend on the weights of the other items entered into the calculation. Thus, when we refer to the assumption of weight constancy in some applications we mean the absolute w's, but we allow the ultimate effective weight of any individual evidence item to vary if other items' weights increase or decrease.

The decision criterion

Applications of the averaging model in the Information Integration framework have typically concluded with the subject's rating on innocent–guilty on a single judgment dimension as the primary dependent variable. We know of no applications of the weighted averaging model that include the "categorical" convict–acquit decision required of an actual juror. Ostrom et al. (1978) proposed that the juror performs a final step in the judgment process by comparing his or her strength of belief in the defendant's guilt to a decision criterion that represents the beyond-reasonable-doubt standard associated with a criminal verdict. To our knowledge, the full process model including evidence evaluation, integration, and comparison to a decision criterion has not been applied. But, in addition to the models of the evidence evaluation and integration processes, there are numerous applications of the algebraic approach to estimate values for the decision criterion (see review below).

The sequential averaging model

The second algebraic model, closely related to the basic averaging model we have just reviewed, is the sequential averaging model. Here the juror's

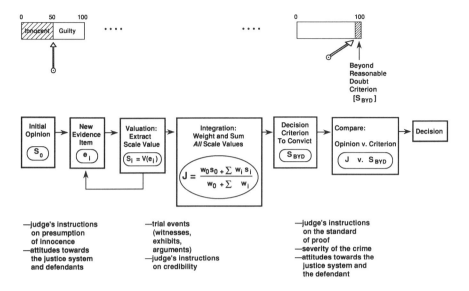

Figure 4.2. Algebraic sequential averaging model. Three parts of the diagram (top to bottom): (a) "opinion meter"; (b) flowchart of processing stages; (c) information relevant at each stage.

decision process is conceptualized as a series of opinion changes rather than as one global integration process (Anderson, 1959; Weld & Danzig, 1940; Weld & Roff, 1938). The trial is treated as a sequential judgment task in which a series of judgments is produced, each based on a combination of the juror's previous judgment and his or her response to new evidence. Opinion change takes place over the course of the trial as the result of many responses to individual pieces of evidence.

The proposed combination rule (Anderson, 1959) represents each new opinion as a linear function of an old opinion, the value of a new piece of evidence, and the weight assigned to the new piece of evidence:

$$J_i = J_{i-1} + w_i(s_i - J_{i-1}) \tag{2}$$

Most of the assumptions of the sequential model are similar to those of the basic weighted average process model. J_{i-1} is the juror's opinion before receiving the new evidence (expressed on a numerical scale of belief that the defendant is guilty, e.g., 0 = certainly innocent and 100 = certainly guilty); J_i is the juror's judgment after the presentation of the new evidence; s_i is the scale value of the evidence on the innocent–guilty scale; and w_i is the weight assigned to each item of evidence (see Figure 4.2).

Although we initially expressed the model (Equation 2) as a sequential operator, it can be rewritten:

$$J_i = (1 - w_i)J_{i-1} + w_i s_i \tag{3}$$

In this form, it is easily seen that the model is equivalent to a special form of the weighted averaging model with weights that sum to 1 applied recursively to integrate new information and the previous judgment. In a sense this is a cumulative or "running" average process that retains a summary of all prior reasoning in a single current average value. It should also be apparent that the process implied by this form of the model is similar to the sequential belief updating process of the Bayesian model. The major difference between sequential weighted averaging and Bayesian processes is the specific computation that is required to adjust a current belief: algebraically additive for the weighted average and algebraically multiplicative for the Bayesian process.

The major differences between the general averaging model and the sequential averaging model concern the sequential averaging model's distinction between processes occurring at different points in time (cf., Figures 4.1 and 4.2). As in the basic weighted averaging model the definition of an information item varies in different applications. But, in the sequential averaging model, the unit of evidence that is subject to valuation is restricted to an item or set of items of evidence that occur contiguously in real time. This time-dependent characterization of processing adds constraints, that are absent from the more general averaging model framework, on what will be counted as an evidence item when the model is applied.

As in the general averaging model, the evaluation operation has been interpreted as the assignment of a single scale value representing certainty in the defendant's guilt or strength of the implication of the item of evidence for guilt or innocence. Thus, again, the multidimensionality of the legal concept of guilt is not represented in the model. This poses a major conceptual problem for the sequential averaging model because in a real trial jurors are often unaware of the specific dimensions of judgment that they will be required to apply until after all the evidence has been presented when they hear the judge's instructions concerning the specific verdicts available. Sometimes the pivotal issues for the juror's decision are apparent from the onset. For example, in some cases the perpetrator's identity is the central issue and the jurors know from the attorneys' opening statements that "Who dun it?" will be the central question they must answer (see the *Commonwealth v. Bryant* case summarized in the Appendix to Chapter 1 of this book). However, in many cases the critical questions that must be addressed by the factfinder are not obvious until the end of the trial (see the *Commonwealth v. Johnson* case summarized in the Appendix to Chapter 1 of this book in which central issues concerning the defendant's state of mind and the conditions for a self-defense verdict are not known by the jurors in advance of the evidence). In these cases, it is difficult to see how the "running guiltiness score" form of reasoning implied by the sequential weighting model could apply as a description of the juror's decision process; because the relevant questions or dimensions of judgment are not known by the juror until the judge instructs the jury on the law. It is difficult to understand how a single dimension of judgment could apply both before and after the judge instructs the jurors concerning "what is to be judged."

In the sequential model, the initial disposition of a juror towards guilt or innocence is represented by the first judgment before any evidence is received: $J_0 = w_0 s_0$. The weighting operation occurs for each evaluated item of information separately. On each updating cycle, two weights are active, one assigned to the new input and the other (complementary) weight assigned to the immediate past judgment summarizing all of the prior judgments made up to that point in time. The weighting reflects the relative impact of new information compared to the immediate past opinion; with the complementary "raw" weights constrained to sum to 1. Again, as in the basic averaging model the weight of the new information is determined primarily by the credibility of its source (witness), relevance to the judgment, and instructions from the judge concerning admissibility. In most applications of the sequential averaging model, the "raw" weights associated with the new and immediate past inputs are assumed to be constant. This means the order of input of items will affect not only the intermediate judgments but the final judgment as well.

Typically, the weights have been selected or estimated to yield predicted recency effects (on the "effective" weights that would describe the ultimate judgment when the sequential process terminates). For example, if two communications, one implying guilt, one implying innocence, are presented, a recency effect is predicted such that the final judgment would favor innocence – the reverse order of evidence would reverse the direction of the final judgment. The magnitude of the recency effect is predicted to increase as the weight assigned to the early evidence decreases and the distance between the implications of the two pieces of evidence increases. Order effects have often been found in jurors' judgments of evidence, although they have not consistently exhibited a recency pattern (Walker, Thibaut, & Andreoli, 1972; cf., Hogarth & Einhorn, 1992).

Application of the sequential averaging model has been associated with a particular research method in which mock jurors are asked to give cumulative successive judgments over the course of a trial (e.g., after each piece of evidence is presented). Individual judgments or average judgments are then examined over the course of time, either summarized graphically or captured by fitting the algebraic model. The average evidence item scale values (s) and weights (w) may be estimated by considering the mean change in judgment between successive judgments ($J_i - J_{i-1}$) as a function of the initial opinion ($J_0 = s_0$; see Anderson, 1959, p. 378). However, Anderson's results suggested that the valuation and weights assigned to evidence over the course of a trial were not constant. He found that later in the trial there was a decreased responsiveness to new information, so the same piece of evidence presented early in the trial would change the judgment more than identical evidence presented late in the trial.

We will not try to resolve the complex question of what sequential weighting pattern best describes the impact of statements, evidence, and arguments on juror decisions. Our own research suggests that a juror often constructs a summary of the evidence in his or her memory and then reviews that summary to make a final decision, the form of that knowledge structure in the juror's memory will predict the impact of individual items of information on his or her decision. Thus, order of presentation will affect the final decision indirectly through its effect on the form of the mediating knowledge structure. If one side of a case has an advantage in controlling the form of the juror's memory of the evidence or if one side presents its witnesses and arguments in an order that promotes their inclusion in the juror's memory, then that side will have an advantage in the ultimate decision. Pennington and Hastie (1987, 1991) have presented empirical demonstrations of substantial evidence order effects on verdict decisions that are consistent with this interpretation of "order of proof" phenomena (see Chapter 8 of this book). This interpretation of order effects in terms of knowledge structures points to a limit on the algebraic approach with its tendency to postulate abbreviated quantitative mental representations (but see Hogarth & Einhorn, 1992, for an algebraic theory of complex order effects).

Assessment of juror and judge applications of the standard of proof and presumption of innocence

A good example of a legal procedure that can be elucidated by empirical research concerns how instructions on the presumption of innocence, burden of proof, and standards of proof are comprehended and applied by jurors. We will focus on the juror's decision, but the same issues arise in the trial judge's exercise of discretion about matters such as whether to admit certain types of evidence (e.g., confessions) or to set aside a jury verdict, as well as in appellate review, and even in the conduct of police officers (e.g., decisions concerning search and seizure or arrest). (Rather than providing a lengthy list of citations to this large area of legal scholarship, we will refer the interested reader to a few reviews that provide detailed references: Ball, 1961; McBaine, 1944, 1954; McCauliff, 1982; Shapiro, 1986; Underwood, 1977.)

The issue of whether or not the standard of proof and other related procedural criteria refer to objective conditions in the real world or to subjective states in the decision maker's mind has been raised repeatedly over the course of jury history. Most modern authorities accept a subjective "strength of conviction" in the mind of the juror interpretation. However, there are traces of early procedures in which the judge was viewed as functioning to insure that sufficient quantities of objective evidence were provided to prove disputed issues or charges. For example, as recently as the seventeenth century, two "good witnesses or a confession" were required for "full proof" in a criminal case, while a single witness with an interest in the outcome of the case was only a one-quarter fraction of legal proof (see Daston, 1987, p. 296; Morano, 1975; Shapiro, 1986, p. 155; Waldman, 1959; Wigmore, 1901). More recently, the notion of probability as a relative frequency of objectively observed events in well-defined categories could be interpreted as an objective foundation for standards of proof (Gigerenzer, et al., 1989). And, some labels (e.g., "preponderance of the evidence") used to define standards of proof are reminders of the former objective interpretation.

A second issue, the usefulness of quantitative versus verbal definitions of presumptions and standards, is currently the focus of heated disputes between advocates of mathematical models and statistical evidence (e.g., Fienberg & Schervish, 1986; Finkelstein & Fairley, 1970; Kaye, 1979; Koehler & Shaviro, 1990; Saks & Kidd, 1980) and advocates of traditional courtroom rituals and nonmathematical instructions and procedures (e.g., Nesson, 1979, 1985; Tribe, 1971a, 1971b). The scope of the disputes between mathematical and traditional advocates is too broad for complete resolution with empirical findings; many of the central issues invoke historical, moral, and philosophical considerations (cf., Goodpaster, 1987). But we believe specific questions concerning juror comprehension of procedural instructions can be answered by applying the algebraic models and measurement techniques discussed below. Even general questions such as those concerning the aspects of the jury trial that make verdicts "acceptable" to the citizenry, would seem to be sharpened and possibly resolved by the application of (empirical) operational definitions and the measurement of concepts such as "acceptability" (e.g., MacCoun & Tyler, 1988).

In our view, the algebraic analysis is extremely useful in providing precise definitions of key concepts for the scholar, the policy maker, the practitioner, and even the juror. The juror's reasoning is represented as movement along a unitary dimension, a dimension that is associated with numbers that can be entered into algebraic calculations, representing the strength of belief in the defendant's guilt or the subjective probability of guilt. Concepts like the "presumption of innocence" that refer to an initial belief state and "beyond reasonable doubt" that refers to a decision criterion sufficient to render a categorical judgment (e.g., guilty–innocent of the charge of first degree murder) are defined as locations on the underlying dimension. Furthermore, the algebraic representation does not appear to distort everyday and legal concepts; to the extent these concepts are coherent and precise, they already employ quantitative metaphors (e.g., *beyond* reasonable doubt, *weight* of the evidence, etc.).

The algebraic approach also comes with useful methods to define, measure, and compare individuals' beliefs about these concepts (e.g., Mosteller & Youtz, 1990; Wallsten, Budescu, Rapoport, Zwick, & Forsyth, 1986). It seems parochial to reject the findings from a sophisticated tradition of empirical analysis, to rely exclusively on the intuitions of law school faculty members to reach conclusions about how jurors and other citizens perform the juror's task or evaluate reports of jury decisions.

Presumption of innocence

The American notion of judicial fairness includes the principle that innocence should be presumed until substantial evidence has been presented to imply guilt. To promote this form of fairness, jurors are given a preliminary instruction to presume innocence. A popular evidence text describes the presumption of innocence as "simply another way of stating the rule that the prosecution has the burden of proving the guilt of the accused" (Cleary, 1972, p. 829). However, the details of the operation of a presumption are complex and there are many disputes about exactly which instructions are true presumptions and what theory describes the essential concept of presumption. Probably the most popular notion is that a presumption is a rule that assigns the burden of producing evidence to one side or the other and, absent the required evidence, prescribes "permissible inferences" that should be made by the factfinder (e.g., infer the defendant is innocent, unless the prosecution presents a substantial case to the contrary). After the required evidence has been produced, the presumption is "spent and disappears" like a "bursting soap bubble."

The application of algebraic models to juror decision making can clarify what the presumption of innocence instruction might mean in terms of the overall decision process summarized in Equation 1 (above). Four distinct views have emerged from various interpretations of the instruction, each of which can be described in terms of the initial belief terms in Equation 1 (w_0 and s_0; Ostrom, Werner, & Saks, 1978).

The most common interpretation of fairness with regards to testing hypotheses is to assume that all tenable hypotheses are equally probable in the absence of relevant evidence. In the context of a binary guilty–innocent decision, this would mean assigning an initial .50 probability of guilt (s_0 equal to .50). Most of the empirical studies provide evidence for subjects' initial inclination to distribute uncertainty approximately in a 50–50 manner between guilty–innocent options, at least as expressed in marks near the midpoint of a judgment rating scale (Anderson, 1959; Helgeson & Shaver, 1990; Kaplan, 1977; Kassin & Wrightsman, 1979; Weld & Danzig, 1940; Weld & Roff, 1938) or by assigning guilt–innocent initial odds in a 1:1 ratio (Martin & Schum, 1987) at the beginning of the decision process. However, we should note that only two of these studies (Helgeson & Shaver, 1990 and Kassin & Wrightsman, 1979) included an explicit instruction on the "presumption of innocence." Kassin and Wrightsman (1979) also varied the timing of the presumption instruction and concluded that the major impact, when presented at the beginning of the trial, was on the initial opinion anchor (s_0) of the jurors' judgments and not on subsequent evidence scale values or weights.

A second interpretation assigns preevidence beliefs or probabilities according to the relevant baserates for events such as convictions in criminal courts (e.g., an s_0 equal to .80). Exactly which baserate is relevant is such a difficult question that many would simply assume maximum ignorance and use the uniform (.50–.50) prior assignment, as in the first interpretation (cf., Keren, 1984; Levi, 1977). However, although no published study reports empirical data in support of a baserate initial probability; research by the author has uncovered a nonnegligible number of mock-juror citizen subjects who justify ratings of initial beliefs about guilt–innocence in terms of their personal estimates of ultimate conviction rates.

A third view would interpret "presume innocent" as an initial probability or strength of belief in guilt at or close to zero (s_0 equal to 0). Ostrom, Werner, and Saks (1978; Saks, Werner, & Ostrom, 1975) reported the results of a carefully-crafted study of preevidence opinions that were consistent with this interpretation (the estimated average prior probabilities of guilt for 3 criminal cases were equal to about .003).

A final view of "presume innocent" would interpret the phrase as an instruction to disregard any opinions held before the first item of relevant evidence is encountered (i.e., to assign a value of zero to w_0). To our knowledge, this interpretation has not received empirical support in any research on juror decision processes, although it seems to be closest in meaning to the legal "bursting bubble" interpretation of the burden of production of an affirmative case by the prosecutor or plaintiff.

Several researchers have entertained the hypothesis that individual differences in the harshness of jurors' verdict decisions can be explained and predicted by their initial beliefs about defendants' guilt. Kaplan (1977) and Kaplan and Miller (1978) separated mock jurors into lenient versus harsh groups on the basis of their general attitudes toward the legal system. Kaplan concluded that an individual difference in harshness (predicted by a questionnaire assessing attitudes toward the justice system) could be "localized" in jurors' predisposition (s_0) to favor guilt or innocence before hearing any of the evidence. Ostrom et al. (1978) used a similar questionnaire approach to separate their subjects into prodefendant versus antidefendant mock jurors. Then, results for the two "types" of subjects were analyzed separately and parameters from the algebraic models were compared. Ostrom et al. (1978) concluded that their prodefendant versus antidefendant jurors differed in the manner in which they weighted the evidence, with jurors favoring the defendant weighting exonerating evidence more heavily than incriminating, with the reverse pattern of weights for the antidefendant mock jurors. The resolution of the apparent conflict between Kaplan and Ostrom is probably that the two types of jurors have a propensity to differ on both their predispositions toward guilt or innocence *and* in the manner in which they weight evidence.

Weld and Danzig (1940) and Weld and Roff (1938) in applications of the sequential averaging model distinguished among individual jurors on the basis of the profiles of their changes of opinion across the sequence of evidence presentation. For example, Weld and Roff examined the judgment patterns of twelve mock jurors whom they considered representative of different subgroups in their larger experimental sample. They identified four judgment profiles that differentiated among jurors: (A) the degree to which a conservative (not guilty) attitude is maintained until late in the sequence of evidence; (B) the degree to which a juror is responsive to new evidence; (C) the degree to which new evidence is balanced in comparison to previous evidence; (D) the degree to which the most recent old evidence influences new evidence. However, after identifying these patterns, Weld and his colleagues did not attempt to apply them to predict or explain additional judgments.

The representation of alternate views of the "presumption" in algebraic terms appears to be extremely productive. We know of no discussion of interpretations or applications that is comparable in conceptual clarity or referential unambiguity to those utilizing the algebraic metaphor. Furthermore the algebraic approach provides empirical methods that can be applied to assess its meaning in the minds of jurors (and other individuals). Granted, the sparse applications to date have been in relatively "low fidelity" simulations of the juror's decision task, but, the empirical methods are readily applicable to richer, naturally-occurring judgment tasks. There is also an intriguing disagreement between laboratories and methods; the Ostrom, Werner, and Saks (1978) estimates are close to 0.0 while all others are near .50. But, thanks to the algebraic approach, the points of disagreement are clear and there is hope for resolution by empirical studies of jurors' reasoning processes, rather than by consulting the miscellaneous ruminations of scholars and other interested parties.

Standard of proof

In the American justice system, the assignment of the burden of proof and a higher standard of proof to the prosecution (and plaintiff) is a further safeguard of the defendant against false conviction. Among policy makers, legal authorities have exhibited remarkable sophistication about the management of error in practical affairs. For example, the Supreme Court has described the trial process as inevitably uncertain, thereby forcing a direct consideration of the two types of error that will occur and the specification of institutions that will distribute the errors appropriately: "Where one party has at stake an interest in transcending value – as a criminal defendant his liberty – this margin of error is reduced as to him by the process of placing on the other party the burden . . . of persuading the factfinder at the conclusion of the trial of his guilt beyond a reasonable doubt" (*Speiser v. Randall*, 1958, p. 525; see also the definitive *in re Winship*, 1970, decision).

The concept of "beyond reasonable doubt," the standard applied to the prosecution in most criminal matters, is difficult to define clearly. A variety of standard verbal instructions have accumulated in the literature of pattern instructions. For example, in Colorado (Colorado Supreme Court Committee on Criminal Jury Instructions, 1983, p. 35):

The burden of proof is upon the prosecution to prove to the satisfaction of the jury beyond a reasonable doubt the existence of all of the elements necessary to constitute the crime charged.

Reasonable doubt means a doubt based upon reason and common sense which arises from a fair and rational consideration of all the evidence, or the lack of evidence, in the case. It is doubt which is not vague, speculative or imaginary doubt, but such doubt as would cause reasonable people to hesitate to act in matters of importance to themselves.

But the communication of a precise, unambiguous meaning of the standard of proof to jurors is a notoriously impossible task (Elwork, Sales & Alfini, 1982; Severance & Loftus, 1982).

As in the case of research on the presumption of innocence, we believe that the algebraic representation clarifies the meaning of the standard of proof instructions. The metaphorical *beyond* in the standard instruction is certainly intended to evoke a geometric image. Indeed, research on the effects of variations in the form of instructions to jurors has found, to date, that only references to a quantitative standard have sensible and reliable effects on mock-jurors' performance (Kagehiro, 1990). In the present context we will focus on various methods that have been applied to estimate numerical values for the point on the judgment continuum that represents the decision criterion assumed in the algebraic models.

Direct rating methods. The obvious method to use to elicit quantitative values for a decision criterion is to ask subjects to express this value directly through ratings on a meaningful numerical scale. The earliest study of this type (that we discovered), Simon (1969), asked subjects to respond with a rating of the number of chances out of ten to indicate: "What would the likelihood or probability have to be that a defendant committed the act for you to decide that he is guilty?" (p. 107). Other researchers have asked similar questions of samples of students, citizens, and judges, and the responses to these questions, concerning the two most common standards "beyond reasonable doubt" and "preponderance of the evidence," from all of the studies we were able to uncover are summarized in Table 4.1. In all of these studies subjects were provided one version or another of a beyond-reasonable-doubt instruction, usually in the context of a specific case summary, and asked to make a rating on a numerical scale to indicate their decision criterion. Different studies and different methods elicited a variety of average ratings from the subjects; for example, estimates of the beyond-reasonable-doubt standard in criminal cases ranged from .51 to .92.

It is important to note that in none of these studies was extensive practice given to subjects with the rating scale, and ratings of likelihoods or probabilities are notoriously variable (see Anderson, 1982, for a useful discussion of rating scales methods and algebraic modeling). Furthermore, the values presented in the table are *averages* on the probability scale and the examination of distributions of individual responses (in the few studies

Table 4.1. *Direct ratings of standard of proof (all expressed on 0.0–1.00 probability scale)*

Study	Subjects	Prepon-derance of evidence	Beyond reasonable doubt
Simon (1969)	Judges	.61	.89
Simon & Mahan (1971)	Citizens	.77	.79
	Students	.76	.89
Kerr, Atkin, Stasser, Meek, Holt, & Davis (1976)	Students		
Stringent criterion instruction		–	.87
Lax criterion instruction		–	.82
Undefined criterion instruction		–	.82
US v. Fatico (1978, Weinstein memorandum) (also "Clear and convincing," .67; and "Clear, unequivocal, and convincing," .74)	Judges	.51	.86
Kassin & Wrightsman (1979)	Students	–	.87
McCauliff (1982) (also "Clear and convincing," .75; and others)	Judges	.55	.90
Hastie, Penrod, & Pennington (1983)	Citizens	–	.92
Cowan, Thompson, & Ellsworth (1984)	Citizens	–	.86
MacCoun (1984)	Students		
Continuous scale		.68	.67
Interval (0, 1, …, 10) scale		.68	.69
Odds ratio scale		.49	.51
Dane (1985)	Students	–	.66
Kerr, Bull, MacCoun, & Rathburn (1985)	Students	–	.79
Kagehiro (1986)	Students	.82	.91
Martin & Schum (1987) Odds ratio scale	Students	–	.91
MacCoun & Kerr (1988) (reported in MacCoun, 1987)	Students	–	.87
	Citizens	–	.83
	Students	.69	.81
Kagehiro (1990)	Students	–	.81–.91

that provide them) yield clear evidence that there are several distinctive response "modes" for each standard of proof. For example, Blackstone's famous maxim on the criminal standard of proof, "it is better that ten guilty persons escape than one innocent suffer" (1769/1962, Book IV, p. 27), would translate into a criterion for conviction of .91, which is one (among several) modal response.

Table 4.2. *Indirect methods – "parallel ranking"*
(all expressed on 0.0–1.00 probability scale)

Study	Subjects	Prepon-derance of evidence	Beyond reasonable doubt
Simon (1970)	Students	–	.70
MacCoun (1984)	Students	.53	.56
Dane (1985)	Students	–	.72

Parallel ranking method. In one of the earliest published reports of a study that assigned numerical values to the decision criterion, Simon (1970) introduced an ingenious method of indirectly estimating a decision criterion. Two independent groups of subjects made judgments after listening to an audiotaped homicide trial; one group made a dichotomous guilty–innocent verdict judgment and the other half of the subjects rated the probability that the defendant committed the crime. The ratings were ranked from highest to lowest and the minimum value for the decision criterion ("beyond reasonable doubt") was obtained by counting down the probability ratings to the rank number corresponding to the proportion of guilty verdicts obtained in the dichotomous decision condition. (A maximum value was also obtained by counting *up* through the ranks. There was a gap between the two estimates, .70–.74, and we provide the minimum value in Table 4.2.) The same method can be applied within-subjects, by asking each subject to make both a probability of guilt judgment and a guilty–innocent dichotomous decision. Dane (1985) and MacCoun (1984) applied the rank order method within-subjects and the resulting estimates are reported in Table 4.2.

A comparison between the direct ratings (Table 4.1) and the rank order method estimates (Table 4.2) suggests that the values obtained from the rank order method tend to be lower than from the direct rating method. Of course, all of the rank order estimates were obtained from students, while the direct ratings were from a more varied sample. However, if we confine our attention to studies of students, the direct ratings are still consistently higher than estimates obtained with the parallel ranking method. We will return to this issue of "rating method effects" in our discussion below.

Decision theory-based methods. The third approach to eliciting numerical values for a decision criterion involves the application of equations derived from decision theory (Luce & Raiffa, 1957; von Neumann & Morgenstern, 1947). Although there are earlier precedents, Kaplan's classic paper (1968) should probably be credited as the seminal source of decision theory applications to the law. There has been a strong reaction to Kaplan's application of decision theory to the juror's fact-finding process (e.g., Tribe, 1971a, 1971b). But, without joining that debate, we will summarize applications of the decision theory approach to estimate numerical values; and discuss the assumptions about juror decision processes that are necessary to take the decision theory estimates seriously. (N.B.: the judgment process model underlying the decision theory approach is algebraic, but different in form from the averaging models we have reviewed in this chapter. We include the decision theory approach for completeness of coverage of the empirical findings concerning the juror's decision criterion. The interested reader should consult the chapters in this book by Schum and Schum & Martin for more detail on the Bayesian judgment model associated with decision theory.)

The decision theory approach characterizes the judgment facing the juror as a problem of how to choose between verdicts to maximize personal satisfaction ("utility") with the mix of uncertain outcomes contingent on conviction or acquittal. Thus, a juror must weight the types of error (convict an innocent defendant, acquit a guilty defendant) associated with each verdict by their perceived probabilities of occurrence. As in the previous algebraic approaches, this is a type of weighted average, but in the decision theory formulation considerations of the satisfaction or utility of the outcome are paramount, while in the earlier averaging model equations, only the implications of evidence for guilt or innocence were the explicit considerations.

There are several variations on the basic equation used to derive a decision criterion in terms of a probability value from numbers representing the utilities and disutilities associated with possible outcomes of a trial decision (Connolly, 1987; Cullison, 1977; Fried, Kaplan, & Klein, 1975; Grofman, 1981; Milanich, 1981; Nagel & Neef, 1979; Tribe, 1971a, 1971b; and others). All of the equations assume that a rational decision maker will convict if and only if the expected utility of convicting is greater than the expected utility of acquitting. The calculation of these ultimate utilities requires assigning probabilities and personal values (elementary utilities) to four events: convicting a guilty defendant, acquitting an innocent defendant, convicting an innocent defendant, and acquitting a guilty defendant. The probabilities cancel out in the proposed equations so that the estimate of the decision criterion (a probability) can be isolated on the left-hand side of an equation with only utilities or personal values on the right-hand side. Fried et al.'s formula is representative:

$$\text{Decision Criterion} = \frac{\text{Utility (Acquit Innocent)} - \text{Utility (Convict Innocent)}}{\begin{array}{c}\text{Utility (Acquit Innocent)} - \text{Utility (Convict Innocent)} \\ + \text{Utility (Convict Guilty)} - \text{Utility (Acquit Guilty)}\end{array}} \quad (4)$$

A common simplification is to assume that the absolute values of the utility and disutility of related correct and erroneous decisions are equal, and the equation becomes

Table 4.3. *Indirect methods – decision theory calculation (all expressed on 0.0–1.00 probability scale)*

Study	Subjects	Preponderance of evidence	Beyond reasonable doubt
Nagel, Lamm, & Neef (1981)	Students	–	.55
Nagel (1979)	Students		
No instruction		–	.60
Beyond reasonable doubt instruction		–	.68
.90 probability instruction		–	.80
"10-to-1 Blackstone error ratio" instruc.		–	.90
MacCoun (1984)	Students	.52	.56
MacCoun (1984) ("Blackstone ratio")	Students	.48	.51
Thompson, Cowan, Ellsworth, & Harrington (1984) (calculated by author)	Citizens		
Prodeath penalty citizens		–	.50
Antideath penalty citizens		–	.58
Dane (1985)	Students	–	.52
MacCoun & Kerr (1988) (reported in	Citizens	–	.55
MacCoun, 1987)	Students	–	.52
	Students	.52	.54
MacCoun & Tyler (1988) (reported in	Citizens	–	.54
MacCoun, 1987)	Students	–	.51

$$\text{Decision Criterion} = \frac{\text{Utility (Convict Innocent)}}{\text{Utility (Convict Innocent)} + \text{Utility (Acquit Guilty)}} \quad (5)$$

Obviously, if a subject is asked to rate the personal values (utilities and disutilities) associated with each of the four outcomes and these are inserted in Equation 1 they may not yield an identical result for the decision criterion if only the disutility terms are inserted as in Equation 2. However, in practice the estimates derived from the two popular forms of the equation are usually similar (MacCoun, 1987) and the values in Table 4.3 are based on the source authors' calculations or on the most complex form of the equation that can be applied post hoc.

The decision theory methods have the advantage of shifting the subjects' task to making judgments of utilities, personal values, or degrees or satisfaction and regret associated with various outcomes which may be easier to reason about than probabilities or probabilities and values. However, it is obvious that estimating the probability based on ratings of personal values requires some extra assumptions and extra steps by the researcher as compared to the relatively direct estimates provided by subjects asked to express a judgment of the decision criterion directly in a probability metric.

The decision theory-based estimates differ from the estimates obtained with direct rating and indirect parallel ranking methods; almost all of the reasonable-doubt values obtained using the decision theory equations are lower and they are close to the preponderance values obtained with direct ratings.

We should note that if Blackstone's 10 to 1 ratio of errors is assumed and the values of convict one innocent defendant and acquit one guilty defendant are set to be equal, we end up with an estimate for the beyond-reasonable-doubt threshold of .91. However, MacCoun (1984) asked his student subjects to make direct ratings of the appropriate ratio and he obtained estimates that were almost exactly 1 to 1 for the two types of errors, yielding a decision criterion of slightly greater than .50.

Summary of findings. There are substantial "methods effects" with estimates of the preponderance standard ranging from .48 to .82 and for the reasonable doubt standard from .51 to .92. In general, the estimates are related to measurement method, with the decision theory calculations yielding relatively low values and the direct ratings relatively high. MacCoun (1984) examined the intercorrelations among alternate rating methods across mock jurors (who made ratings on several types of response scales). He concluded that the odds ratio method was most difficult for subjects to use, was correlated with the other methods to only a moderate degree, and was probably the most errorprone of the methods.

Dane (1985) and MacCoun (1984) have proposed an analysis of the validity of the decision criterion estimates based on their ability to predict individual jurors' verdict decisions. For each mock juror in their research they compared the estimated decision criterion with the individual's judgment of the defendant's guilt. A "correct prediction" was counted for each individual who convicted when the judgment of guilt was greater than his or her estimated decision criterion (and, conversely, acquitted when the guilt judgment was lower than the criterion). The proportion of mock jurors whose verdicts were "correctly predicted" is an index of the validity of the decision criterion estimates. Interestingly, the indirect methods, parallel ranking and decision theory-based, yielded the most accurate predictions of individual verdicts (over 80% correct); although all methods predicted well above a chance level of 50% accuracy.

The discrepancy between the direct and decision theory estimates of the standard of proof; the suggestion that the lower decision theory values are more valid; and the typical finding that the presumption of innocence is manifested in an even-handed 50–50 initial attitude toward guilt suggests an intriguing speculation. Perhaps the "quantity" of evidence required to convict a defendant of most criminal charges is less than expert and juror intuitions (expressed in the direct ratings) imply. Rather than requiring "enough" evidence to move a juror from disbelief (close to 0%) to near certainty (over 90%), perhaps the typical "winning" prosecution case moves a juror from equivocal (50%) to a strong, but not overwhelming, preponderance (about 65%). For the present, this suggestion must be labeled highly speculative because so few of the empirical studies conducted to date have utilized realistically complex trial simulations. But the methods necessary to evaluate this speculation are clearly illustrated in the examples we have reviewed (also see the discussion of this issue in Kerr, this book).

Differences between individuals. The quantitative measures of the decision criterion provide comparisons among types of subjects that are suggestive of differences in the decision process manifested in shifts in the decision criterion. The earliest studies (Simon, 1969; Simon & Mahan, 1971) compared the decision criteria employed by judges (including a within-judge comparison of elected versus appointed judges), citizens eligible for jury duty, and students. The studies summarized in Table 4.1 suggest that judges have somewhat higher decision criteria for the reasonable doubt standard and somewhat lower criteria for the preponderance standard than other groups of subjects. Ellsworth and her colleagues have been interested in differences in jurors' judgments associated with their attitudes toward the death penalty (see chapter by Ellsworth, this book). Their results consistently suggest that jurors who favor the death penalty (who might serve on death-qualified juries) tend to have lower criteria for conviction in criminal cases than jurors with antideath penalty attitudes (who are likely to be excluded from death-qualified juries). Another interesting comment on individual differences (probably associated with differences in case types as well) is the result reported by Nagel and his colleagues of a lower decision criterion to convict in a rape case for women students than for men students (.50 versus .70) under conditions where no explicit instructions were provided. These results are suggestive of important and substantial individual differences in comprehension of the standard-of-proof instruction.

Case type effects. In several of the studies summarized in Table 4.1, subjects were asked to make decisions for more than one type of case. Again, interesting and suggestive differences appear as the severity of the case varies. For example, Martin and Schum (1987) and Simon (1969) found that higher criteria were associated with more severe charges, a result consistent with the motivation implicit in decision theory that erroneous conviction involving a more serious charge produces a greater disutility than the same error for a less severe crime. Thus, a plausible strategy to avoid the greater loss associated with erroneous convictions of more severe crimes is to shift the decision criterion "up," in a more stringent direction (of course, this also increases the probability of the erroneous acquittal events which are also more consequential for more severe crimes).

The effects of instructions. It would be surprising if variations in the form and nature of the instruction communicating the standard of proof to the inexperienced juror did not have effects on estimates of his or her decision criterion. Kagehiro (summarized in 1990) has pursued an extensive research program to examine the effects of variations in the form of the instruction on judgments. The theme that emerges from her research is that verbal instructions expressing alternate standards of proof (e.g., the "preponderance" instruction contrasted with a "reasonable doubt" instruction) have surprisingly small effects on the decision criterion. Kerr, et al. (1976) found that a stringent verbal instruction raised the criterion over a lax instruction or no instruction, although the difference was only .05 on a probability scale (similar results were reported by Cornish & Sealy, 1973). However, Kagehiro found that instructions that refer to a numerical standard (e.g., an instruction to convict only if the probability of guilt is greater than .90) have substantial effects. Nagel (1979) reached a similar conclusion comparing verbal instructions with quantitative instructions (a .90 probability instruction and a "10-to-1 Blackstone error ratio" instruction).

Again, the results suggest important differences and illustrate a method to investigate the effects of alternate forms of instructions. To date, no one has thoroughly explored the effects of a verbal but comparative instruction that informs jurors that there is a range of levels of confidence required for a decision and then expresses the scale in an ordinal fashion by listing and contrasting the alternate verbal standards, concluding with a statement of the relative degree of confidence representing the applicable standard of proof.

The algebraic modeling research paradigms and their relation to the trial jurors' task

One of the major advantages of the algebraic modeling approach is its close association to a measurement method that solves the problems of scaling the meaning of evidence and assessing the goodness of fit of valuation and integration operation models. The Functional Measurement Theory that is associated with Information Integration Theory requires that factorial analysis of variance experimental designs be used to fit and test the algebraic models. Typically, these designs are within-subject designs where a single subject performs judgments on a set of legal cases in which two or three characteristics of the evidence (independent variables such as positive versus negative descriptions of the defendant's character, presence or absence of an eyewitness, judge's instructions, etc.) are varied systematically. The advantages of this approach are that parameters of the model can be estimated rigorously and that the combination rules and functions prescribed by the process model for integration and the valuation operations can be inferred and tested in a proper manner.

However, from another perspective, the close link between Information Integration models and the factorial within-subject experimental design seriously limits the practical applicability of this approach. Experimental studies carried out under the aegis of Information Integration Theory have been limited to stimuli that are artificially constructed using many possible combinations of different levels of factors, so that the stimulus cases to which subjects are exposed bear little resemblance to the cases that a juror would normally encounter in the courtroom. Stimulus cases have been dramatically simplified (e.g., containing only incriminating evidence and being composed of 10 to 20 sentences), presented in a written format, and highly contrived (e.g., to guarantee that different statements and evidence are conceptually independent).

Another simplification has been the requirement that the response scale be unidimensional, continuous, and interval. This also departs from the juror's response choices in a real trial where he or she is required to make a judgment of category membership (e.g., armed robbery, first-degree murder, not guilty, etc.). There is a dramatic tradeoff between what is gained by control and "leverage" to estimate experimental parameters, against a loss in realism (Ellsworth, 1977).

The basic sequential averaging model has formal similarities to the global weighted averaging model, but the research paradigm within which it has been explored is somewhat different. The focus of research has been on the effects of variations in the order in which evidence was presented. The obvious difference between the two paradigms is that the global averaging model has been tested by evaluating the goodness of fit of the model to a single final judgment of guilt or innocence, while the sequential averaging model has focused on evidence-item-to-evidence-item changes over the entire sequence of evidence items presented in a stimulus case.

Although the elicitation of intermediate judgments has the advantage of providing a fine-grained picture of the judgment process, it is also possible that requiring these judgments alters the judgment process from the manner in which it would unfold in an actual legal trial where only the ultimate judgment is required. Weld and Danzig (1940) and Kassin and Wrightsman (1979) compared these two conditions (intermediate judgments versus final judgment only) for simplified legal trials, and concluded that the final decision was not affected (but Pennington & Hastie, 1992, report a counterexample).

Another problem with the sequential averaging model is that it does not appear to precisely fit the quantitative data from mock-juror judgments. Anderson (1959; Anderson & Farkas, 1973) has suggested that the process is more complex and that there are actually two components of the judgment concerning guilt or innocence at any point in time. First, a "basal" component is established at some point during the trial evidence that is resistant to change. Second, a "surface" component that is labile and changes as new evidence is presented, conforming to the predictions of the sequential averaging model. When a juror is asked his or her opinion about the evidence, it reflects either or both of these components, with the contribution of each component changing as a function of the time intervening between the presentation of evidence and the request for a judgment.

Discussion and conclusions

The long and productive history of algebraic models of psychological processes provides a compelling warrant for the application of the approach to juror decision making. The potential advantages of the conceptual clarity, intuitive appeal, and flexibility in application of the averaging model have not yet been fully realized. To date, the most visible accomplishments have been byproducts of the algebraic application; e.g., useful individual-level numerical indices of the importance of evidence, presumptions of innocence, and standards of proof. Furthermore, of the three meter models that have been applied to legal decision making, the weighted averaging model has the strongest record of success in comparative analyses (e.g., Pennington & Hastie, 1992; Schum & Martin, 1980).

Our major reservation concerning the algebraic approach derives from the limits on the methods and case materials that have been employed in research to date. Each study has included only a subset of the component judgment tasks (e.g., those that estimate the decision criterion, usually leave out evidence evaluation) and all major applications have studied judgments based on limited, unrealistic case materials (e.g., 10- to 20-sentence cases with artificially contrived independent relations among pieces of evidence). There is no reason to believe that the models will not "scale up" successfully, perhaps in the form of hybrids of algebraic processes and cognitive (semantic) memory representations (e.g., Anderson, 1989; Hastie, 1988).

References

Anderson, N. H. (1959). Test of a model for opinion change. *Journal of Abnormal and Social Psychology, 59*, 371–381.

(1980). Information integration theory in developmental psychology. In F. Wilkening, J. Becker, & T. Trabasso (Eds.), *Information integration by children* (pp. 1–45). Hillsdale, NJ: Erlbaum.

(1981). *Foundations of information integration theory.* New York: Academic Press.

(1982). *Methods of information integration theory.* New York: Academic Press.

(1983). Intuitive physics: Understanding and learning of physical relations. In T. J. Tighe & B. E. Shepp (Eds.), *Perception, cognition, and development: Interactional analyses* (pp. 231–265). Hillsdale, NJ: Erlbaum.

(1989). Functional memory and on-line attribution. In J. N. Bassili (Ed.), *On-line cognition in person perception* (pp. 175–220). Hillsdale, NJ: Erlbaum.

Anderson, N. H., & Farkas, A. J. (1973). New light on order effects in attitude change. *Journal of Personality and Social Psychology, 28*, 88–93.

(1975). Integration theory applied to models of inequity. *Personality and Social Psychology Bulletin, 1*, 588–591.

Ball, V. C. (1961). The moment of truth: Probability theory and standards of proof. *Vanderbilt Law Review, 14,* 807–830.

Bigelow, J. (Ed.). (1887). *The complete works of Benjamin Franklin.* New York: Putnam.

Blackstone, W. (1962). *Commentaries on the laws of England of public wrongs.* Boston: Beacon. (Original work published 1769)

Boring, E. G. (1963). The beginning and growth of measurement in psychology. In R. I. Watson & D. T. Campbell (Eds.), *History, psychology, and science: Selected papers by Edwin G. Boring* (pp. 140–158). New York: Wiley.

Brehmer, B., & Joyce, C. R. B. (Eds.). (1988). *Human judgment: The SJT view.* Amsterdam: North-Holland.

Brunswik, E. (1943). Organismic achievement and environmental probability. *Psychological Review, 50,* 255–272.

Cleary, E. W. (1972). *McCormick's handbook of the law of evidence* (2nd ed.). St. Paul, MN: West.

Colorado Supreme Court Committee on Criminal Jury Instructions. (1983). *Colorado jury instructions: Criminal.* St. Paul, MN: West.

Connolly, T. (1987). Decision theory, reasonable doubt, and the utility of erroneous acquittals. *Law and Human Behavior, 11,* 101–112.

Cornish, W. R., & Sealy, A. P. (1973). Juries and the rules of evidence. *Criminal Law Review, 17,* 208–223.

Cowan, C. L., Thompson, W. C., & Ellsworth, P. C. (1984). The effects of death qualification on jurors' predisposition to convict and on the quality of deliberation. *Law & Human Behavior, 8,* 53–79.

Cullison, A. D. (1977). The model of rules and the logic of decision. In S. S. Nagel (Ed.), *Modeling the criminal justice system* (pp. 225–246). Beverly Hills, CA: Sage.

Dane, F. C. (1985). In search of reasonable doubt: A systematic examination of selected quantification approaches. *Law and Human Behavior, 9,* 141–158.

Daston, L. J. (1987). Rational individuals versus laws of society: From probability to statistics. In L. Kruger, L. J. Daston, & M. Heidelberger (Eds.), *The probabilistic revolution: Vol. 1. Ideas in history* (pp. 295–304). Cambridge, MA: MIT Press.

Ebbesen, E. B., & Konečni, V. J. (1975). Decision making and information integration in the courts: The setting of bail. *Journal of Personality and Social Psychology, 32,* 805–821.

Ellsworth, P. C. (1977). From abstract ideas to concrete instances: Some guidelines for choosing natural research settings. *American Psychologist, 32,* 604–615.

Elwork, A., Sales, B. D., & Alfini, J. J. (1982). *Making jury instructions understandable.* Charlottesville, VA: Michie.

Fechner, G. T. (1966). *Elements of psychophysics* (H. E. Adler, Trans.). New York: Holt, Rinehart & Winston. (Original work published 1860)

Fienberg, S. E., & Schervish, M. J. (1986). The relevance of Bayesian inference for the presentation of statistical evidence and for legal decisionmaking. *Boston University Law Review, 66,* 771–798.

Finkelstein, M. O., & Fairley, W. B. (1970). A Bayesian approach to identification evidence. *Harvard Law Review, 83,* 489–517.

Fried, M., Kaplan, K. J., & Klein, K. W. (1975). Juror selection: An analysis of voir dire. In R. J. Simon (Eds.), *The jury system in America: A critical overview* (pp. 49–66). Newbury Park, CA: Sage.

Gigerenzer, G., Swijtink, Z., Porter, T., Daston, L., Beatty, J., & Krueger, L. (1989). *The empire of chance: How probability changed science and everyday life.* New York: Cambridge University Press.

Goodpaster, G. (1987). On the theory of the American adversary criminal trial. *Journal of Criminal Law and Criminology, 78,* 118–154.

Grofman, B. (1981). Mathematical models of juror and jury decision-making: The state of the art. In B. D. Sales (Ed.), *The trial process* (pp. 305–351). New York: Plenum.

Hammond, K. R. (Ed.). (1966). *The psychology of Egon Brunswik.* New York: Holt, Rinehart & Winston.

Hastie, R. (1988). A computer simulation model of person memory. *Journal of Experimental Social Psychology, 24,* 423–447.

Hastie, R., Penrod, S. D., & Pennington, N. (1983). *Inside the jury.* Cambridge, MA: Harvard University Press.

Helgeson, V. S., & Shaver, K. G. (1990). Presumption of innocence: Congruence bias induced and overcome. *Journal of Applied Social Psychology, 20,* 276–302.

Himmelfarb, S. (1975). On scale value and weight in the weighted averaging model of integration theory. *Personality and Social Psychology Bulletin, 1,* 580–583.

Hogarth, R. M., & Einhorn, H. J. (1992). Order effects in belief updating: The belief-adjustment model. *Cognitive Psychology, 24,* 1–55.

in re Winship, 397 U.S. 358 (1970).

James, W. (1950). *The principles of psychology.* New York: Dover. (Original work published 1890)

Kagehiro, D. K. (1986). *Defining the standard of proof in jury instructions.* Paper presented at the meeting of the Midwestern Psychological Association, Chicago.

   (1990). Defining the standard of proof in jury instructions. *Pscyhological Science, 1,* 194–200.

Kaplan, J. (1968). Decision theory and the factfinding process. *Stanford Law Review, 20,* 1065–1092.

   (1978). *Criminal justice: Introductory cases and materials* (2nd ed.). Mineola, NY: Foundation Press.

Kaplan, M. F. (1975). Informational integration in social judgment: Interaction of judge and informational components. In M. F. Kaplan & S. Schwartz (Eds.), *Human judgment and decision processes* (pp. 139–171). New York: Academic Press.

   (1977). Discussion polarization effects in a modified jury decision paradigm: Informational influences. *Sociometry, 40,* 262–271.

Kaplan, M. F., & Kemmerick, G. D. (1974). Juror judgment as information integration: Combining evidential and nonevidential information. *Journal of Personality and Social Psychology, 30,* 493–499.

Kaplan, M. F., & Miller, L. E. (1978). Reducing the effects of juror bias. *Journal of Personality and Social Psychology, 36,* 1443–1455.

Kassin, S. M., & Wrightsman, L. S. (1979). On the requirements of proof: The timing of judicial instruction and mock juror verdicts. *Journal of Personality and Social Psychology, 37,* 1877–1887.

Kaye, D. (1979). The laws of probability and the law of the land. *University of Chicago Law Review, 47,* 34–56.

Keren, G. (1984). On the importance of identifying the correct "sample space." *Cognition, 16,* 121–128.

Kerr, N. L., Atkin, R. S., Stasser, G., Meek, D., Holt, R. W., & Davis, J. H. (1976). Guilt beyond a reasonable doubt: Effects of concept definition and assigned decision rule on the judgments of mock jurors. *Journal of Personality and Social Psychology, 34*, 282–294.

Kerr, N. L., Bull, R. H. C., MacCoun, R. J., & Rathborn, H. (1985). Effects of victim attractiveness, care and disfigurement on the judgments of American and British mock jurors. *British Journal of Social Psychology, 24*, 47–58.

Koehler, J. J., & Shaviro, D. N. (1990). Veridical verdicts: Increasing verdict accuracy through the use of overtly probabilistic evidence and methods. *Cornell Law Review, 75*, 247–279.

Levi, I. (1977). Direct inference. *Journal of Philosophy, 74*, 5–29.

Luce, R. D., & Raiffa, H. (1957). *Games and decisions: Introduction and critical survey.* New York: Wiley.

MacCoun, R. J. (1984). *Modeling the impact of extralegal bias and defined standards of proof on the decisions of mock jurors and juries.* Unpublished doctoral dissertation, Michigan State University.

  (1987). *Perceptions of accuracy and error in legal judgments.* Paper presented at the annual meeting of the Law and Society Association, Washington, DC, June 12, 1987.

MacCoun, R. J., & Kerr, N. L. (1988). Asymmetric influence in mock jury deliberation: Jurors' bias for leniency. *Journal of Personality and Social Psychology, 54*, 21–33.

MacCoun, R. J., & Tyler, T. R. (1988). The basis of citizens' perceptions of the criminal jury: Procedural fairness, accuracy, and efficiency. *Law and Human Behavior, 12*, 333–352.

Martin, A. W., & Schum, D. A. (1987). Quantifying burdens of proof: A likelihood ratio approach. *Jurimetrics Journal, 27*, 383–402.

McBaine, J. P. (1944). Burden of proof: Degrees of belief. *California Law Review, 32*, 242–268.

  (1954). Burden of proof: Presumptions. *UCLA Law Review, 2*, 13–31.

McCauliff, C. M. A. (1982). Burdens of proof: Degrees of belief, quanta of evidence, or constitutional guarantees? *Vanderbilt Law Review, 35*, 1293–1335.

McFatter, R. M. (1978). Sentencing strategies and justice: Effects of punishment philosophy on sentencing decisions. *Journal of Personality and Social Psychology, 36*, 1490–1500.

Milanich, P. G. (1981). Decision theory and standards of proof. *Law and Human Behavior, 5*, 87–96.

Morano, A. A. (1975). A reexamination of the development of the reasonable doubt rule. *Boston University Law Review, 55*, 507–528.

Mosteller, F., & Youtz, C. (1990). Quantifying probabilistic experiences. *Statistical Science, 5*, 2–34.

Nagel, S. S. (1962). Judicial backgrounds and criminal cases. *Journal of Criminal Law, Criminology and Police Science, 53*, 333–339.

  (1979). Bringing the values of jurors in line with the law, *Judicature, 63*, 189–195.

Nagel, S. S., Lamm, D., & Neef, M. G. (1981). Decision theory and juror decision-making. In B. D. Sales (Ed.), *The trial process.* (pp. 353–386). New York: Plenum.

Nagel, S. S., & Neef, M. G. (1979). *Decision theory and the legal process.* Lexington, MA: Lexington Books.

Nesson, C. R. (1979). Reasonable doubt and permissive inferences: The value of complexity. *Harvard Law Review, 92,* 1187–1225.

(1985). The evidence or the event? On judicial proof and the acceptability of verdicts. *Harvard Law Review, 98,* 1357–1392.

Oden, G. C. (1977). Fuzziness in semantic memory: Choosing exemplars of subjective categories. *Memory and Cognition, 5,* 198–204.

(1979). A fuzzy logical model of letter identification. *Journal of Experimental Psychology: Human Perception and Performance, 5,* 336–352.

Ostrom, T. M., Werner, C., & Saks, M. J. (1978). An integration theory analysis of jurors' presumptions of guilt or innocence. *Journal of Personality and Social Psychology, 36,* 436–450.

Pennington, N., & Hastie, R. (1987). Explanation-based decision making. *Proceedings of the Ninth Annual Meeting of the Cognitive Science Society* (pp. 682–690). Hillsdale, NJ: Erlbaum.

(1991). A cognitive theory of juror decision making: The Story Model. *Cardozo Law Review, 13,* 519–557.

(1992). Explaining the evidence: Tests of the Story Model for juror decision making. *Journal of Personality and Social Psychology, 62,* 189–206.

Saks, M. J., & Kidd, R. F. (1980). Human information processing and adjudication: Trial by heuristics. *Law & Society Review, 15,* 123–160.

Saks, M. J., Werner, C. M., & Ostrom, T. M. (1975). The presumption of innocence and the American juror. *Journal of Contemporary Law, 2,* 46–54.

Schum, D. A., & Martin, A. W. (1980). *Probabilistic opinion revision on the basis of evidence at trial: A Baconian or a Pascalian process* (Research Rep. 80-02). Houston, TX: Rice University, Department of Psychology.

Severance, L. J., & Loftus, E. F. (1982). Improving the ability of jurors to comprehend and apply criminal jury instructions. *Law and Society Review, 17,* 153–197.

Shapiro, B. J. (1986). "To a moral certainty": Theories of knowledge and Anglo-American juries 1600–1850. *Hastings Law Journal, 38,* 153–193.

Simon, R. J. (1969). Judges' translations of burdens of proof into statements of probability. In J. J. Kennelly & J. P. Chapman (Eds.), *The trial lawyer's guide* (pp. 103–114). Mundelein, IL: Callaghan.

(1970). "Beyond a reasonable doubt" – An experimental attempt at quantification. *Journal of Applied Behavioral Science, 6,* 203–209.

Simon, R. J., & Mahan, L. (1971). Quantifying burdens of proofs: A view from the bench, the jury, and the classroom. *Law and Society Review, 5,* 319–330.

Speiser v. Randall, 357 U.S. 513, 525–526 (1958).

Thompson, W. C., Cowan, C. L., Ellsworth, P. C., & Harrington, J. C. (1984). Death penalty attitudes and conviction proneness: The translation of attitudes into verdicts. *Law and Human Behavior, 8,* 95–113.

Tribe, L. H. (1971a). Trial by mathematics: Precision and ritual in the legal process. *Harvard Law Review, 84,* 1329–1393.

(1971b). A further critique of mathematical proof. *Harvard Law Review, 84,* 1810–1820.

Ulmer, S. S. (1963). Quantitative analysis of judicial processes: Some practical and theoretical applications. *Law and Contemporary Problems, 28,* 164–184.

Underwood, B. D. (1977). The thumb on the scales of justice: Burdens of persuasion in criminal cases. *Yale Law Journal, 86,* 1299–1348.

U.S. v. Fatico, 458 *Federal Supplement* 388 (1978).

von Neumann, J., & Morgenstern, O. (1947). *Theory of games and economic behavior* (2nd ed.). Princeton, NJ: Princeton University Press.

Waldman, T. (1959). Origins of the legal doctrine of reasonable doubt. *Journal of the History of Ideas, 20,* 299–316.

Walker, L., Thibaut, J., & Andreoli, V. (1972). Order of presentation at trial. *Yale Law Journal, 82,* 216–226.

Wallsten, T. S., Budescu, D. V., Rapoport, A., Zwick, R., & Forsyth, B. (1986). Measuring the vague meanings of probability terms. *Journal of Experimental Psychology: General, 115,* 348–365.

Weld, H. P., & Danzig, E. R. (1940). A study of the way in which a verdict is reached by a jury. *American Journal of Psychology, 53,* 518–536.

Weld, H. P., & Roff, M. (1938). A study in the formation of opinion based upon legal evidence. *American Journal of Psychology, 51,* 609–628.

Wigmore, J. H. (1901). Required numbers of witnesses: A brief history of the numerical system in England. *Harvard Law Review, 15,* 83–108.

(1937). *The science of judicial proof, as given by logic, psychology, and general experience, and illustrated in judicial trials* (3rd ed.). Boston: Little, Brown.

5 Stochastic models of juror decision making

Norbert Kerr

Stochastic models, models that characterize processes as probabilistic or chance events, have been applied fruitfully to describe many psychological phenomena. The word stochastic derives from a Greek root that means random, chance, or haphazard. In scientific usage, the antonym for stochastic would be certain or deterministic. While a deterministic model (for example, an algebraic model such as those based on Information Integration Theory) predicts a single response from a given stimulus situation, a stochastic model predicts a set of possible responses weighted by their probabilities of occurrence. It is often useful to think of stochastic models as represented metaphorically by mechanical devices such as decks of cards, roulette wheels, or dice.

Models that describe some aspects of human behavior in probabilistic terms have been applied to simple choice behavior (Luce, 1959), elementary perception and judgment phenomena (Green & Swets, 1966), and simple learning (Estes, 1959). These applications have been extremely successful in describing and predicting human behavior. The probabilistic components in the models may at some basic level of analysis (perhaps physiological) provide an accurate depiction of the underlying physical process. Furthermore, the stochastic component serves as a vehicle to generalize an account of behavior across diverse processes, individuals, or stimulus conditions (Cotton, 1982). For example, in the legal domain, it seems natural to conceptualize the diverse range of cases to which a juror might be assigned as a distribution of potential stimulus events that vary in strengths of evidence favoring one side or the other of each case. Similarly, a theorist might conceive of a distribution of possible decision strategies or individual differences in case-relevant knowledge that are sampled stochastically when jurors are assigned to cases.

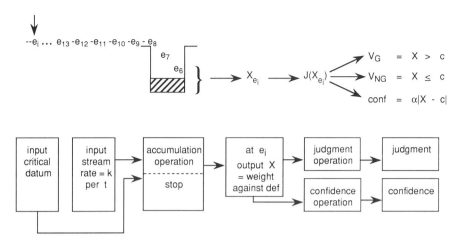

Figure 5.1. A process representation of the Poisson model (conf = confidence, def = defendant; based on Pennington & Hastie, 1981, p. 271, Figure 6).

The Thomas and Hogue Poisson process model

Thomas and Hogue (1976) have been the primary advocates for the application of stochastic models to juror decision making and Kerr (1978a, 1978b; Kerr, Harmon, & Graves, 1982) has applied the model to infer properties of jurors' decisions such as their evaluations of weight of evidence and decision criterion. Inspired by signal detection theory, Thomas and Hogue (1976) proposed that the juror's task could be separated into two stages. A first stochastic stage in which the juror derived the implications of the evidence in the case for the defendant's guilt or innocence. The output of this stage is a single value (X) representing the perceived weight of the evidence against the defendant. And, a second deterministic stage, in which the juror determines whether or not the value of the evidence exceeds a decision criterion (c) to render a verdict. If X exceeds the c, the juror decides "guilty"; otherwise the juror decides "innocent."[1] A by-product of the processing in the second stage is a judgment of confidence in the verdict that is determined by the difference between the decision criterion and the weight of the evidence value. See Figure 5.1.

Thomas and Hogue (1976) proposed a family of models with members defined by alternate versions of the stochastic process in Stage One that produced the weight of evidence value and the algebraic relation in Stage

[1] One may also think of X as the perceived weight of evidence in the defendant's favor and of c as the criterion for acquittal. The two versions of the model are not equivalent. We have chosen to present here the version which corresponds most naturally to legal conventions (e.g., criminal trial jurors must be convinced beyond a reasonable doubt to convict) and which has been most often used in applications of the model.

Two that produced degree of confidence values from the difference between the weight of evidence value and the decision criterion. Although at least six possible models were considered in the Thomas and Hogue investigation, one was repeatedly favored by the results of empirical research. We will only discuss this "winning" combination in the present review (see Thomas & Hogue, 1976; or Pennington & Hastie, 1981, for the full set of models).

Thomas and Hogue assumed that the apparent weight of evidence against the defendant could be described as a random variable distributed across the population of potential jurors who heard all of the evidence for a single case. The psychological process corresponding to the stochastic model proposed by Thomas and Hogue can be described as follows (see Figure 5.1). Information comes to the juror at trial from two sources: evidence and nonevidential factors. Each of these sources affects the apparent weight of evidence against the defendant by increasing it at a constant rate until a critical event (perhaps a dramatic piece of evidence) occurs, at which time the apparent weight of evidence from one source is fixed. This "freezing" process occurs twice yielding fixed values of the weight of evidence (and "nonevidence") against the defendant. The individual juror's belief that the defendant is guilty is determined by the sum of the values of the evidentiary and the nonevidentiary sources with their inputs "frozen" at the points in time when the critical events for each source occurred. For any particular trial, the probability that the critical event will occur for each source at any point in the trial is constant. If k is the rate of accumulation of evidence and k' is the constant probability of the accumulation halting per time unit, the $M' = k/k'$ (where M' is the mean, across all jurors) apparent weight of evidence against the defendant. A similar relation is assumed to hold for the accumulation of nonevidentiary information. Thus, in mathematical terms each component process is a Poisson process and their sum, the distribution of possible weights of evidence (Xs) across individual jurors, $f(x)$ takes the form of a generalized gamma probability density function (see Figure 5.2). The stochastic process of generating a single value summarizing the weight of all the evidence and decision-relevant nonevidence for each juror is Stage One of the model.[2]

The application of a random process to describe the extraction of meaning from evidential and nonevidential sources of information is one effective and legitimate approach to capturing variation in jurors' reactions to

---

[2] Although one may simply apply the generating logic for the generalized gamma to the process of jurors' determination of the apparent weight of evidence, the validity and utility of this version of the Thomas and Hogue model need not hinge upon such a literal interpretation. For example, even if the weight of evidence does not accumulate through two independent Poisson processes, the generalized gamma distribution could possess distributional features (e.g., single-peaked and asymmetrical pdf, bounded below but not above) which characterize the true distribution of apparent weight of evidence, generated through some very different psychological process. Thus, one might just consider this model version to be a useful theoretical baseline, deviations from which might inform future model development (cf. Davis, 1969).

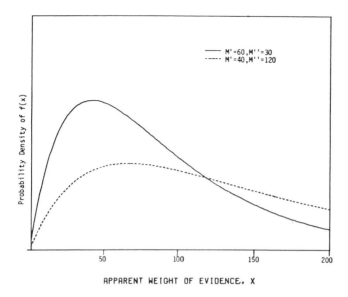

Figure 5.2. Example probability density functions for the generalized gamma distribution that describes the distribution of apparent weight of evidence values across jurors for a single case in Stage One of the Poisson process model. M' and M'' are the expected values the evidentiary and nonevidentiary sources of information, combined in this figure to yield a single value of x for each juror.

the trial stimulus. Presumably these processes comprise some knowable causes, such as individual differences among jurors in case-relevant knowledge, initial presumptions of innocence, attitudes toward the defendant and other actors in the trial, and perhaps individual differences in capacities to comprehend and reason about the evidence. As our knowledge advances concerning the potent individual differences in juror decision making, the application of the Poisson process model can be refined. This would probably mean separate applications of the model to partitions of the sample of jurors, when enough is known to identify subsets of jurors with different proclivities to evaluate weight of the evidence for a single case. It might also mean elaboration of the basic model to include multiple component Poisson processes in Stage One that can be combined to yield a single average estimate of the weight of evidence parameter. In any case, the current model with two component random processes is a fair representation of our ignorance of the individual differences that affect evidence evaluation (see chapter by Ellsworth, this book).

The central component of the second stage is a comparison between the weight of evidence value (produced by the first stage) and a decision criterion. The decision criterion is presumably primarily determined by the judge's instructions on the standard of proof necessary to return a verdict, although there is evidence that standards of proof derive from jurors'general understanding of common law (MacCoun & Kerr, 1988) and there are individual differences in such concepts (e.g., Simon & Mahan, 1971). In the present model the decision criterion is assumed to be constant across jurors (*not* sampled from a probability distribution). An individual juror's strength of belief in the verdict will be determined by the distance between the (shared) decision criterion and his or her individual weight of evidence value (X). Thus, confidence will be distributed across individual jurors because weight of evidence is probabilistically distributed although the criterion is not. A final ingredient in the most plausible version of the Thomas and Hogue model is an assumption (supported empirically) that the function, g, relating the difference between the apparent weight of the evidence and the decision criterion to confidence is linear (i.e., confidence = $g(|x-c|)$ = alpha$|x-c|$, where alpha is a scaling constant).

There are three important parameters of the model that must be estimated to fit it to the data from a group of jurors rendering individual verdicts for a single case under uniform instructions. First there is a parameter (m) representing the mean weight of the evidence (m') plus non-evidence (m'') factors against the defendant (mean of the distribution of Xs). Second, there is a fixed value (c) representing the decision criterion, the value that must be exceeded by the apparent weight of the evidence to render a guilty verdict. Third, there is a parameter (alpha) that "scales" the subjective distance between the criterion and the weight of the evidence to fit it to the rating scale values used by the experimenter to measure confidence in the verdict decision. The alpha parameter is not given a psychological interpretation, but has simply been set to a convenient value so that the remaining parameter estimates will assume values that range around 1. These parameters occurring in the equations for Stage One (Figure 5.2) and Stage Two (Figure 5.3) can be estimated from judgment data collected from jurors asked to judge a single case. The data needed for such estimation are the proportion of jurors who acquit, mean confidence of jurors acquitting, and mean confidence of jurors convicting (Figure 5.3).

The Poisson process model has several important advantages. First, obviously its expression in mathematical form yields the benefits of clear unambiguous statement, deductive power, and predictive precision. Second, the underlying parameters are clearly identified and methods for their empirical identification have been developed by statisticians. Third, the central estimated parameters, mean weight of evidence and decision criterion, have legal and intuitive interpretations that make sense. Fourth, in the domain of juror decision making models, the Poisson model stands out as the only approach that rigorously includes a specification of a decision threshold (criterion), its implication for the decision and confidence judgments, and a method for simultaneous measurement of the weight of the evidence and the criterion. As we shall see, many legally important and theoretically interesting judgment phenomena may have their causál locus in the decision criterion and not elsewhere in the judgment process.

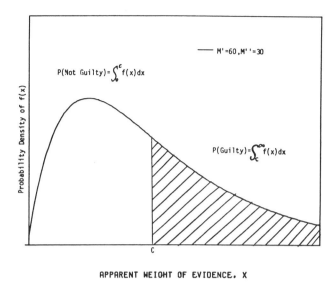

Figure 5.3. An example of a distribution of individual apparent weight of evidence values generated by Stage One and a decision criterion indicating the threshold rule for deciding on *guilty* or *not guilty* verdicts.

The model has been criticized by Pennington and Hastie (1981) and others on several grounds. The model's stochastic component represents variation across individuals, thus it does not attempt to model the decision made by a single juror. The sampling distributions of the estimated model parameters have not been determined, so statistical comparison of estimates obtained under different conditions is problematic. Values for the parameters do not always have plausible interpretations nor do external task variables always affect them in a consistent, intuitively plausible manner. Furthermore, Thomas and Hogue's (1976) initial applications of a family of six possible models were not strongly motivated by empirical or theoretical considerations. Initially all six members of the family had an equal intuitive appeal and in several applications, at least two members fitted the data equally well but provided different estimates of parameters. Nonetheless, on balance the model's advantages outweigh its disadvantages. Specific fits of the unitary model introduced in this chapter describe juror behavior well and yield important insights into the independent effects of decision task conditions on the weight of evidence and decision criterion. Perhaps the only aspect of the model that is clearly unrealistic is the assumption that for a particular set of trial conditions, all individual jurors share a common decision threshold (c).

Empirical research

Initial work by Thomas and Hogue (1976) developed the theoretical foundation and form of the theoretical model. The first empirical research was designed to select the particular combination of Stage One and Stage Two functions (f and g) that would constitute the most successful model. As we noted above, the Thomas and Hogue and subsequent Kerr research have favored the combination of a generalized gamma probability density function plus a linear function relating the apparent weight of evidence – decision threshold difference to confidence. With this basic model in hand, the research tactic that has dominated subsequent work has been to fit the model to data collected under various experimental conditions (usually variations in legal instructions or case materials) to see whether and how parameter estimates vary with these conditions, thereby providing an interpretation of observed verdict effects in terms of shifts in jurors' perceived weight of evidence and standards of proof.

Standard of proof instructions

In one of the earliest applications by Thomas and Hogue, (1976, Criminal Case 1, p. 454), the model was fitted to experimental data collected by Kerr et al. (1976). The experimental treatment of interest was a manipulation of the judge's instructions concerning the standard of proof to be applied to individual juror's decisions. The a priori prediction was that the effects of the standard of proof instruction should be reflected in estimates of the decision criterion parameter (c) and to a lesser extent, if at all, in the estimated mean apparent weight of the evidence (m). The results of fitting the model (see Figure 5.4) are in essential agreement with these predictions. Estimates of the decision criterion showed a much bigger impact of the standard-of-proof instruction than did the weight of evidence estimates.

The second independent variable in the experiment involved the point of time at which subjects made the ratings of verdict choice and verdict confidence: after hearing the case materials and the judge's instruction but before deliberation ("pre" in Figure 5.4) or after a brief deliberation ("post" in Figure 5.4).

When the original Kerr et al. (1976) study was conducted, no predictions were made about the likely effects of deliberation (the pre- versus post-rating comparisons in Figure 5.4) on the parameter estimates. However, recent research summarized in MacCoun and Kerr (1988) provides an interpretation of the finding that the decision criterion (c) appears consistently to rise from before to after deliberation (at least when the conviction criterion is high, as is typical and legally prescribed).

MacCoun & Kerr conducted a meta-analysis of several studies of jury decision making and documented a pervasive tendency for criminal juries to shift from a balanced preference for conviction versus acquittal to be relatively more likely to convict than acquit (cf. Stasser, Kerr, & Bray, 1982). The effect of this phenomenon across a broad range of trials is to produce a "Leniency Shift." This effect and the pre- post- difference in decision criteria (see estimates in Figure 5.4) may be manifestations of the same

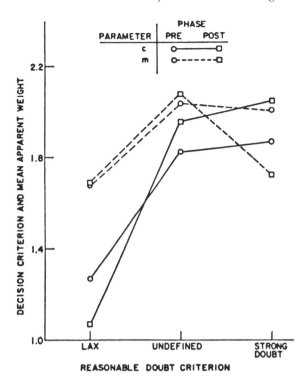

Figure 5.4. Estimates of decision criterion (*c*) and mean apparent weight (*m*) for the Kerr et al. (1976) criminal case for each temporal phase and reasonable doubt instruction condition.

underlying judgment process. First, we know from previous research (e.g., Thompson, Cowan, Ellsworth, & Harrington, 1984) that jurors place a relatively high cost on the error of convicting an innocent defendant. Second, we assume that group discussion tends to intensify ("polarize") strength of individual feelings about the modal belief (cf. Myers & Lamm, 1976). Thus, after deliberation jurors should feel even more strongly that conviction of the innocent is to be avoided. Perhaps the most plausible consequence of this feeling will be an increase in jurors' decision criterion (recall our analogy to statistical decision theory above). This is exactly what we observed in the estimates of the decision criterion in the present study (Figure 5.4). Note that when the criterion was relatively low (the "lax" condition), deliberation seems to have lowered it still further. The general conclusion from this analysis is that the Thomas and Hogue approach is supported and that its predictions were confirmed, viz., the weight of evidence parameter (*m*) was unaffected by the experimental manipulations while the decision criterion (*c*) was affected by a manipulation of the reasonable doubt instruction and time of rating.

This general research strategy of convergent and divergent validation of the constructs represented by the model parameters was pursued in a subsequent series of experiments in which independent variables were manipulated that were expected to have effects on verdicts. To the degree that key constructs (verdict criterion and mean apparent weight of evidence) mediate such effects, the parameter estimates should be sensitive to these independent variables.

Victim's attractiveness and conduct

The character, appearance, and behavior of the victim of a crime are almost always legally irrelevant to the juror's decision. However, intuition and a small number of social psychology experiments suggest that characteristics of the victim of a crime can influence verdicts in an extralegal manner (see Dane & Wrightsman, 1982, for a review). Laboratory experiments by Landy and Aronson (1969) and Jones and Aronson (1973) found effects of victim's character on judgments of defendant's guilt. Kalven and Zeisel's (1966) judges believed that jurors' susceptibility to considerations of victims' attractiveness, status, and character explained some of the cases in which jurors and judges disagreed on the proper verdict. And, perhaps the most extreme attitude is expressed in a famous trial attorney's maxim, "The best defense in a murder case is the fact that the deceased should have been killed, regardless of how it happened" (Percy Forman, quoted in Smith, 1966, p. 96).

Kerr (1978a) reported an experiment to study the effects of manipulation of the victim of a crime's physical attractiveness and precautiousness, on mock-juror's verdicts. Students read transcripts of an automobile theft case, rendered verdicts, provided ratings of their confidence in their verdicts, and made several other collateral ratings. The attractiveness of the victim was manipulated by attaching a photograph of either a very attractive or a relatively unattractive woman to the transcripts. The victim's precautiousness was manipulated by varying (within the transcript) the manner in which the victim left the car that was stolen. In a high-care condition, the victim attached a security lock to the steering wheel, removed her keys, and locked her car prior to the theft; in the low-care condition the victim failed to attach the lock, failed to remove her keys, and left the car unlocked. In the case materials, the defendant's criminal record established that even in the high-care condition, theft of the car would pose no practical problem. Furthermore, legal instructions established that the victim's level of carefulness had no evidential value.

Log-linear analysis of the guilty verdict data showed an interaction effect of victim attractiveness and carefulness such that when the victim was both attractive and careful, probability of a guilty verdict was at its maximum; the other three conditions were equal and lower in guilty verdict rates (see Figure 5.5). Again, as in the first experiment, an application of the Thomas

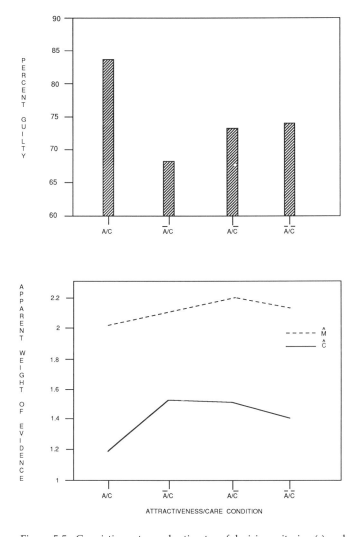

Figure 5.5. Conviction rates and estimates of decision criterion (c) and mean apparent weight (m) for Kerr (1978a) (A = attractive victim, not-A = unattractive victim, C = careful conduct, not-C = careless conduct).

and Hogue model elucidates the judgment process that produced these results. When the careful victim was also attractive (and well-liked), a lower threshold for conviction (c) was applied than when the victim was unattractive. However, when the victim's behavior was careless, victim attractiveness had no effect on the conviction criterion. The analysis, through the model, also suggested that the experimental variables had relatively little effect on juror's perception of weight of evidence (m) (see Figure 5.5). These results support an interesting speculation, that at least some legally proscribed biases which reflect sensitivity to extralegal factors tend to have their effects on the judgment criterion (c), not on evaluations of the weight of the evidence (m).

Severity of penalty

In a third experiment, the effects of another factor, severity of the penalty prescribed for a crime were studied. Prescribed penalty would generally be considered an extralegal factor with reference to the verdict decision.[3] However, there are several grounds for expecting information about severity of penalty to affect jurors' verdicts. One reason derives from a parallel between the juror verdict decision and the test of a statistical hypothesis (e.g., Feinberg, 1971). In both conceptualizations, the decision maker is confronted with a choice between two hypotheses: null hypothesis versus alternative hypothesis for statistical decision theory; innocence versus guilt for the juror. In both tasks, one hypothesis (null, innocence) is presumed and retained unless evidence is sufficiently inconsistent with it. And, just like the statistical decision maker, a juror risks committing one of two types of errors: convicting an innocent person (Type I error) or acquitting a guilty person (Type II error). The probabilities of committing each of these types of errors depend on hypothetical decision criteria: the statistician's level of significance, or the juror's conception of standard of proof (beyond reasonable doubt for criminal cases). The two types of errors trade off, such that any movement of the decision criterion increases one type and decreases the other type. In statistical decision theory, choice of a decision criterion is usually dependent on the costs associated with each type of error, with a criterion chosen to minimize the expected loss associated with the overall decision process. Similar reasoning is applied in the legal domain, and the historical convention of setting a high criterion to convict (beyond reasonable doubt) is justified by the general desire to avoid the juridic Type I error (i.e., convicting an innocent person) more than the Type II error (i.e., acquitting a guilty person; Blackstone, 1769/1962). Presumably because the appropriate costs associated with the two types of errors are already incorporated in the legal convention of standard of proof, jurors are instructed that their verdict decision should not be swayed by consideration of associated penalties.

In spite of the injunction against consideration of penalty in guilt–innocence decisions, there is considerable empirical evidence that jurors are affected by penalty. Attorneys, judges, and legislators believe that as penalty increases, all other things being equal, jurors will become less likely to convict (Galliher, McCartney, & Baum, 1974; Kalven & Zeisel, 1966). Legal

---

[3] There are some contexts, though, where jurors' attitudes towards possible penalties have been held to be a legitimate basis for evaluating their fitness to sit as triers of fact (e.g., exclusion of prospective jurors expressing strong reservations about the death penalty from capital trials, *Lockhart v. McCree*, 1986).

historians have concluded that harsh penal codes are mitigated in part by the refusal of jurors to convict of a capital offense (Radzinowicz, 1948; Tobias, 1967). And analyses of data from field experiments and surveys has shown that severe penalties for traffic violations are sometimes associated with increased acquittal rates (Campbell & Ross, 1968; Robertson, Rich, & Ross, 1973).

When we turn to the experimental research literature, we find less consistent support for the hypothesis of penalty effects on verdicts. First, there are a number of experiments that explore the effects of juror's belief that their verdict will have actual consequences contrasted with role-playing mock jurors who do not anticipate that their judgment will have an effect. Zeisel and Diamond (1978), found that actual jurors were less likely to convict than mock jurors who viewed a case after having been challenged during the voir dire jury selection procedure. However, this result has not been replicated in other experiments (Wilson & Donnerstein, 1977; Kerr, Nerenz, & Herrick, 1979).

Second, are a set of immediate precedents for the present work in which, within a mock-juror decision task, severity of penalty was manipulated directly. Davis, Kerr, Stasser, Meek, and Holt (1977) and McComas and Noll (1974) did not find effects of penalty severity on verdicts. However, Vidmar (1972) did find effects, although he notes his manipulations confounded severity of penalty with legal standards for conviction.

The conclusions of past research, particularly of experimental research, are equivocal with reference to the question of whether penalty severity affects verdicts. However, the volume of literature and speculation clearly establishes the significance of the question to both professional and academic audiences. Kerr (1978b) conducted an experiment designed to cleanly manipulate severity of penalty and to examine the effects, through applications of the Thomas and Hogue model, on juror's judgments of weight of evidence and decision criterion.

The experimental design and materials were based on the Vidmar (1972) and the McComas and Noll (1974) methods. The crime circumstances involved the killing of the proprietor of a store during a robbery. Six experimental conditions were created by varying the crime with which the defendant was charged and the penalty associated with the crime. The manipulations were between subjects so that one-third heard the defendant charged with first degree murder, one-third second degree murder, and one-third manslaughter. Two levels of penalty were described; half of the subjects were told the penalty might range from one to twenty years imprisonment (lenient), the other half were told the penalty might range from 25 years imprisonment to capital execution (severe). Subjects read the case materials, selected a verdict, rated their confidence in the verdict, and also provided a rating of probability of guilt on the same scale as that used by McComas and Noll.

Penalty severity (mild vs. severe) was expected to be inversely related to probability of conviction. A one-tailed t-test on arc sine transformed proportions of subjects convicting the defendant was significant, supporting this hypothesis. In the severe penalty conditions, 62% of the subjects voted to convict, and in the mild penalty conditions, 69% voted to convict. Similarly, the seriousness of the charge against the defendant was predicted to be inversely related to probability of conviction. The proportions of subjects voting to convict the defendant in the three charge conditions were ordered as predicted, first degree murder 41% convictions, second degree murder 75% convictions, manslaughter 79% convictions. Pairwise t-tests generally supported the hypothesis, although the difference between manslaughter and second degree murder was not statistically significant.

In the previously described experiments, the Thomas and Hogue model was applied to determine the effects of the independent variables on the two hypothesized substages of the decision process. By analogy to the statistical decision theory characterization of juror decision making, it was predicted that penalty severity and subjects' decision criterion for conviction would be inversely related. As predicted, the criterion for conviction was significantly higher (i.e., the weight of evidence had to be higher to prove guilt) when the prescribed penalty was severe than when it was mild. The effects of penalty severity on the weight of evidence parameter (m) were also tested. Surprisingly, it, too, was affected by the penalty severity manipulation. However, the magnitude of the effect on the parameter estimates was much smaller than the effect on the decision criterion parameter (c), (see Figure 5.6).

The Thomas and Hogue model advances our understanding of the effects on verdicts of another extralegal factor, penalty severity. Essentially, as in the experiments on victim attractiveness, the impact of the manipulation is primarily on the second stage of juror decision making, where the subjects set and apply their decision criteria. The results of the present study are more equivocal than our earlier experiments because the weight of evidence parameter also showed a small but significant effect of the penalty severity manipulation.

A commonly expressed remedy for high crime rates is the imposition of more severe penalties. Although this remedy might have the intended effect of increasing deterrence or incapacitation, its effect upon decision makers who exercise considerable discretion (e.g., arresting officers, prosecutors, jurors) might be to make arrest, prosecution, and conviction *less* likely by increasing the perceived cost associated with mistakes involving innocent suspects and defendants. Furthermore, this reasoning suggests many other factors which could be expected to affect the perceived costs of juridic errors. Thus, any factor which increases the cost of the juridic Type II error, acquitting a guilty defendant, should lower conviction criteria and raise conviction rates. Anything which makes the prospect of acquitting a genuinely guilty defendant more abhorrent should have this effect (e.g.,

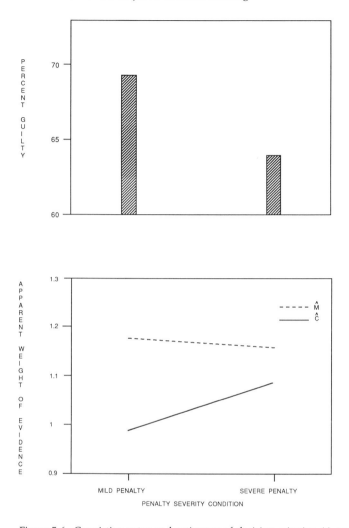

Figure 5.6. Conviction rates and estimates of decision criterion (*c*) and mean apparent weight (*m*) for Kerr (1978b).

indications that the true culprit is particularly dangerous or likely to be a recidivist). Likewise, any other factor which, like penalty severity, increases the perceived cost of the juridic Type I error, convicting an innocent defendant (e.g., the harshness of prison conditions, an inability to compensate a wrongly convicted person) should raise criteria and reduce convictions.

Strength of evidence in prior cases

A final experiment investigated another phenomenon that, if present, would have to be labeled an extralegal bias. A fundamental assumption of criminal and civil law is that a juror will consider only evidence presented at trial in rendering a verdict. This means, among other things, that a juror who sits on more than one case should insulate each decision from the influence of evidence and decisions in previous cases. In many jurisdictions this is a practical matter because jurors sit for terms from one week to six weeks duration and frequently serve on more than one case. Attorneys have many theories about the forms of nonindependence that will occur when jurors serve on more than one case. One general principle we have heard frequently is that, early in their service, jurors tend to favor the prosecution side in criminal cases; but later in their service, the defense is favored. Another theory, with a contrary implication, was proposed by Owen (1973, p. 98) who concluded that, "if jurors vote to convict once, it is easier the next time."

In fact, with a little thought, it is possible to generate and believe that several different forms, sometimes contradictory, of nonindependence might hold. For example, positive assimilation, or "halo" relationships are plausible if we suppose (like Owen above) that conviction is a habit that needs to be learned but persists once practiced. Or, we might suppose that there are conviction and acquittal prone jurors and that whichever tendency an individual juror represents is expressed more and more intensely as his or her experience as a juror proceeds. Another possibility suggested by Erwin, Greenberg, and Minzer (1971, p. 68) is that, "a juror who is completing his service and has been a known convictor is likely to be a good defense juror on his last case." Other, more general contrast hypotheses have been proposed by social scientists such as Broeder (1965), Pepitone and DiNubile (1976), and Parducci (1968).

In response to this rich collection of dissonant hypotheses, Kerr, Harmon, and Graves (1982) conducted an experiment to cleanly test the effects of prior case context on subsequent juror decisions. It focused on the effect of prior case strength of evidence against the defendant on judgments in a subsequent test case. The strength of evidence was manipulated in two pairs of context cases, followed by one test case. The cases were constructed to produce four types of prior context: four strong cases preceding the test case, four weak cases, a pair of strong cases followed by a pair of weak cases, and a pair of weak cases followed by a pair of strong cases. A fifth control condition was also included, in which only the test case, with no context preceding it, was decided. Mock jurors read the case materials for four context armed robbery cases, followed by the test case; or in the control condition, only the test case. Then they indicated their choice of verdicts and the confidence with which they held their verdicts.

The strength of evidence in the context cases had a large effect on the test case verdicts, with a clear contrast effect pattern emerging. If the four context cases were strong, conviction rates in the test case were at their lowest (50%, see Figure 5.7); when the context cases provided weak strength of evidence for the prosecution, conviction rates in the test case were at their

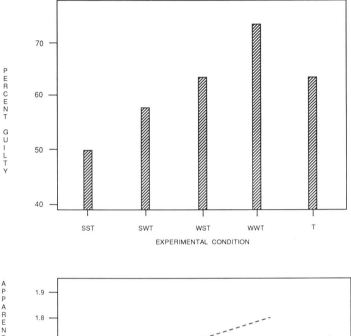

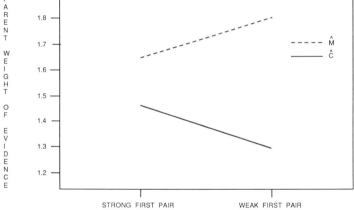

Figure 5.7. Conviction rates and estimates of decision criterion (*c*) and mean apparent weight (*m*) for Kerr et al. (1982) (S = a pair of cases with strong evidence against the defendant, W = a pair of cases with weak evidence against the defendant, T = a test case with balanced evidence).

highest level (74%). For the mixed context cases, strong followed by weak and weak followed by strong prosecution evidence, conviction rates were at an intermediate level. Omnibus statistical tests suggested that strength of evidence in the first pair of cases was the primary determinant of conviction rate on the final (test) cases. The no context control case judgments of verdicts fell in the middle in the range of conviction levels (64%).

The Thomas and Hogue model was applied to estimate weight of evidence (m) and decision criterion (c) parameters, expecting that the context case strength of evidence manipulation would have its greatest impact on the subjects' perceptions of the weight of evidence in the test case. Because the statistical analyses suggested that the first cases in the context set were the critical determinant of judgments on the test case, the two context conditions with strong case pairs in the first position (strong–strong and strong–weak contexts) were combined and compared to the two context conditions with weak case pairs in the first position (weak–strong and weak–weak). As predicted, the parameter representing subjects' subjective evaluations of strength of evidence in the test case showed a clear effect context cases in the form of a contrast pattern. If the first context case pair presented strong prosecution evidence, weight of evidence for the prosecution (m) for the test case was seen as relatively weak. If the first context case pair presented weak evidence for the prosecution, then the test case weight of evidence was seen as relatively strong for the prosecution (see Figure 5.7).

Unexpectedly, the strength of evidence in context cases also affected the decision criterion parameter (c) for the test case. The pattern of effects tended to reinforce the effects we have already noted on weight of evidence to produce a consistent joint impact on mock-jurors' conviction rates. Strong prosecution evidence on the first context case pair tended to move the subjects' decision criterion for the test case up, thereby making the requirement for conviction more strict or difficult to meet. Recall that the effect of strong context case evidence for the prosecution was also to reduce the perceived weight of evidence for the test case, so that the two effects together on weight of evidence and decision criterion would both favor decreased conviction rates on the test case. In contrast, when the first context case was weak for the prosecution, the decision criterion was lowered. Again, in combination with the effect on perceived weight of evidence for the test case (it was increased by weak prosecution context cases), the joint effect would be consistent, with both factors favoring increased conviction rates on the third test case.[4]

Conclusions

We have introduced the currently most popular stochastic model for juror decision making and presented four examples of applications to juror behavior. The model is unique in providing simultaneous estimates of the

---

[4] Kerr et al. (1982) interpret these criterion shifts in terms of jurors' attempts to achieve an appropriate overall conviction rate. For example, when jurors are exposed to four context cases with extremely weak evidence, they are likely to acquit for most if not all of them. These jurors may believe that this conviction rate is unusually low and attribute it in part to their application of a decision criterion that is too high. The chances of obtaining more convictions in later cases and thus a more reasonable overall rate of conviction are improved by lowering this criterion.

effects of legally significant task variations on jurors' evaluations of the evidence and on their decision criterion. More specifically, the results consistently indicate that the primary impact of many extra-legal factors such as victim attractiveness, penalty severity, and previously decided cases is on the juror's decision criterion and not on his or her evaluation of the evidence. This is not to suggest that the effects of *all* extralegal biasing factors are mediated primarily by criterion shifts. There are many such factors which seem to exert their influence through changes in the apparent weight of evidence (e.g., inadmissible but relevant testimony; Sue, Smith, & Caldwell, 1973; prior conviction for a similar offense; Wissler & Saks, 1985).

This research has important theoretical implications: A decision criterion must be included in any plausible theoretical model. And, interpretations of juror decision phenomena in terms of evidence evaluation processes are not warranted unless the role of the decision criterion as a mediator is considered in the same analysis. The conclusion also has important implications for legal policy and practice. Essentially, it suggests that trial procedures should insure that the burden of proof and standard of proof instructions are clearly understood and correctly applied. Such precautions may be the best protection against extra-legal biases in juror judgment.

In closing I would like to reiterate the significant advantages of the mathematical modeling approach. The Thomas and Hogue model is stated clearly and unambiguously. The deductive power of mathematical analysis is easily applied to derive quantitative, testable implications and to fit the model to empirical data. And, finally, the inclusion of stochastic components in the model is a reasonable method to express precisely the bounds on our limited knowledge of juror decision making.

References

Blackstone, W. (1962). *Commentaries on the laws of England of public wrongs.* Boston: Beacon. (Original work published 1769)

Broeder, D. W. (1965). Previous jury trial service affecting juror behavior. *Insurance Law Journal, 506,* 138–143.

Campbell, D. T., & Ross, H. L. (1968). The Connecticut crackdown on speeding: Time-series data in quasi-experimental analysis. *Law and Society Review, 3,* 33–53.

Cotton, J. W. (1982). Where is the randomness for the human computer? *Behavior Research Methods and Instrumentation, 14,* 59–70.

Dane, F. C., & Wrightsman, L. S. (1982). Effects of defendants' and victims' characteristics on jurors' verdicts. In N. L. Kerr & R. M. Bray (Eds.), *The psychology of the courtroom* (pp. 83–115). New York: Academic Press.

Davis, J. H. (1969). *Group Performance.* Reading, MA: Addison-Wesley.

Davis, J. H., Kerr, N. L., Stasser, G., Meek, D., & Holt, R. (1977). Victim consequences, sentence severity, and decision processes in mock juries. *Organizational Behavior and Human Performance, 18,* 346–365.

Erwin, R. E., Greenberg, L. A., & Minzer, M. K. (1971). *Defense of drunk driving cases: Criminal – civil* (3rd ed.). New York: M. Bender.

Estes, W. K. (1959). The statistical approach to learning theory. In S. Koch (Ed.), *Psychology: A study of a science: Vol. 2. General systematic formulations, learning and special processes* (pp. 380–491). New York: McGraw-Hill.

Feinberg, W. E. (1971). Teaching the Type I and Type II errors: The judicial process. *The American Statistician, 25*(3), 30–32.

Galliher, J. F., McCartney, J. L., & Baum, B. E. (1974). Nebraska's marijuana law: A case of unexpected legislative innovation. *Law and Society Review, 8,* 441–455.

Green, D. M., & Swets, J. A. (1966). *Signal detection theory and psychophysics.* New York: Wiley.

Jones, C., & Aronson, E. (1973). Attribution of fault to a rape victim as a function of respectability of the victim. *Journal of Personality and Social Psychology, 26,* 415–419.

Kalven, H., & Zeisel, H. (1966). *The American jury.* Boston: Little, Brown.

Kerr, N. L. (1978a). Beautiful and blameless: Effects of victim attractiveness and responsibility on mock jurors' verdicts. *Personality and Social Psychology Bulletin, 4,* 479–482.

——— (1978b). Severity of prescribed penalty and mock jurors' verdicts. *Journal of Personality and Social Psychology, 36,* 1431–1442.

Kerr, N. L., Atkin, R. S., Stasser, G., Meek, D., Holt, R. W., & Davis, J. H. (1976). Guilt beyond a reasonable doubt: Effects of concept definition and assigned decision rule on the judgments of mock jurors. *Journal of Personality and Social Psychology, 34,* 282–294.

Kerr, N. L., Harmon, D. L., & Graves, J. K. (1982). Independence of multiple verdicts by jurors and juries. *Journal of Applied Social Psychology, 12,* 12–29.

Kerr, N. L., Nerenz, D. R., & Herrick, D. (1979). Role playing and the study of jury behavior. *Sociological Methods and Research, 7,* 337–355.

Landy, D., & Aronson, E. (1969). The influence of the character of the criminal and his victim on the decision of simulated jurors. *Journal of Experimental Social Psychology, 5,* 141–152.

Lockhart v. McCree, 106 S. Ct. 1758 (1986).

Luce, R. D. (1959). *Individual choice behavior: A theoretical analysis.* New York: Wiley.

MacCoun, R. J., & Kerr, N. L. (1988). Asymmetric influence in mock jury deliberation: Jurors' bias for leniency. *Journal of Personality and Social Psychology, 54,* 21–33.

McComas, W. C., & Noll, M. E. (1974). Effects of seriousness of charge and punishment severity on the judgments of simulated jurors. *Psychological Record, 24,* 545–547.

Myers, D. G., & Lamm, H. (1976). The group polarization phenomenon. *Psychological Bulletin, 83,* 602–627.

Owen, I. (1973). *Defending criminal cases before juries: A common sense approach.* Englewood Cliffs, NJ: Prentice-Hall.

Parducci, A. (1968). The relativism of absolute judgments. *Scientific American, 219*(6), 84–90.

Pennington, N., & Hastie, R. (1981). Juror decision-making models: The generalization gap. *Psychological Bulletin, 89,* 246–287.

Pepitone, A., & DiNubile, M. (1976). Contrast effects in judgments of crime severity and the punishment of criminal violators. *Journal of Personality and Social Psychology, 33,* 448–459.

Radzinowicz, L. (1948). *A history of English criminal law and its administration from 1750: Vol 1. The movement for reform.* London: Stevens.

Robertson, L. S., Rich, R. F., & Ross, H. L. (1973). Jail sentences for driving while intoxicated in Chicago: A judicial policy that failed. *Law and Society Review, 8*, 55–67.

Simon, R. J., & Mahan, L. (1971). Quantifying burdens of proof: A view from the bench, the jury, and the classroom. *Law and Society Review, 5*, 319–330.

Smith, M. (1966). Percy Forman: Top trial lawyer. *Life, 60*(13), 92–96, 98, 101.

Stasser, G., Kerr, N. L., & Bray, R. M. (1982). The social psychology of jury deliberations: Structure, process, and product. In N. L. Kerr & R. M. Bray (Eds.), *The psychology of the courtroom* (pp. 221–256). New York: Academic Press.

Sue, S., Smith, R. E., & Caldwell, C. (1973). Effects of inadmissible evidence on the decisions of simulated jurors: A moral dilemma. *Journal of Applied Social Psychology, 3*, 345–353.

Thomas, E. A. C., & Hogue, A. (1976). Apparent weight of evidence, decision criteria, and confidence ratings in juror decision making. *Psychological Review, 83*, 442–465.

Thompson, W. C., Cowan, C. L., Ellsworth, P. C., & Harrington, J. C. (1984). Death penalty attitudes and conviction proneness: The translation of attitudes into verdicts. *Law and Human Behavior, 8*, 95–113.

Tobias, J. J. (1967). *Crime and industrial society in the 19th century.* New York: Schocken Books.

Vidmar, N. (1972). Effects of decision alternatives on the verdicts and social perceptions of simulated jurors. *Journal of Personality and Social Psychology, 22*, 211–218.

Wilson, D. W., & Donnerstein, E. (1977). Guilty or not guilty? A look at the "simulated" jury paradigm. *Journal of Applied Social Psychology, 7*, 175–190.

Wissler, R. L., & Saks, M. J. (1985). On the inefficacy of limiting instructions: When jurors use prior conviction evidence to decide on guilt. *Law and Human Behavior, 9*, 37–48.

Zeisel, H., & Diamond, S. S. (1978). The effects of peremptory challenges on jury and verdict: An experiment in a federal district court. *Stanford Law Review, 30*, 491–531.

6 Formal and empirical research on cascaded inference in jurisprudence

David A. Schum and Anne W. Martin

Introduction

This paper[1] contains an introduction to some of the results and observations we have accumulated from a series of studies on the task of assessing the probative value of inconclusive or probabilistic trial evidence. Some of these studies are formal or logical in nature and concern the manner in which the probative value of evidence *should be* assessed coherently. The other studies are empirical and behavioral in nature and concern the manner in which persons *actually do* assess the probative value of evidence. Our dual concern was voiced by Wigmore (1937, p. 8), who expressed interest in ". . . the reasons why a total mass of evidence does or should persuade us to a given conclusion, and why our conclusions would or should have been different or identical if some part of that total mass of evidence had been different." Our formal and empirical studies have proceeded hand-in-hand. Formal research helps to identify meaningful variables and measures for empirical research; empirical research, interesting in its own right, is also useful in testing the adequacy of the foundations for formal studies.

A major focus of our research has been upon inductive inference tasks, which Wigmore termed "catenated"; the modern terms for these tasks are "cascaded" or "hierarchical" (Wigmore, 1937, p. 13). Wigmore was the first to point out the fact that most inferential reasoning tasks are cascaded in nature. A cascaded inference task is composed of one or more reasoning

This chapter originally appeared in *Law and Society Review,* 1982, *17,* 105–151. Copyright © 1982 by the Law and Society Association. Reprinted by permission.

[1] The research reported in this paper was supported by The National Science Foundation under Grants SOC 77-28471 and SES 80-24203 to Rice University. The authors gratefully acknowledge the advice and assistance during the planning of our research of Professor Richard Lempert, University of Michigan School of Law, and Professor L. Jonathan Cohen, The Queen's College, Oxford University. The authors also wish to thank Dr. Felice Levine, National Science Foundation, for her encouragement and support.

stages interposed between evidence observable to the factfinder and the ultimate facts-in-issue. An example of a cascaded inference is presented by testimony from a witness of less than perfect credibility that the defendant was at the scene at the time of the crime. The testimony requires one first to assess the likelihood that the defendant was, in fact, at the scene/time. This foundational stage involves evaluation of the witness's credibility. Then, assuming the defendant at the scene/time of the crime, one must assess how strongly this event bears on the issue of whether or not the defendant committed the crime. Further difficulty is presented by intricate patterns of reasoning which require the joint consideration of current evidence with one or more previously given pieces of evidence.

The formal research discussed in this paper concerns the logical requisites of cascaded inference tasks and the manner in which these requisites should be combined. Wigmore acknowledged that logicians had found canons of reasoning in simple situations; however, he lamented the fact that (at that time) there were no such canons of reasoning from an entire mass of evidence "mixed" with respect to logical form (Wigmore, 1937, p. 8). Our formal work shows that, though the process is tedious and difficult, canons of reasoning can be derived for masses of mixed evidence.

The present article is meant to introduce the reader to ways in which formal analysis can be used to understand the logical demands of inference from the types of evidence presented in legal settings. As a result, the detailed mathematical arguments that form the bases for the analyses will not be described here. Interested readers are directed to our monographs dealing with these mathematical arguments. Our focus in this article is on the major conclusions of our formal studies as they bear upon commonly encountered evidentiary issues in inferences made at trial. A technical appendix is included in which we illustrate the essentials of our formal process using three examples. The reader choosing to disregard this appendix is in no way disadvantaged in reading the text of this paper.

The benefits of formal research on legal inference have not gone unnoticed by current scholars in jurisprudence (e.g., Eggleston, 1978; Lempert, 1977; Lempert & Saltzburg, 1977). Such research assists in efforts to illuminate and sharpen legal reasoning. The reader is, of course, interested in how our current research adds to this process.

Our empirical research concerns the reasoning processes of the ordinary citizens upon which so much depends in court trials. In fact, very little is known about human inferential reasoning, partly because of the lack of knowledge about the tasks people are asked to perform. Our formal research concerns what these tasks demand, and our empirical research concerns how well persons seem to meet these demands. Previous studies have suggested that everyone is subject to biases and errors in inferential behavior (e.g., Saks & Kidd, 1980). Unfortunately, many conclusions about human biases and error rest upon studies incorporating ill-posed problems or problems which are quite abstract. An objective in our empirical research was to present carefully posed concrete inferential problems which begin to approach the complexity of those faced by the factfinder in a court of law.

Formal research: Foundations

The inference tasks performed by the factfinder commonly involve the interplay of inductive and deductive reasoning processes; this fact was noted by Wigmore in his analysis (1937, p. 20). Our formal research generally focuses upon inductive inference, the task of revising one's opinion about the relative likelihood of rival facts-in-issue on the basis of inconclusive or probabilistic evidence. In evaluating or "weighing" evidence in an inferential task, one recognizes that items of evidence differ in strength; for various reasons some items are persuasive and allow for substantial revision in our opinions, while other items seem to justify little or no opinion revision. Thus, a major task in inductive inference consists of evaluating the inferential or probative strength of evidence. Given more than one item of evidence, one must somehow aggregate or combine the probative weights given to each item. One major complication is that the probative weight given to one item frequently depends strongly upon our recollection of other items. We explore the tasks of evaluating the probative strength of individual items of evidence and of collections of all the items. In essence, this research is concerned with relevance issues.

Federal Rule of Evidence FRE 401 defines *relevant* evidence as "evidence having any tendency to make the existence of any fact that is of consequence to the determination of the action more probable or less probable than it would be without the evidence." As others have noted (Lempert & Saltzburg, 1977), there appear to be "natural" measures within conventional probability theory for the relevance or probativity of evidence. These measures are termed "likelihood ratios," and they provide an indication of the necessary opinion revision prescribed by FRE 401 for relevant evidence. In our context, a likelihood ratio expresses the probability of an item of evidence assuming the defendant's guilt, relative to the probability of this same item of evidence assuming defendant's innocence.[2] We use an upper-case Greek lambda [Λ] to symbolize a likelihood ratio and add a subscript when Λ applies to a certain evidence item e; thus, Λ_e means the likelihood ratio for evidence item e. When $\Lambda_e = 1.0$, evidence e has equal probability assuming guilt or assuming innocence, and so e is nonprobative. When Λ_e is greater than 1.0, then e is probative evidence favoring defendant's guilt; when Λ_e is less than 1.0, then e probatively favors defendant's innocence.

Our first formal objective has been to formulate and study likelihood ratio expressions for various identifiable logical species of evidence. We have termed these species of evidence *inference structures* and have used

---

[2] Likelihoods and likelihood ratios appear as ingredients in Bayes' rule. Essentially, these ingredients prescribe the amount of revision, from prior opinion to posterior opinion, which an item of evidence justifies.

these inference structures as the basic "building blocks" in thinking about complex masses of evidence representing entire cases. The complexity of a likelihood ratio depends upon the form of the evidence and the nature of the reasoning process established by the evidence. Once derived for the evidence in some inference structure, likelihood ratio expressions tell us what probabilistic ingredients are required at each step in the reasoning process and how they should be combined in a coherent manner.

To many persons, equations seem sterile and, when applied as representations for human tasks, seem almost certain to fail in capturing all of the behavioral essentials that intuition and experience suggest are features of the tasks. Consequently, the second objective in our formal research has been the study of what we have termed the "behavioral richness" of our likelihood ratio expressions (Schum, 1977a). This term does not refer to the extent to which any of our formal expressions describes or predicts the actual behavior of any person. In our usage, a likelihood ratio is behaviorally rich if it captures the essentials and subtleties of probative value assessment that recorded experience with the evidence of concern suggest are there.

A third objective in our formal research has been to relate the study and analysis of likelihood ratio expressions for various inference structures to the rules and prescriptions of evidence law, noting both similarities and differences between the prescriptions of our formal expressions and corresponding established legal prescriptions. In general we have been impressed by the many similarities, a full accounting of which appears in our specific monographs. We view this correspondence between formal and legal prescriptions concerning relevance issues as evidence for a convergence to coherence in the development of evidentiary rules and procedures.[3] In addition, our formal research provides some basis for the sharpening of the definition of legal terms. As laypersons in jurisprudence, we have observed apparent difficulties among jurists in obtaining crisp definitions of certain terms (e.g., redundancy, corroborative and cumulative evidence). Formal research forces one to be precise, or at least to settle upon definitions.

One of our strong hopes has been that our formal research will assist us in efforts to perform empirical research of greater interest and relevance to

[3] We note that our formal approach provides just one set of standards against which the coherence of legal prescriptions can be evaluated. There are other standards which we both recognize and appreciate. Our formal research is grounded on the axioms of "conventional" mathematical probability theory. There are other axiom systems which lead to other prescriptions for "coherent" inductive reasoning. One in particular is Cohen's system of "inductive" probabilities (Cohen, 1977). Cohen claims this system to be more congenial to application in legal matters than the mathematical systems which we use; much current debate on this issue has resulted (e.g., Cohen, 1981; Kaye, 1979, 1981; Schum, 1979c). Other systems include the "belief functions" of Shafer (1976), and the "possibility" measures of Zadeh (1978). We continue to work within the mathematical system, because it is our belief that this system is the only one extant which offers the flexibility necessary to capture the rich array of subtleties in evidence.

jurists. Laboratory research on human inference is often criticized for being too abstract and for not including enough relevant aspects of tasks as they occur in natural settings (Winkler & Murphy, 1973). In our empirical research, subjects evaluated evidence having a variety of subtle properties. Likelihood ratios, derived for the evidence our subjects evaluated, contain ingredients which, far from being mathematically arcane, in fact lay bare the logical steps or stages in reasoning from the evidence to the major facts-in-issue.

Formal studies: Results and observations

On inference structures

Substantively, evidence varies in near-infinite fashion. Fortunately, however, there appears to be a manageably finite number of logically distinct forms of evidence. Various classification schemes are found in evidence law treatises, but no one scheme seems to enjoy universal acceptance. Our formal work has basically involved circumstantial evidence with a testimonial foundation; Wigmore noted that such evidence is the form most frequently encountered at trial (1937, p. 13). Our formal process works equally well for "real" evidence; in fact, formalizations for the probative value of such evidence are simpler than for testimonial evidence (Schum, 1980). Our interest in testimonial evidence arises partly because of an abiding interest in the nature of the relationship between the credibility of the source of evidence and the inferential or probative value of what the source reports (Schum & DuCharme, 1971).

There appears to be a relatively small number of generic types of evidence which we have termed *inference structures.* We distinguish between simple, complex, and mixed inference structures. A *simple* inference structure is a chainlike reasoning process "set in motion" by a single item of testimony. The foundation of the reasoning chain is a testimonial assertion; later stages or links in the chain represent circumstantial reasoning steps from the matter asserted to the ultimate or major facts-in-issue. In such structures the number of reasoning steps can vary. A further characteristic of a simple inference structure is that neither the testimonial assertion nor the events at subsequent reasoning stages are assumed to be probabilistically linked to previous evidence or events in their reasoning chains. Shown in Figures 6.1-A and 6.1-B below are diagrammatic representations of two simple inference structures involving testimonial evidence. The one in Figure 6.1-A, termed a "first-order cascaded inference," is the simplest possible case of cascaded or catenated inference. Witness W_i asserts that event D happened – for example, that the defendant was at the scene of the crime. The event D^c is the event that D did not occur. We represent the testimonial assertion that D occurred as D_i^* to distinguish it from the event D itself. Failure to distinguish between testimony about an event (D_i^*) and the event

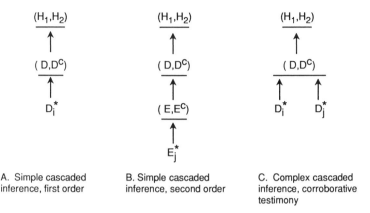

A. Simple cascaded
inference, first order

B. Simple cascaded
inference, second order

C. Complex cascaded
inference, corroborative
testimony

Figure 6.1. Example inference structures.

itself (D) has caused no end of difficulties in many previous studies of the impact of witness credibility upon the probative value of testimonial evidence (e.g., Eggleston, 1978). The first stage of reasoning is from testimony D_i^* to events D, D^c; this is the foundation stage of reasoning and, as formalizations for the probative value of D_i^* show, involves assessment of the credibility of W_i. The next stage of reasoning is from events D and D^c to events H_1 and H_2, representing the major or ultimate facts-in-issue (e.g., that defendant committed the crime, H_1, or did not, H_2). In this stage of reasoning the probative importance of the defendant's being at the scene of the crime is assessed. Equation 1 in the Technical Appendix of this chapter shows the expression for the likelihood ratio for testimony D_i^*.

Figure 6.1-B shows a "second-order cascaded inference." Witness W_j asserts E_j^*, that event E occurred. Suppose E is the event that the defendant's car was at the scene of the crime at the time in question. The first stage of reasoning, from E_j^* to events, E, E^c, is an assessment of the credibility of W_j. The next stage involves circumstantial reasoning from E, E^c to events D, D^c whether or not defendant was at the scene. The final stage involves circumstantial reasoning from events D, D^c to events H_1, H_2. Equation 2 in the technical appendix shows the likelihood ratio for testimony E_j^*. Simple inference structures like these two can have any number of reasoning stages or "levels" of cascading or catenation.

In *complex* inference structures there is always foundation testimony from more than one witness. Often there are probabilistic linkages among events in the reasoning chains based on each item of testimony. We have identified four basic classes of complex inference structures: those representing *contradictory* testimony, *corroboratively redundant* testimony, *cumulatively redundant* testimony, and *nonredundant* testimony. In contradictory testimony, one witness asserts that event D occurred and another asserts that D did not occur. Corroboratively redundant testimony concerns the assertions of two or more witnesses that the (same) event D occurred. Figure 6.1-C depicts a complex inference structure involving corroboratively redundant testimony. In this structure, two witnesses W_i and W_j assert that event D occurred; their testimonies are D_i^* and D_j^*. That the testimony here is possibly redundant is obvious, since they both testify to the same event. If the first witness has perfect credibility, then testimony from the second usually adds nothing. Suppose, however, we thought that the first witness could not actually determine whether or not D occurred. Then, testimony from the second witness does have probative value depending, in part, on the credibility of this second witness. This situation introduces the important feature of *conditional nonindependence*. Two or more items of evidence or events at reasoning stages suggested by evidence are conditionally *non*-independent if, considered jointly, they mean something probatively different than they do if considered separately. If not, then they are said to be conditionally independent.[4] Equation 3 in the appendix shows the likelihood ratio for the second and possibly redundant testimony. There are terms in this expression which allow one to account, in a formally ideal way, for the degree of redundance involving these two witnesses.

In *cumulatively* redundant testimony, there is an assertion from one witness that event E occurred. A later assertion that a different event F occurred comes from either the same or a different witness. Suppose that even E, if it occurred, made event F highly probable in the nature of things (i.e. regardless of what else you know), and therefore testimony that F occurred yields little if any probative value if the first witness is believed. For example, the first witness asserts that defendant was at the scene/time of the crime. The second asserts that he/she found the defendant's coat at the scene/time. If the first witness is believed, testimony from the second adds little to our determination about whether or not the defendant was at the scene/time. The redundance of cumulative testimony of this sort can be

---

[4] At various points we use the expression conditional independence or nonindependence of events, because with it we can represent a remarkable array of subtleties in evidence. Two events A and B are said to be unconditionally independent or simply *independent* if knowledge of one of the events does not cause you to change your mind about the probability of the other; if such knowledge does cause a change, then the events are said to be nonindependent. Suppose we have knowledge of a third event C. Events A and B are said to be *conditionally independent*, given event C, if knowledge of one of the events A or B does not cause you to change your mind about the probability of the other, provided that event C is true. If knowledge of event A causes you to change your mind about the probability of B, when event C is known or assumed, then A and B are said to be *conditionally nonindependent*, given event C. Very often, two or more evidence items or events at reasoning stages suggested by these items mean something probatively different when considered jointly than they do if considered separately. The concept of conditional independence/nonindependence allows you to express this probative difference. Unfortunately, the concepts of independence and conditional independence are often confused; they are related concepts, but they are not the same. Examples of subtleties which find expression via patterns of conditional nonindependence include a variety of credibility-related effects, redundance in testimony, the significance of weak links and rare events in reasoning stages, a reasoning stage relation called transitivity, and the locus of probative value in equivocal testimony or the nonproduction of testimony.

represented, along with other subtleties, in an appropriate expression of conditional nonindependence.

If two or more items of testimony are redundant, earlier items tend to decrease the probative value of later items. Alternatively, testimony can be *facilitative* so that one item makes a later item seem more probatively valuable. In *nonredundant* testimony, either the assertion of one witness causes no change in the value of a later assertion, or it acts to enhance the value of a later assertion. For example, the first of two witnesses reports finding the defendant's revolver beside the victim's body in the defendant's apartment. The second witness reports the sound of a revolver shot coming (apparently) from the window of this apartment. On the issue of whether or not the defendant is guilty, the first testimony seems to have a facilitative effect upon the probativity of the second.

Finally, a *mixed* inference structure represents various combinations of the above structures. As an example, two witnesses testify that event E occurred; their testimony is corroboratively redundant. Then, three witnesses give joint corroborative testimony that event E did not occur, thus contradicting the testimony of the first two. The reader who is interested in a complete collection of the inference structures we have studied, including a derivation of likelihood ratio expressions for each structure, may refer to Schum and Martin (1980a; 1981).

Cases or collections of evidence can be thought of as collections of inference structures. Testimony or other evidence upon which these structures are based open up specific lines of reasoning which the structures indicate. Such evidence may be thought of as "mainframe" evidence, having direct probative value. Other evidence may be thought of as "ancillary" evidence in the sense that it allows the factfinder to evaluate the strength of linkages among events at various stages in the reasoning suggested by an inference structure. Ancillary evidence may be said to have "acquired" or "derived" probative value. For example, Witness W_j asserts that the observational conditions were good on the day that a previous witness W_i observed E, an event linked circumstantially to major facts-in-issue. The testimony of W_j is not probative on these facts by itself; it does, however, acquire probative value since it bears on the credibility of W_i, whose testimony about E does have direct probative significance. Thus, all evidence at trial can be grossly categorized as "mainframe" or "ancillary" evidence. Had Wigmore realized this, he might have been able to simplify some of his very complex diagrammatic illustrations of case evidence, and he might also have been able to see how specific formalization of such evidence could be derived.

On witness credibility

The credibility of the source or sources of the evidence forms the foundation for cascaded reasoning from testimonial evidence. Likelihood ratio expressions for the process of assessing the probative value of testimonial evidence reveal several important logical characteristics of this process. First, established grounds for impeaching or supporting the credibility of witnesses find expression in these likelihood ratios (Schum, 1977a; Schum & Kelly, 1973). These grounds include observational capacity, bias, prior inconsistent statements, influence among witnesses, and character (Cleary, 1972). Second, our formal process makes clear the fact that the behavior of a witness, as revealed by the witness or by other evidence, is often a source of probative value in addition to that provided by the events reported by the witness. Finally, our studies show the precise nature of the important interaction between the credibility of a witness and the rarity of the event reported by the witness in determinations of the probative value of witness testimony (Schum, 1977a).

In studying the probative value of witness testimony we have found it useful to use two constructs from signal detection theory, a theory which has had great impact on sensory psychophysics and a variety of other research areas (e.g., see Egan, 1975; Swets, 1964). This theory provides the means for separating two basic dimensions of testimonial behavior. The first dimension, which concerns the observational sensitivity or capacity of a witness, is indexed by a measure labeled d'. The second dimension concerns motivational and other factors that influence the decisions by a witness about what event to report following an observation. This decision criterion, $L(x_0)$, can be determined from information about the observer's expectations, goals, and motives.

The hit and false-positive probabilities in our Λ formulations, together with other directly related probabilities called "misses" and "correct rejections" are key elements in signal detection theory; in fact, these labels come from this theory. For some observational task, if we know or assume the conditional probability of an event being reported not true (a false positive), we can determine d' and $L(x_0)$. Moreover, we can vary d'-related information independently of $L(x_0)$-related information in the formal study of how such classes of information influence the probative value of testimonial evidence.

In our formal studies we first examined situations in which credibility-related hit and false-positive probabilities were not conditioned by other events in a reasoning chain. When this is true, straightforward tradeoffs are possible between observational sensitivity and decision-related factors in determining the probative value of testimony. For example, testimony from a witness with low observational sensitivity but a strong bias against offering the testimony can have as much value as testimony from a highly sensitive witness who is biased in favor of giving such testimony. We also attempted to clarify the meaning of "biased" testimony in relation to testimony that lacks veracity. In our context, bias refers to a witness's apparent preferences for or against offering the testimony. Such preferences can sometimes be inferred from other evidence such as information about the relationship between witness and defendant. Suppose a witness is a close friend of defendant; this witness may have a distinct bias in favor of reporting an event favorable to the defendant's case. We may easily believe the witness to be biased without also believing that the witness is lying when he/she reports the occurrence of this event. Our formal process shows why biased testimony need not be untruthful, and how testimony which lacks veracity need not be biased. Generally, bias is a factor in the determination of the probative *strength* of testimony, while veracity determines the probative *direction* of testimony (i.e., which of the two rival facts-in-issue the testimony favors).

We also examined a variety of situations in which observational capacity and/or decision-related factors were made conditional upon events representing rival facts-in-issue. This is another way of saying that credibility-related factors for a witness provide probative value over and above the value of the event being reported. As an example of how factors underlying the observational and decision-related factors influence the value of testimonial evidence, we have examined a case in which a witness testifies against preference. In such a case one expects a "gain" in probative value over identical testimony from a witness who has no such preferential bias. Our formal studies show that this gain is justified and show the precise formal locus of such gain. In general, the observational and testimonial behaviors of a witness by themselves are important sources of probative value. These studies show just how important these sources are, since our formulations are remarkably sensitive to apparently minor alterations of credibility-related ingredients when they are made conditional upon one or the other facts-in-issue.

Redundance issues

Redundance is among the most interesting but formally difficult evidentiary issues. Our interest in the formal study of the redundance of testimonial evidence was stimulated by Lempert's (1977) concern about the "double-counting" of such evidence. In our studies (Schum, 1979b) we distinguished between "cumulative" and "corroborative" redundance since we observed a formally necessary distinction between the instances in which two or more witnesses say the same thing and the instance in which two or more witnesses give different testimony but on obviously related matters. Our usage of the term *redundance* corresponds with the common interpretation that redundant evidence is superfluous and supplies little, if any, probative value in addition to previous evidence. We explored the various uses of the terms "corroborative" and "cumulative" and observed some confusion; some jurists make sharp distinctions between these terms, while others use them interchangeably. In our study we found it necessary to make a distinction since, formally, corroborative redundance is a special case of cumulative redundance. In our studies of the factors which influence the redundance of testimonial evidence, it is apparent that there are more factors

influencing cumulative redundance than there are influencing corroborative redundancy.

In a strict sense *redundance* is a property of the *events* being reported and
not the testimony of these events. To see that this must be so, consider the
testimony of two witnesses who both report that event D occurred. The
first witness, we are convinced, could not tell whether or not D occurred,
and therefore we assign *no* probative value to this testimony. The second
witness seems reasonably credible, and we are justified in assigning probativity to this second testimony to the extent that the second witness is
credible and to the extent that event D is probatively valuable.[5] Equations 4
and 5 in the technical appendix express our measures of event redundance
in the cumulative and corroborative cases.

The following six factors influence the *cumulative* redundance of testimony F_j^*, given prior testimony E_i^*: The strength of the redundance of
events E and F (as measured by R_{cum} in Equation 4 in the technical appendix), the credibilty of W_i and of W_j; the probative value of event F, given E^c
(the first witness may be untruthful); the rarity of events E and F; and the
number of reasoning stages between E and F and major facts-in-issue. Four
factors determine the redundance of *corroborative* testimony E_i^* and E_j^*: the
credibility of W_i and of W_j; the rarity of event E; and the number of reasoning stages between E and the major facts-in-issue. Careful study reveals a
large number of interesting consequences to probativity assessment when
redundancy is ignored. For example, ignoring redundancy of E and F will
sometimes, but not always lead to the overvaluation of testimony F_j^*. Certain combinations of credibility-related ingredients for witnesses W_i and
W_j cause one to *undervalue* testimony F_j^* even when events E and F are
strongly redundant. In the corroborative case, ignoring the natural redundance of such testimony is most serious when the credibility of the prior
witness W_i is strong; i.e., "double-counting" of evidence in the corroborative case is most serious because, when the prior witness is highly credible,
the value of testimony from the second witness is, formally, nearly valueless. The rarity of events exerts an interesting influence in the corroborative case. When the event being reported is rare, a stronger level of credibility of the first witness is required to make the value of the testimony
of the second witness vanish when natural corroborative redundance is
ignored.

Reasoning chain issues

In the analysis of inductive reasoning chains, a variety of issues arouse considerable interest. Following are three issues which we have examined using

[5] Concepts from *statistical communications theory*, often called *information theory*, allow us to
measure the probative redundancy of events in well-defined reasoning chains. In this theory, measures of redundancy are crucial in assessing the efficiency of ideal and actual communications channels (e.g., Staniland, 1966). Our measure of *event* redundance has essentially the same properties as does the redundancy measure in information theory.

various analyses of likelihood ratio formulations for simple inference structures based upon a single item of foundation testimony (Schum, 1979a). The first issue concerns a formal relation called *transitivity*. Suppose foundation evidence A probatively favors B, and B probatively favors C; this chain of reasoning is said to be *transitive* if A probatively favors C. If A does not favor C, the relation in the chain of reasoning is *intransitive*. We have examined a variety of conditions under which such transitive relations are either formally allowable or denied. The second issue concerns the effects upon the probative value of foundation testimony of locating a "weak link" at various points in an inferential reasoning chain. The third issue concerns the effects upon the probative value of foundation testimony of locating a "rare" event at various points in a chain of inferential reasoning. Transitivity and weak link issues and their analysis within the conventional probability system were critically examined by Cohen (1977). Our study of these issues was prompted, in part, by Cohen's analysis, since we did not believe that all problems raised were adequately posed.

Study of conditions favoring transitive relations among stages of inductive reasoning are particularly important in civil cases in which at least some courts enforce different proof standards at different stages of an inferential chain (Cohen, 1977, p. 69). For example, a foundation stage may require a more stringent standard of proof in order to support a subsequent stage whose proof standard is "on balance of probabilities" or "preponderance of the evidence." Our analysis shows that whether or not transitive relations occur formally in a chain of reasoning depends entirely upon the pattern of conditional independence/nonindependence relations among events in a reasoning stage. Suppose there is a complete pattern of conditional independence relations among events in a reasoning stage; this means that any event is conditioned only by events at the next higher stage of reasoning. When this is true, if foundation A probatively favors B, and B probatively favors C, then A will probatively favor C. However, under various patterns of conditional nonindependence in which an event at one stage may be linked with those at several higher stages, transitive relations, though intuitively expected, are frequently denied by appropriate formalization. Thus, it is not true in general that, if argument at each reasoning stage favors side A, then the overall argument favors A.

As an example, suppose testimony that the defendant was at the scene (D_i^*) favors the event that the defendant actually was at the scene (D) and, in turn, the defendant being at the scene (D) favors the event that the defendant is guilty as charged (H_1). Our formal process shows why it is not necessarily the case that testimony that defendant was at the scene (D_i^*) probatively favors defendant's guilt (H_1). This probative relation may be transitive or intransitive, depending on what we know about the witness.

Analysis of "weak links," "rare events," and their location in a reasoning chain also reveals the importance of conditional independence/nonindependence patterns among events in a reasoning chain. Some may expect that a weak link at the foundation stage of an argument is more damaging than one located at the "top" of a chain. Grounds for this expectation seem to be that a strong foundation for a weak argument is preferable to a weak foundation for a strong argument. Our formal analysis shows that neither is preferable provided that there is a pattern of complete conditional independence among events in a reasoning chain. This says that the location of a weak link does not matter under these conditions and that the chain cannot be stronger than its weakest link wherever it is located. The location of "rare" events in a chain *does* matter. Rare events are more damaging to the probative value of foundation testimony if they occur at the top of the chain, whether or not there are conditional nonindependence patterns in the chain.

On several special types of evidence

Following is a brief account of formal issues encountered in our examination of three well-known types of evidence. Study of these types of evidence, all of which can involve cascaded inference, has required us to examine several issues of more general importance in the analysis of complex reasoning chains.

Hearsay evidence. One of the most difficult tasks in the formal study of evidence concerns a type of evidence that each one of us evaluates on a regular basis; in jurisprudence such evidence is termed "hearsay"; more generally it is called "second-hand" evidence. This latter designation is more general than it appears, since it is usually applied to instances in which one receives a report or testimony passed through several intermediate sources; often, the original source is unknown. In evidence law there is an abundant literature on the admissibility of various forms of hearsay but a sparse literature on the probative value of such evidence. Suppose a "simple" situation in which A, a witness at trial, reports testimony allegedly given by out-of-court assertor B. There are, of course, complex credibility-related issues concerning both A and B; so, at the very least, we have more than one foundation stage in reasoning from such evidence.

Our formal studies of hearsay (Martin, 1979) represent elaboration and extension of Tribe's model for the "triangulation" of hearsay in which only admissibility issues were of concern (Tribe, 1974). Likelihood ratio representations for the probative value of hearsay are made difficult by the fact that there are several possible different stages of reasoning involved. We may ask: did B actually observe the event in question; did B in fact report anything to A? (A may have "put words into B's mouth".) Derivation of Λ for alternative forms of reasoning from hearsay evidence led to the discovery of some very important *recursive* algorithms which occur in all Λ formulations. A recursive rule is one that is defined in terms of itself. Such discovery led to the development of a *general* algorithm for the analysis of inference structures of virtually any degree of complexity and involving any pattern of conditional independence assumptions involving events in the structure (Martin, 1980). A computer program called CASPRO has been developed which uses this algorithm and which facilitates analysis of complex inference structures.

Equivocal testimony or no testimony on a relevant issue at trial. We now consider three species of "evidence" which some, at least, would judge to be, by their very nature, probatively vacuous regardless of the facts-in-issue (Schum, 1981a). Formal study, however, convinces us that there is the possibility of very strong probative value in each case. The first concerns *equivocal testimony* given by a witness who, when asked whether or not the event D occurred, replies "I don't know," "I don't remember," "I couldn't tell," etc. In some instances this may simply indicate a form of self-impeachment by the witness who, in fact, is truthful in giving any of these responses. Formally, such testimony is probatively valueless. In other instances, depending upon what else we may know about the witness, we may infer that the witness is "sandbagging" and actually knows more than his/her testimony indicates. In such instances, formal analysis shows that the probative value of such equivocation can be even more probative than *certain* knowledge of the occurrence of one of the events about which the witness equivocates.

The second case concerns *silence* as evidence; queried about whether or not event D occurred, the witness stands mute or exercises privilege. In this case other facts brought to light at trial can, under some conditions, formally justify stronger opinion revision about facts-in-issue than would specific testimony by the witness. The same also applies to a third case involving the *nonproduction* of evidence (testimonial or otherwise). Such nonproduction can be at least as probative as specific evidence on the matter at issue given by a witness of any level of credibility.

Opportunity and alibi testimony. The array of subtleties in evidence make the formal study of evidence rather like walking through a minefield; one wrong step, however minor, can cause subsequent discomfort. We experienced such discomfort in applying our formal processes to opportunity evidence and its logical negation, alibi evidence. Probatively, opportunity evidence, even if given by a perfectly credible source, is inconclusive that the defendant committed the act as alleged. Alibi evidence, if given by a perfectly credible source, is conclusive evidence of defendant's nonparticipation in the act as alleged. We assume here that the act in question would, if performed by defendant, require his/her physical presence. Unless Λ equations are formulated with extreme care, certain embarrassing indeterminacies can arise in equations whose ingredients seem entirely plausible unless carefully examined (Schum, 1981b).

As a final word on formal issues we mention Wigmore's desire for "mental probative equations" (Wigmore, 1937, p. 8). Whether or not our Λ formulations bear any resemblance to the equations Wigmore had in mind, we can never tell. Our formal study reveals the intricacies of cascaded or catenated inference even for simple items of evidence. The process of "connecting up" the evidence is, formally, frightening to contemplate. We have done so, however, for small evidence sets. This process, we have noted, bears no small resemblance to the sensory-perceptual tasks of observing an object against a background. Prior evidence exerts a "contrast" effect on current evidence in the same way as the color of a background influences the perceived color of an object presented against this background (Schum, 1977b). Before considering empirical research issues, we note our realization that formal study of evidence by itself can never prescribe what the "rules of evidence" ought to be. However, as one jurist (Keyser, 1929) remarked: "An ensemble of experience-given propositions (like those constituting any existing branch of law) never gets so thoroughly examined and criticized and understood as when the ensemble is submitted to the severe processes of mathematicization."

Empirical studies: Background, objectives, and methods

Our empirical research was designed to provide information about human capabilities and limitations in the task of assessing the probative or inferential value of evidence. In a series of related studies whose results are summarized below, research subjects provided specific numerical responses as indications of their assessments of the probative strength of individual items of evidence and of collections of evidence items. Examination of these responses in various ways is one means of studying certain characteristics of human behavior in the task of reasoning from inconclusive evidence. In actual court proceedings, however, factfinders are not encouraged to make public their judgments about the evidence. At the outset we note that no part of our study was designed to convince jurists that the factfinding process ought to require specific quantitative assessments of evidence strength or that forensic standards of proof ought to be specifically quantified. This disclaimer seems necessary in light of controversy among jurists about the use of various probabilistic representations in actual court trials (e.g., Finkelstein & Fairley, 1970; Tribe, 1971).

It is commonly believed that the quantitative reasoning skills of ordinary persons are not very strong and that quantitatively expressed human judgments are neither accurate nor reliable. In a variety of research contexts, psychologists and others have obtained useful results by relying heavily upon numerical judgments expressed by their research subjects; we do so here.[6]

---

[6] In the study of sensory and perceptual processes, for example, there is a large collection of *psychophysical* measurement procedures, many of which require numerical judgments from subjects. In sensory psychophysics, it is common practice to take seriously the numerical

Background and specific objectives

Our present studies of human capabilities and limitations in the task of assessing the probative weight of evidence have three major roots: Wigmore's work on the analysis of complex masses of mixed evidence, basic and applied research performed by psychologists and others concerning the design of more efficient ways to allocate tasks among persons and devices in various information-processing systems, and our recent work on the formal analysis of cascaded inference. We have already acknowledged our debt to Wigmore, who began the formidable task of decomposing complex inferences. Within psychology, study and analysis of complex inference tasks dates from the early 1960s with Ward Edwards' suggestions about how such inference tasks ought to be decomposed so that a person, confronted with a mass of evidence, could be relieved of the task of mentally aggregating large amounts of probabilistic evidence (Edwards, 1962). As Edwards discussed, Bayes' rule is suggestive of ways in which such task decomposition ought to be performed. These ideas generated a substantial amount of research on matters concerning human performance on inductive or probabilistic reasoning. Most of this research was performed in laboratory settings involving tasks of varying complexity; excellent reviews are to be found in papers by Slovic and Lichtenstein (1971) and Rapoport and Wallsten (1972). Research on inferential processes continues; recent research on various attributes of human probabilistic judgments of concern to jurists has been reviewed by Saks and Kidd (1980). Our own formal research on cascaded or hierarchical inference was designed to extend the applicability of Bayes' rule to complex forms of evidence.

In planning our studies of cascaded inference in jurisprudence we had a number of objectives. Three of these objectives concern our basic interest in the task of assessing the probative weight of evidence, and the results presented in the next section bear upon these.

1. In the study of many human tasks a natural question is: How accurately or correctly can a person perform the task? Unfortunately, as we recognize, we can *never* ask how correct or accurate is a person's assessment of the probative weight either of an item of evidence or a collection of evidence given at trial. Such evidence involves unique or one-of-a-kind events, and each factfinder evaluates the evidence according to personal

judgments individuals provide as indications of various attributes of their sensory experience. Such faith has not been unrewarded; a variety of useful metrics and measurement procedures based upon subjective quantitative assessments are employed on a regular basis in very practical applications related to vision and audition. Behaviorally useful measures of light and sound are all based upon psychophysical measures (e.g., Stevens, 1975). Our present studies are within the tradition of psychophysics in the sense that we take seriously the numerical judgments about evidence strength provided by our subjects. We do in fact, construe these judgments as psychophysical judgments and, in so doing, are consistent with the philosopher Hume's assertion that all probabilistic reasoning is a species of sensation; the weight given to alternative arguments involves subjective feelings about the relative intensity or strength of the arguments (Hume, 1888).

strategies based upon a unique matrix of prior experience. In short, there is no "true" or "correct" probative weight for any item or collection of evidence; still, even though we cannot measure the accuracy of probativity assessment, we can under certain circumstances evaluate the consistency or coherence of such assessments. One such circumstance occurs when a person can be asked to perform the same task in different but equivalent ways. As we shall see, a probativity assessment task can be decomposed to varying degrees; we can ask how consistent or coherent are assessments across various levels of task decomposition. In a word, this objective concerns the extent to which a person's assessment of the value of "parts" of an evidence collection are consistent with this person's assessment of the "whole" collection of the evidence. Our formal process supplies the essential basis for showing how probative value assessment tasks can be decomposed in formally equivalent ways; this process also, of course, shows us how the decomposed "parts" ought to be put back together again.

2. The evidence items evaluated by our research subjects are classifiable into the logically distinct categories that we have termed "inference structures." Our second objective was to study characteristics of responses to these forms of evidence. One might expect that the consistency with which persons evaluate evidence would depend upon the logical form of the evidence.

3. Study of the internal consistency of probativity assessment involves a focus on the performance of individual persons. We were concerned, however, about the extent of the agreement or concordance across subjects in probativity assessment for various forms and collections of evidence.[7]

Methodological choices and tradeoffs

At a fairly early stage in our empirical research planning, we abandoned hope of being able to present precise descriptions of our methodology in any journal-length account of our work. Our solution to this problem was to prepare a monograph in which we provided a detailed account of all aspects of our empirical studies, including precise descriptions of the subjects' tasks, the exact instructions that they were given in each part of the

---

[7] Other objectives also guided some of our research. One objective concerned a test of the relative adequacy of Pascalian (mathematical) and Baconian (inductive) systems in charting the general course of probability revision based upon inconclusive trial evidence. A novel methodology is required for such a comparison, because the two competing systems have almost no comparable numerical properties. The reader interested in our approach to and results of such a comparison can refer to our recent preliminary report (Schum & Martin, 1980c).

Another objective of the research concerned how subjects' perceptions of the value of trial decision consequences for a defendant may influence their assessment of the probative value of evidence. Our analysis of results bearing upon this objective, though at this time incomplete, suggests that value influences are very slight. This should be good news to decision and inference theorists in general, since most decision theories assume an absence of interaction among inference-related and value-related judgments.

study, the evidence they evaluated, the formal basis for selecting the evidence, the nature of the subjects' responses to the evidence, and the means by which these responses were to be analyzed. The report is available to persons interested in these details (Schum & Martin, 1980a). The reader of this report may conclude that we over-reacted to criticism about the simplicity of "laboratory" studies of human inference (e.g., Winkler & Murphy, 1973), and that we sought complexity for its own sake, but this assessment would be inaccurate. We sought to study, in a reasonably systematic way, human inferential reasoning processes in an evidentiary context which begins, at least, to approach the evidentiary complexity of actual court trials. Quite simply, there is a price to be paid for the incorporation in research on human inferential reasoning of the subtleties in evidence upon whose recognition and evaluation in actual trials so much depends.

Following is a brief account of the necessary tradeoffs we were forced to consider in the design of our empirical research. If one wishes to study a person's evaluation of collections of formally identifiable classes of evidence, one must either find actual cases whose evidence fits into these classes, or one must contrive evidence which does fit in these classes. After an unsuccessful attempt at the former, we chose the latter. Our study of the consistency with which individuals evaluate evidence requires that a person evaluate the same evidence over again on several occasions; possible "carry-over" effects from one evaluation to another, though they cannot be eliminated, can be minimized. We were forced to rule out two ingredients which may have increased at least the "surface validity" of our studies. The first concerns the use of a "random" sample of juror-eligible persons. Our study demanded lengthy subject participation over a period of 5½ weeks, ability of subjects to understand fairly detailed instructions, and absolute subject commitment to participate in all parts of the study. We considered the use of actors in a video presentation of "trial testimony"; this was rejected for reasons of time and expense. Consequently, our subjects received written accounts of "testimony." Since our major purpose was to examine individual evaluations of evidence, our studies did not involve a group deliberation process similar to actual jury deliberation. Finally, to make certain evidentiary events occur "on cue," we were forced to take some liberties with the natural order of evidence presentation as it might occur at trial. Following is a brief account of the details of our method.

Research subjects. Twenty jury-eligible persons, ten males and ten females, from the undergraduate population at Rice University completed all phases of our study. None of these persons had taken a college-level course in probability theory (the only stated requirement), and all were paid at an hourly rate with a bonus for completion of all phases of the study. At the completion of our studies, we had compiled a data base of over 16,000 numerical assessments provided by the twenty subjects in response to the evidence they were asked to evaluate.

The evidence. Our subjects evaluated *testimonial* evidence in 12 separate *contrived* felony "cases." Evidence from each case was presented in written "transcripts," each of which consisted of a description of the defendant and the crime with which he/she was charged, followed by several separate blocks of evidence. Evidence presented in each case was not intended to represent a complete case; this is not a crucial issue, since our research subjects were never asked to make judgments about the guilt or innocence of the "defendant" in any case. In fact, their only task was to assess, in various ways, how strongly case evidence favored the guilt or the innocence of the "defendant" in each case.

Each block of evidence in a case consisted of two basic forms of information. The first, which we have called "mainframe" evidence, is a testimonial assertion by a witness whose assertion opens up a line of reasoning to major facts-in-issue. The second, which we referred to as "ancillary evidence," concerns other evidence which bears upon the task of evaluating the strength of linkages in the reasoning chains suggested by "mainframe" testimony. Such ancillary evidence included evidence regarding the credibility of the witness and other explanatory evidence such as that brought out in cross-examination or by other rebuttal witnesses. In Wigmore's terms, each block of evidence consisted of *proponent's assertion* followed by *opponent's explanation and/or denial.* Each of the twelve "cases" contained either four, five, or six blocks of evidence.

The most important characteristic of each block of evidence was that it was contrived to fit into one of 15 well-defined inference structures such as the ones shown above in Figure 6.1. Thus, the essential logic of each "case" was represented as a collection of inference structures; the substance of the evidence in a case was contrived to fit the logic of each case. These twelve cases, together with their "logic diagrams" and likelihood-ratio equations appropriate in each inference structure in the logic diagram, are also available upon request to the authors. Our formal research has provided the means for developing likelihood ratio expressions (Λ) for the evidence in each inference structure used. There were five basic classes of inference structures, those representing: "simple" inference structures, contradictory testimony, corroboratively redundant testimony, cumulatively redundant testimony, and nonredundant testimony. The substance of the "mainframe" testimony concerned either means, motive, or opportunity evidence relevant to each case. We drew heavily upon Wigmore's examples in contriving the evidence in each structure (Wigmore, 1937), especially his many examples of the number of reasoning stages typically necessary for means, motive, and opportunity evidence. Typically, for instance, motive evidence requires more reasoning stages than does opportunity evidence, since a motive is inferred from past behavior. Finally, the likelihood ratios developed for each inference structure show the necessary probabilistic ingredients and the manner of their coherent combination in the task of assessing the probative value of evidence in each inference structure. As we now discuss, such formalizations, together with other elements of Bayes' rule suggest three equivalent formal means for assessing the probative value of the evidence in each case.

Research subjects' tasks and responses. Subjects provided assessments of the probative value of evidence in three formally equivalent ways; these three response methods allow us three ways of assessing the internal consistency of evaluations of evidence for entire cases or collections of evidence and one way of assessing the internal consistency of evaluations of individual items of evidence. Two of these three response methods involve the estimation by subjects of likelihood ratios; the third involves the estimation of conditional probabilities. Following are the three response methods for probative value assessment used by every subject for each "case."

Zero task-decomposition (ZTD). In this response method, subjects estimated a single likelihood ratio for the *entire* collection of evidence in a case. In giving such an estimate, a subject is asked to assess the likelihood of case evidence assuming defendant's guilt relative to the likelihood of this same evidence assuming innocence. Subjects' actual responses consisted of a letter-number pair which indicated both the probative *direction*, i.e., whether the case evidence favored guilt G or innocence I, and probative *force*. For example, the pair G-10 indicates that the subject thinks the evidence 10 times more probable assuming guilt than assuming innocence; the pair I-5 indicates that the subject believed the evidence 5 times more probable assuming innocence than assuming guilt. A response "N" meaning "neutral" was allowed if the subject believed the evidence was probatively neutral and favored neither fact-in-issue G nor I. Our computer converted these pairs to ratios according to the following definition of the likelihood ratio for case evidence C: $\Lambda_C = P(C|G)/P(C|I)$. For a G-10 response, for example, $\Lambda_C = 10$; for an I-10 response $\Lambda_C = 1/10$; for an N response $\Lambda_C = 1.0$. This letter-number pair response was used to prevent subjects from being confused by the ratios involved where $\Lambda_C > 1$ means C favors "G" and $\Lambda_C < 1$ means C favors "I".

This ZTD response is the result of a subject's holistic or global assessment of the probative value of an entire collection of evidence. Subjects made these responses following the thorough reading of the entire collection of evidence in each case. In this ZTD condition of our study, subjects made one such judgment for each of the twelve cases. The condition is called "zero task-decomposition" since the subjects performed the entire process of aggregating the evidence mentally and provided a single judgment indicating the probative force and direction of the evidence.

Partial task-decomposition (PTD). In this condition, subjects made exactly the same kinds of likelihood ratio estimates as in the ZTD condition, except that they made one such judgment for each item of "mainframe" testimony in each case. Such judgments were supported by the ancillary evidence in each block of evidence. On occasion, subjects were asked to refer to previous items of mainframe testimony in a case when there was some linkage between the items; for example, if the second of two items was contradictory with the first, subjects were asked to recall the first testimony in assessing the likelihood ratio for the second. Thus, if there were K items of "mainframe" testimony in a case, each subject made K assessments, one for each item.

Consider Case C_j which has some number K of evidence items. Bayes' rule prescribes a multiplicative procedure for combining the probative value for individual items to find the probative value of the entire case C_j. Thus, for case C_j, $\Lambda_{C_j} = \prod_{k=1}^{K} \tilde{\Lambda}_{jk}$, where $\tilde{\Lambda}_{jk}$ is the estimated likelihood ratio for the kth item of mainframe testimony in case C_j. We can compare $\tilde{\Lambda}_{C_j}(ZTD)$, a person's estimated likelihood ratio in the zero task-decomposition condition, with $\Lambda_{C_j}(PTD)$, a value calculated by simply multiplying together $\tilde{\Lambda}_{jk}$ values for the individual testimonies in case C_j. Comparison between $\tilde{\Lambda}_{C_j}(ZTD)$ and $\Lambda_{C_j}(PTD)$ is one indication of internal consistency; are the probative value assessments of parts of a "case" consistent with the overall assessment of the entire case? This condition is called "partial task-decomposition," since the subject is now relieved of aggregating probativity assessments over the K evidence items in a case.

Complete task-decomposition (CTD). In this condition, subjects' probativity-assessment tasks were decomposed to the "finest-grained" level of analysis allowed by our formal methods. This part of the study was conceptually the most difficult and required the most extensive instructions. As an illustration of the subjects' task in this condition, consider Equation 1 in the Technical Appendix. This shows the composition of a likelihood ratio, $\Lambda_{D_i^*}$, which describes the process of assessing the probative value of testimony D_i^* about event D, where D is circumstantial evidence of major facts-in-issue H_1 and H_2. Observe in Equation 1 that there are six conditional probability ingredients in $\Lambda_{D_i^*}$. Suppose D_i^*, from witness W_i, was an item of mainframe testimony in one of the cases the subjects evaluated. The subject's task was to estimate each of the six ingredient conditional probabilities required for a determination of $\Lambda_{D_i^*}$. For example, suppose that D represents the event that the defendant was at the scene/time of the crime. Subjects assessed the relative likelihood of this event under the asumption of guilt (H_1) and innocence (H_2) by means of the conditional probability ingredients $P(D|H_1)$ and $P(D|H_2)$. The remaining four ingredients in Equation 1 all concern the credibility of witness W_i, each of which the subject assessed. For example, $P(D_i^*|DH_1)$ asks: how probable is the witness testimony that defendant was at the scene/time, assuming that defendant was at the scene *and* guilty. The term $P(D_i^*|DH_2)$ asks: how probable is defendant's testimony, assuming defendant was at the scene *and* innocent. Subjects estimated such ingredient values on a probability scale $[0, 1]$ for Λ_{jk} values for each mainframe item of testimony in every case C_j.

In the actual estimation tasks in CTD, subjects reponded to verbal descriptions of required conditional probabilities whose events corresponded to those in the case of concern. From these conditional probability estimates, we are able to calculate a value Λ_{jk} for any item of testimony in any case. These calculated values, for any subject, can be compared with that subject's estimate $\tilde{\Lambda}_{jk}$ for the same evidence item. In addition, for an entire case C_j we can determine $\Lambda_{C_j}(CTD)$, a calculation of the probative value of entire case C_j based upon Λ_{ij} values calculated, in turn, from a subject's conditional probability estimations.

In summary, our method allows three determinations of the probative value of each case for each subject; $\tilde{\Lambda}_{C_j}(ZTD)$, $\Lambda_{C_j}(PTD)$, and $\Lambda_{C_j}(CTD)$; these three values can be compared in consistency studies. In addition, our methods allow a comparison, for any subject and any evidence item k, between $\tilde{\Lambda}_{jk}(PTD)$ and calculated $\Lambda_{jk}(CTD)$. Thus, we have consistency measures for whole-case probative value assessment and for individual evidence item assessment. As a final note, the three "levels" of task decomposition can be thought of as three sets of instructions of increasing specificity about the task or probativity assessment. The ZTD task leaves the entire aggregation and assessment burden on the subject. The PTD task requires holistic or global responses, but only to individual evidence items. The CTD task involves very specific instructions about the formally necessary linkages between events in reasoning chains established by foundation testimony. As we now relate, comparison of responses in these three conditions provides some interesting insight into human response characteristics in the task of weighing evidence.

Empirical studies: Results and observations

Following is a brief summary of major results obtained in those parts of our studies which concerned the assessment of the probative value of evidence. The accumulated data base is very large, and we have performed a variety of analyses on these data. A thorough account of the analyses and an extensive interpretation of the results are to be found in two recent research reports which, like others, are available to the reader interested in details (Schum & Martin, 1980b; 1981). Two types of results are presented here: those concerning the consistency of alternative ways of assessing the probative value of evidence for entire cases and for individual evidence items and those bearing upon several interesting response patterns observed in the evaluation of several different species of evidence or inference structures. A few comments on our measurements and analyses are necessary before we begin.

Estimated or calculated values of likelihood ratio Λ are *vectors* having both probative *decision* and probative *force* properties. Probative direction specifies which major rival fact-in-issue (guilt or innocence) the evidence favors or "points toward" in an inferential sense. Probative force indicates the strength with which the evidence points toward the favored fact-in-issue.

Some forms of statistical analyses are grossly misleading unless these two properties are examined separately. Consequently, we will talk about two "forms" of consistency. *Directional consistency* among two or more assessment methods means that the assessments in all methods agree in favoring the same fact-in-issue. *Force consistency* is measured by the degree to which two or more assessment methods assigned the same probative strength to the same evidence. For force consistency, we use a measure F, which indicates the factor by which two Λ values (estimated or calculated) differ. For example, if $\Lambda_1 = 10$ and $\Lambda_2 = 5$, then $F = 2$. All measures of directional and force consistency are within-subject measures; that is, they compare two or more responses made by the same subject. One useful measure of between-subject consistency or agreement in probativity assessment is the familiar *concordance coefficient*. Applied to whole-case Λ_C it measures the extent to which the 20 subjects agree in rank-ordering the 12 cases in terms of their aggregate probative value. Applied to individual evidence items, this coefficient shows the agreement among the 20 subjects in rank-ordering the evidence items in a particular case in terms of their probative value.

Consistency among alternative methods for assessing the probative value of evidence

Table 6.1 contains a summary of results bearing upon the consistency of the three alternative response methods (ZTD, PTD, and CTD) and two other results of interest. Blank cells in Parts A and B simply indicate that the ZTD procedure produces no results for individual evidence items, since it involves a single estimate for an entire case; F is a pairwise measure. Part A shows directional consistency results for the four possible types of comparisons among ZTD, PTD, and CTD for whole-case Λ_C (Row A-1), and for individual evidence items Λ_{jk} (Row A-2). For example, 183 of the 240 possible Λ_C comparisons involving PTD and CTD were directionally consistent. Part B, rows B-1 and B-2 show probative force consistency measures F for whole-case Λ_C comparisons in which the assessments agreed directionally (B-1) and when they did not (B-2). Such separate analysis is necessary because F suppresses directionality. For example when Λ_C values in ZTD and PTD agreed in probative direction, they typically differed in probative force by a factor of 2.5. The number in parentheses under each F value indicates the number of comparisons over which a median F value was calculated. Rows B-3 and B-4 show median F for individual evidence item Λ_{jk} comparisons. For example, in the 729 instances in which PTD and CTD assessments of Λ_{jk} were directionally consistent, they differed typically by a factor of just 1.58.

Part C simply shows the typical (median) size of Λ_C estimated in ZTD or calculated in PTD or CTD; Row C-1 contains results when Λ_C favored guilt (G) and C-2 when Λ_C favored innocence I. Notice how Λ_C typically increases in size, whether it favors G or I, as the assessment task is decomposed

Table 6.1. General consistency results summary

	ZTD, PTD, CTD	ZTD, PTD	ZTD, CTD	PTD, CTD
A.				
1. Directional consistency, A_C, 12 per subject	117/240 = 48.8%	132/240 = 55%	156/240 = 65%	183/240 = 76.3%
2. Directional consistency, A_{jk}, 60 per subject	—	—	—	732/1200 = 61%
B.				
1. Force consistency, A_C, Median F, directional agreement	—	2.5[a] (132)	4.3 (156)	4.1 (183)
2. Force consistency, A_C, Median F, directional disagreement	—	10.0 (108)	30.0 (84)	20.0 (57)
3. Force consistency, A_{jk}, Median F, directional agreement	—	—	—	1.58 (729)
4. Force consistency, A_{jk}, Median F, directional disagreement	—	—	—	2.30 (471)

C.

	ZTD	PTD	CTD
1. Median A_C (G)	2.0 (183)	5.0 (163)	10.0 (207)
2. Median A_C (I)	4.0 (37)	5.0 (77)	8.0 (33)
3. Concordance: Ranking entire cases	0.17	0.54	0.29

D. Concordance, individual items

Cases:	1	2	3	4	5	6	7	8	9	10	11	12
PTD	.35	.25	.07	.18	.29	.60	.58	.24	.48	.32	.41	.56
CTD	.61	.60	.39	.55	.75	.61	.63	.53	.06	.61	.59	.39

[a] The lower the value, the greater the consistency.

to finer-grain levels. Row C-3 shows the concordance across the 20 subjects in rank-ordering the 12 cases in terms of Λ_C produced by each of the three methods; Λ_C in the PTD condition produces the greatest concordance among subjects. Finally, Part D shows the concordance or agreement among the 20 subjects in rank-ordering the evidence in each case using either PTD or CTD assessments. In all but two cases (9 and 12) the CTD procedure yielded Λ_{ij} values which were most in agreement across subjects.

ZTD. In this response method, subjects had the task of assigning a single letter/number pair which indicated the probative strength and direction of the entire set of evidence in a "case." Though required to make only a simple response to each case, subjects had the complete burden of integrating or aggregating all of the evidence in a case. In determinations of the overall probative value of a case, ZTD fares worst in comparison with other methods. This method produces, pairwise, the weakest directional consistency with the other two methods, is most variable across subjects and across cases in directional comparisons, applies the weakest probative force, and has the lowest degree of concordance among subjects in ordering cases in terms of their probative value.

These results are not surprising. Similar results have been observed in other research on holistic assessments in comparison with other procedures (Edwards, Phillips, Hays, & Goodman, 1968). There are several explanations for the typically weak force assessments provided by ZTD. The common explanation is the *misaggregation hypothesis.* This simply says that subjects, left to their own devices in combining large amounts of probabilistic evidence, use judgmental algorithms (or heuristics) which tend to let probative value inherent in evidence "leak out." By this hypothesis, we are all seen as "wasteful" processors of information. Another explanation is that the typically small Λ estimates used by subjects in ZTD simply reflects a *response bias* against using large numbers, particularly in situations in which there is ample evidence, even though conflicting, contradictory, and unreliable (DuCharme, 1970). Equally plausible is the notion that, in ZTD, subjects are free to discard any evidence for any reason. One could simply focus on a few "salient" features of evidence or only upon that evidence which agrees with prior expectations. This says that subjects are free to make the overall assessment task easier by reducing the number of items being considered. This strategy eliminates inconsistencies and reduces processing load; it may also yield weaker assessments if the subject is aware of the fact that evidence is being discarded.

PTD. In this response method, subjects were forced to consider the probative value of the testimony of each major witness in a case. In this method Λ_C for an entire case is established by aggregating (multiplicatively) a subject's assessment of the probative value of each "mainframe" testimonial assertion. In such a method subjects are *partially* unburdened of aggrega-tion, since they are never required to combine their assessments across other testimony. They do, however, have an increased response burden, being now required to provide one assessment for each of the "mainframe" items of testimony in a case. In directional consistency comparisons, PTD fares better than ZTD. There is a high directional consistency rate for PTD/CTD comparisons (A-1, A-2). These results are partially explainable by the fact that both use a common rule for aggregating probative value *across* the evi-dence items in a case (namely, multiplication). The closeness of these pro-bative force results is also due to the apparent consistency of the ingredients subjects estimated in the CTD procedure, since a common between-item aggregation rule would not produce good agreement unless the ingredients in CTD were assessed in reasonable accordance with factors considered by subjects in the holistic PTD assessments. The PTD method produced the highest degree of concordance among subjects in ordering the 12 cases in terms of their probative value.

For individual evidence items, PTD agrees well with CTD in directional consistency and in force consistency (Part B). Concordance among sub-jects in ordering the evidence in individual cases is generally lower for PTD than for CTD. The PTD procedure, because it requires a focus on each indi-vidual witness, allows incorporation of factors which may be overlooked, discarded, or "integrated out" in the ZTD procedure. However, the PTD assessments for individual witnesses are holistic when compared to those assessments in CTD. Our results generally support the conjecture that addi-tional features of probativity assessment required in CTD are overlooked, discarded, or "integrated out" in PTD.

CTD. Most surprising to the authors was the overall consistency and ade-quacy of the many detailed probabilistic assessments made by subjects in the CTD procedure. Each subject made a total of 332 such assessments. In this response mode, subjects had a minimal aggregation burden but a max-imal response or judgmental burden. In CTD, subjects were required to make judgments about the subtle linkages among events involved in the often-complex chains of reasoning from testimony to major facts-in-issue in each case. Judgments of the conditional probabilistic ingredients formally required in these chains, when aggregated by formally appropriate means, result in probativity assessments for entire cases and individual items which agree very well with assessments made by other, more holistic, means. This can only mean that the meticulous conditional probability assessments which CTD requires were performed in very reasonable and consistent ways by our subjects. As seen in Table 6.1-C, both directional and force consistency comparisons involving CTD are strongest for entire cases and for individual items. In addition, the degree of concordance among sub-jects in rank-ordering cases is second to PTD; in rank ordering individual items in a case, concordance among subjects is greatest using CTD procedures. CTD forces a person to look at the very fine-grained details of an inference task. Our study shows that persons required to bear the burden of such detailed analysis can perform the task in a manner very consistent with performance using other methods.

As the task of probativity assessment is decomposed into finer levels of analysis, a larger amount of the probative value latent in evidence is extracted and reflected in the assessment. This is explainable by at least two means. First, one locus of probative value in evidence is the possible conditional nonindependence of evidence items. Such nonindependence may easily be unrecognized or unaccounted for in ZTD. The PTD procedure alerts the subject to the existence of such nonindependence and simply tells the subject to account for it. In the CTD procedure, however, the method not only alerts the subject to such nonindependence, but also is instructive in how to reflect such nonindependence in assessments. Second and more obvious, as tasks are further decomposed, there is no chance that crucial evidence items, or factors concerning evidence items, will be overlooked, discarded, or "integrated out." For these reasons one expects more probative value in assessments in which more of the evidence in a collection is, in fact, incorporated and in which more of the subtle linkages among evidence items are reflected in the assessments.

We have also seen that there is greater concordance or agreement among individuals in probativity assessments as these tasks are further decomposed. The finer the level of decomposition, the more specific are the instructions required. It comes as no surprise to learn that agreement in judgment among persons is greater the more specific are the instructions about these judgments. We did, however, believe that the very specific conditional probabilistic judgments required in CTD would be difficult for our subjects to make. Results indicate that these judgments were made effectively, if not easily. The essence of task-decomposition in inference is that it forces consideration of finer-grained details of the task and ensures that such consideration is incorporated in overall assessments. Under procedures such as ZTD, where specific attention to these details is not enforced, entire evidence items or features of these items and their probabilistic linkages are easily discarded or overlooked by persons who may be unaware of their existence or who simply choose to ignore them.

Probative assessment characteristics for different inference structures

Following is a collection of results obtained in a comparison of the PTD and CTD procedures for assessing the probative value of individual mainframe evidence items in each case. We first discuss results for evidence belonging to *simple* inference structures and then consider results for evidence in *complex* inference structures in which there were patterns of con-

Table 6.2. *Directional and force consistency: PTD and CTD conditions*

	Logical remoteness			
	0	1	2	3
A. *Simple inference structures*				
1. Directional consistency	65%	73%	79%	73%
	104/160	146/200	253/320	88/120
2. Force consistency (median F)	2.2	2.4	1.7	1.4
	CON	COR	CUR	NR
B. *Complex inference structures*				
1. Directional consistency	41%	61%	65%	63%
	49/120	49/80	52/80	76/120
2. Force consistency (median F)	2.0	2.1	1.9	2.0

tradictory, corroboratively redundant, cumulatively redundant, or nonredundant evidence.

Simple inference structures. These structures are characterized by the number of intermediate reasoning stages separating a single item of mainframe testimony and the ultimate facts-in-issue. A direct testimonial assertion about a major fact has no intermediate reasoning stages; therefore, its "level" of cascading is *zero*. The value of such testimony depends only on the witness's credibility. In our simple inference structures there were three other "levels" of cascading representing either one, two, or three intermediate reasoning stages. Evidence of opportunity typically may have either one or two intermediate reasoning stages, while evidence of means or motive typically have more as Wigmore noted (1937). So our essential results concern the effects, upon probative value assessment in the PTD and CTD condition, of the degree of logical remoteness between testimony and major facts-in-issue. Table 6.2-A summarizes probative direction and force consistency between assessments in PTD and CTD.

Row A-1 shows that logical remoteness has little effect upon the proportion of *directionally* consistent assessment in PTD and CTD. Row A-2, however, shows that logical remoteness does influence the force consistency of these assessments; such consistency typically improves as the remoteness of testimony and facts-in-issue increases. The reason is quite apparent; assessed values of Λ_{jk} in PTD and those based upon subject ingredient estimates in CTD both decreased in size as the remoteness of testimony and major facts-in-issue increased. Abraham Lincoln's assessment of inference-upon-inference thus applies formally as well behaviorally; he is quoted as saying that inference-upon-inference frequently has the same strength as "soup made by boiling the shadow of a pigeon that has been starved to death" (Maguire, Weinstein, Chadbourn, & Mansfield, 1973).

Complex inference structures. "Complex" inference structures feature the testimony of more than one witness and involve various probabilistic linkages among events in the reasoning stages suggested by the testimony. All complex inference structures in our study involved two items of testimony, and inference structures were defined for various instances in which the second testimony was either contradictory (CON), corroboratively redundant (COR), cumulatively redundant (CUR), or nonredundant (NR) with the first item of testimony. Part B of Table 6.2 above contains results bearing upon the directional and force consistency of assessments of Λ_{jk} in PTD and CTD; the Λ_{jk} of concern in each case is for the *second* testimony in each structure, the one which either corroborates or is redundant or nonredundant with the first. As shown in Table 6.2, Part B, there is little difference in probative force consistency across complex inference structures. Directional consistency, however, is lower for contradictory structures than for the others. The explanation of this result requires a more detailed analysis, which we now present for each inference structure.

(1) *Contradictory testimony.* Subject's probative response patterns to contradictory testimony in the PTD and CTD conditions are among the most interesting in this study. In the evidence evaluated by subjects there were six instances of contradictory testimony from two witnesses of apparently equal credibility; across 20 subjects we thus observed 120 pairs of PTD/CTD assessments relative to contradictory testimony. Of these 120 assessment pairs, 57 (48 percent) exhibited the following pattern. In the holistic PTD assessments, subjects either ignored the second and conflicting testimony (i.e., they assigned it no probative value) *or* they gave it value but made it agree directionally with the first item with which it was contradictory. Thus, in nearly half the contradictory evidence occasions subjects either ignored contradictory testimony or treated such testimony as if it were corroborative. However, on these *same* occasions, their assessed ingredients in CTD for the Λ_{jk} values for contradictory testimony resulted in calculated Λ_{jk} values which were directionally the opposite of those for the first item of testimony. In short, asked to examine the fine-grain details of the tasks, subjects' assessments "brought out" the contradictory nature of evidence either overlooked or suppressed in their holistic PTD assessments.

This result brings to mind the so-called "primacy" effects others have observed in human holistic reactions to conflicting or contradictory evidence (e.g., Peterson & DuCharme, 1967; Pitz, 1969). The mind is set in motion in one direction by early evidence and somehow resists being moved in the other direction following later contradictory or conflicting evidence. In our study two items of contradictory testimony were always temporally adjacent. We have labeled the suppression of contradiction in such instances a "local" primacy effect to distinguish it from more global primacy effects

Table 6.3. *Subject policies for assessing redundant evidence in the PTD and CTD conditions*

	PTD		CTD	
	r	b	r	b
A. *Corroborative*				
1. Instance 1	.96	.93	.72	.17
2. Instance 2	.97	1.07	.72	.23
3. Instance 3	.93	1.16	.65	.66
4. Instance 4	.83	.84	.42	.42
B. *Cumulative*				
1. Instance 1	.93	1.11	.34	.26
2. Instance 2	.79	.78	.25	.22
3. Instance 3	.73	1.00	.33	.27
4. Instance 4	.94	.99	.33	.19

which may persist over longer periods of time and over much intervening testimony (Schum, 1980). The interesting result in our present study is that such primacy or contradiction-suppression is removed when subjects assess fine-grain logical details of evidence. It is important to note that such removal is not due to the aggregation models themselves, since calculated Λ_{jk} values depend entirely upon values of assessed ingredients. A subject's assessed ingredients, when coherently aggregated, "brought out" contradictions that this same person ignored or suppressed in holistic assessments. In making holistic or global assessments of any kind, individuals obviously resort to simplification strategies. Unfortunately, one such strategy may be the removal of contradiction or, worse yet, the incorporation of contradiction as if it were corroboration.

(2) *Redundant evidence structures.* We now examine the subjects' PTD and CTD response patterns to corroboratively or cumulatively redundant testimony. We have mentioned Lempert's (1977) concern about the extent to which jurors "double count" redundant testimony. Our results, taken seriously, suggest that his concern is certainly well founded. The systematic holistic PTD tendency to "double count" testimony from the second of two corroborative witnesses is shown in Table 6.3-A, and the holistic PTD tendency to overvalue cumulatively redundant testimony is shown in Table 6.3-B. Also shown in these tables is that such double-counting and overevaluation tendencies do not appear in the CTD procedure for probativity assessment. These results are best illustrated and summarized using the correlational statistics which we now describe.

In the case evidence subjects evaluated, there were four instances of testimony from two witnesses of nearly equal-appearing credibility who said the same thing. In Part A, for each of these four instances, are correlation coefficients (r), and regression coefficients (b), in both PTD and CTD assessment conditions. To see how they were determined, take ZTD and instance 1 as an example. The value of $r = 0.96$ results from correlating, across all 20 subjects, the Λ_{jk} value assigned by a subject to the first testimony and the Λ_{jk} value assigned by the subject to the second (corroborating) testimony; values of b are found in the process. A value of r close to 1.0 means consistency across subjects in their policies for Λ assignment. The value b essentially tells what this policy was; if $b = 1.0$, this means that the subjects' values for the first and second items were identical; $b < 1$ means that Λ for the second item was smaller than Λ for the first; and $b > 1$ means that Λ for the second item was greater than for the first.[8] So, for instance 1 in ZTD, the 20 subjects were nearly perfectly consistent in assigning the same probative weight to the second (corroborative) testimony as they assigned to the first. As can be seen, essentially the same thing happens in all four instances; in PTD (holistic assessment) subjects systematically double-counted corroboratively redundant testimony.

In the CTD condition the generally lower r values mean less consistency in policy; this is to be expected given the very large number of conditional probability ingredients involved in determining the Λ_{jk} value being correlated. Notice however that b is much less than 1.0 in every instance; this means that the probative weight assigned to the corroboratively redundant testimony was typically smaller than the weight assigned in the original testimony. In short, subjects' CTD estimates, when formally aggregated, "bring out" the redundance apparently overlooked in the holistic PTD assessments.

Part B of Table 6.3 shows the same analysis for the four instances of cumulatively redundant testimony in our evidence. Essentially the same results occur across subjects though it is evident that there is less consistency in estimating Λ_{jk} ingredients than there is in holistic estimates of Λ_{jk}. Cumulative redundance is a more subtle effect than is corroborative redundance, and Λ_{jk} models for cumulatively redundant testimony have many more ingredients than those for corroboratively redundant testimony. Nevertheless, cumulative redundancy overlooked in PTD is "brought out" in the fine-grained analysis in CTD. Once again we emphasize that the "bringing out" in CTD of subtleties due to contradiction or redundance are not necessarily due to the formal aggregation models for Λ_{jk}; it is the subject-assessed ingredients which allow these calculations to bring out these subtleties.

(3) Nonredundant structures. In the evidence that subjects evaluated there were six instances in which the first of two testimonial assertions was contrived to be probatively facilitative on the second. Apparently, our contrived evidence failed to appear facilitative since, in both PTD and CTD, the second testimony was weighted essentially the same as the first. The

---

[8] These stated policies assume that the calculated intercepts are zero or near zero, which they were in all but one condition in Part A. An intercept of zero says that subject's Λ values have no initial bias toward guilt or innocence.

formal distinction between redundant and nonredundant testimonial evidence is subtle and involves no sharply defined boundary. In fact, measures of the redundance of evidence suggest a continuum along which evidence may be placed in terms of whether it is redundant or facilitative (Schum, 1979b).

Conclusion

The formal research summarized in this paper provides examples of the method whereby various identifiable forms of evidence can be subjected to a fine-grained analysis in which the subtleties in evidence can be identified and systematically examined. The stimulus and guidance for such research have come in large measure from existing evidence scholarship in jurisprudence, there being no similar body of scholarship to be found in other areas in which reasoning from inconclusive evidence is commonly encountered. Our formal research has concerned some matters of which jurists are already aware, such as the complex interplay between witness credibility and the value of what the witness says in a determination of the probative value of testimony by the witness. In fact, some of our specific formal studies on such areas as testimonial redundance have been enhanced by careful examination of evidentiary distinctions which jurists commonly recognize or, in a few instances, fail to recognize. It is generally the case that difficulty in the formal analysis of some forms of evidence (e.g., hearsay, cumulatively redundant evidence) parallels the difficulty jurists experience in formulating specific prescriptions concerning the relevance and admissibility of such evidence.

Our formal research also concerns matters about which there is only infrequent or oblique reference in evidence scholarship – event rarity and transitivity issues being examples. One distinct virtue of the formal analysis of various evidentiary patterns is that it allows one to observe the way in which a variety of evidence-related formal systems can be brought to bear in the study and analysis of evidence subtleties. Thus, we are able to show how the theory of "signal detection" provides very useful concepts and methods in the study of credibility-related ingredients in the analysis of the probative value of testimonial evidence. Similarly, concepts from "statistical communication theory" (or "information theory") allow one to be more precise in formulating problems relating to possible redundance in certain evidence.

How exciting or informative are the results of the empirical studies we summarize depends to some extent on the reader's expectations. Some of our results are very similar to those found in other, more abstract, laboratory studies; other results are unique because of the complexity of the tasks our research subjects performed. In these concluding comments about our empirical results we do *not* wish to leave the reader with the impression that these studies are simply further examples of psychological research demonstrating the inadequacy of human performance on inference-related tasks. In fact, our results show how well persons who are given adequate instructions about reasonably well-formulated problems can respond to a variety of subtle aspects of evidence and reflect these subtleties in their responses. Demonstrating human inadequacy at an inferential task presupposes uncontroversial performance standards, well-posed tasks, and adequate instructions. *No* empirical study of inference (including ours) has the first, and regrettably few have the other two.

A general result of our study is that individuals can capture in their probativity-assessment responses an assortment of subtle aspects of evidence provided that their probativity-assessment tasks are decomposed to a level at which these subtleties are exposed. Further, the concordance or agreement among the probativity assessors in our study was highest for decomposed assessment tasks. Finally, global, holistic, or nondecomposed assessments of the probative value in a collection of evidence are the most variable across persons and frequently disagree directionally with assessments made by other methods involving task decomposition. One suggestion is that individuals asked to mentally aggregate a large collection of evidence may ignore, discard, or integrate over contradictory evidence and otherwise overlook other subtleties in evidence. Our message to jurists cannot, for obvious reasons, be that factfinders' tasks ought to be decomposed in the manner in which they were in our study. Presumably, the deliberation process following a trial encourages a factfinder to consider factors which others have noted but which he/she has discarded or ignored; such mutual enlightenment, however, cannot be guaranteed.

Perhaps the most striking results of our study concern the manner in which our research subjects assessed the value of contradictory and of redundant testimony. Quite startling is the frequently observed holistic tendency to make contradictory testimony either probatively valueless or, what seems worse, corroborative; such behavior, however, is certainly not unheard-of in more abstract studies of human inference. Our studies show the existence of local as well as global "primacy" effects in which, apparently, the mind resists changes in the direction of opinion revisions. The most systematic result in our study concerns the holistic tendency to "double count" corroboratively redundant testimony. Neither tendency is apparent when subjects are allowed to examine and respond to the fine-grained details of evidence having these characteristics.

If, as asserted earlier, the factfinder's task cannot be decomposed and the posttrial deliberation process cannot guarantee appropriate assessment of various forms of evidence, then it is left to the skill of one counsel in "decomposing" the arguments made by the other. Our formal research strongly suggests the essential formal adequacy of the rules and procedures for this process of "beating and boulting out the truth" (Hale, 1739/1971). Our empirical studies suggest that attentive factfinders with reasonable intellectual skills can incorporate the many subtleties in evidence if, at least, they are alerted to the existence of these subtleties. Thus, the double-counting of redundant testimony and the "local primacy" of earlier testimony that is contradicted later are examples of common reasoning inconsistencies exhibited by many people which can, perhaps, be overcome by an equally attentive counsel.

Technical Appendix

Three examples of likelihood ratio Λ determination for the three inference structures shown in Figure 6.1 in the text

Figure 6.1-A in the text shows the simplest possible case of cascaded inference. Witness W_i testifies that event D occurred; event D is circumstantial evidence bearing on major rival facts-in-issue H_1 and H_2. As a factfinder, what we have is W_i's testimonial assertion D_i^* that event D occurred. D_i^* and D are not the same events, and we shall be misled if we treat them so. The reason is that, unless we believe W_i to be perfectly credible, testimony D_i^* is consistent both with D, the actual occurrence of the event, and D^C, the nonoccurrence of this event. In this case, what can condition or change our opinion about the relative likelihood of H_1 and H_2 is the event D_i^* representing the testimony of W_i. In this inference structure the likelihood ratio for testimony D_i^* is as follows:

$$\Lambda D_i^* = \frac{P(D_i^*|H_1)}{P(D_i^*|H_2)}$$
$$= \frac{P(D|H_1)[P(D_i^*|DH_1) - P(D_i^*|D^CH_1)] + P(D_i^*|D^CH_1)}{P(D|H_2)[P(D_i^*|DH_2) - P(D_i^*|D^CH_2)] + P(D_i^*|D^CH_2)} \qquad (1)$$

In this expression the conditional probabilities $P(D|H_1)$ and $P(D|H_2)$ express the strength of the linkage between D and H_1 and H_2; in words, these probabilities prescribe how probatively valuable is event D. They indicate the strength of the linkage between D and H_1, H_2. All other terms concern the credibility of witness W_i and refer to the linkage between testimony D_i^* and D, the matter asserted. So far, intuition is supported by $\Lambda_{D_i^*}$; the value of an item of testimony depends upon the importance of what the source has to say and upon the credibility of the source.

There are two additional features of $\Lambda_{D_i^*}$ which we must also notice. Observe that the terms $P(D|H_1)$ and $P(D|H_2)$ occur separately in Equation 1 and not together as the ratio $P(D|H_1)/P(D|H_2)$. This fact tells us that the probative value of testimony also depends upon the *rarity* of D, the event being reported. The reason is that the ratio of two numbers suppresses information about the precise values of the numbers; e.g., $4 = 0.40/0.10 = 0.04/0.01$. In $\Lambda_{D_i^*}$ we must have the precise values of $P(D|H_1)$ and $P(D|H_2)$ and not simply their ratio; such precision preserves the rarity of events, to which Λ is sensitive. In general, the rarer the event reported, the stronger credibility we may require from the source of information about the source.

The other feature concerns the four credibility-related ingredients of $\Lambda_{D_i^*}$ in Equation 1. Take $P(D_i^* | DH_1)$ for example. By itself, the conditional probability $P(D_i^* | D)$ is called a "hit" probability or a "true positive," and it expresses how likely testimony D_i^* is if event D actually occurred. The addition of the conditioning term H_1 in $P(D_i^* | DH_1)$ tells us essentially that W_i's "hit probability" may depend upon H_1. A similar process applies to another ingredient $P(D_i^* | D^C H_1)$, which is called "false positive," and also to these hits and false positives when H_2 is true. Here is the essential message; in assessing the probative value of testimony D_i^* we must consider whether or not the likelihood of testimony D_i^* depends upon factors other than the occurrence or nonoccurrence of the events being reported. Our formal process makes clear that the observational and reporting behavior of a witness may contain probative value over and above the probative value of the event being reported. In short, the witness's behavior can be probative in a number of ways. The manner in which credibility-related ingredients occur in Λ expressions allows us to incorporate a wide variety of subtleties associated with the behavior of witnesses including their observational sensitivity and many motivational considerations.

Figure 6.1-B represents a situation in which witness W_j offers testimony E_j^* that event E occurred; the occurrence of E is circumstantial on D which, in turn, is circumstantial on major facts-in-issue H_1 and H_2. Equation 2 shows $\Lambda_{E_j^*}$ in a special case which we shall identify:

$$\Lambda_{E_j^*} = \frac{P(E_j^* | H_1)}{P(E_j^* | H_2)}$$

$$= \frac{P(D|H_1)[P(E|DH_1) - P(E|D^C H_1)] + P(E|D^C H_1) + \left[\frac{P(E_j^*|E)}{P(E_j^*|E^C)^{-1}}\right]^{-1}}{P(D|H_2)[P(E|DH_2) - P(E|D^C H_2)] + P(E|D^C H_2) + \left[\frac{P(E_j^*|E)}{P(E_j^*|E^C)^{-1}}\right]^{-1}} \quad (2)$$

This structure reveals three reasoning stages: from testimony E_j^* to events E, E^C; from events E, E^C to events D, D^C; and from events D, D^C, to ultimate facts-in-issue H_1, H_2. Examination of Equation 2 shows probative ingredients for each stage of reasoning. The "special-case" nature of this expression concerns the foundation reasoning stage from testimony E_j^* to events E, E^C. In the more general expression for $\Lambda_{E_j^*}$, the hit and false-positive $P(E_j^* | E)$ and $P(E_j^* | E^C)$ have other conditioning terms, namely, the four possible combinations of one of D, D^C and H_1, H_2. The special case arises when one assumes that these hit and false positives do not depend upon any events "higher" in the chain of reasoning. The elimination of these higher-order conditioning events is accomplished by conditional independence assumptions. For example, $P(E_j^* | EDH_1) = P(E_j^* | E)$ is the assumption that testimony E_j^* is independent of D and H_1, given event E. In short, this is an assumption that the credibility-related hit probability $P(E_j^* | E)$ does not depend upon other events in the reasoning chain.

Figure 6.1-C shows a case in which two witnesses W_i and W_j both testify that event D occurred. Here is an instance in which the probative value of one item of testimony depends upon previous evidence; our Λ formulations account for such dependency, allowing us to represent a variety of subtle effects of one evidence item on another. This example allows us to show the degree to which testimony D_j^* is probatively redundant, since W_j reports the *same* event as did earlier Witness W_i.

The probative value of testimony from the first witness W_i is given by Equation 1. Now consider W_j who also testifies that D occurred. We must now examine testimony D_j^* *in light of* prior testimony D_i^*, since there is an obvious logical relationship – namely, both witnesses say the same thing. Formally, the likelihood ratio for D_j^*, given D_i^*, is prescribed by:

$$\Lambda D_j^* | D_i^* = \frac{P(D_j^* | H_1 D_i^*)}{P(D_j^* | H_2 D_i^*)}$$

$$= \frac{P(D | D_i^* H_1)[P(D_j^* | DD_i^* H_1) - P(D_j^* | D^C D_i^* H_1)] + P(D_j^* | D^C D_i^* H_1)}{P(D | D_i^* H_2)[P(D_j^* | DD_i^* H_2) - P(D_j^* | D^C D_i^* H_2)] + P(D_j^* | D^C D_i^* H_2)} \quad (3)$$

This formalization shows that there are two interesting factors in the relationship between D_i^* and D_j^*. The first concerns the terms $P(D | D_i^* H_1)$ and $P(D | D_i^* H_2)$. Basically, these terms prescribe the "residual" probative value in D remaining after W_i's testimony; how much is left depends upon W_i's credibility. If W_i is perfectly credible, then there is no probativity left for the testimony of W_j; if you believe W_i, then testimony by W_j should tell you nothing more in inference about H_1 and H_2. The other factor concerns the possible conditioning of testimony D_j^* by testimony D_i^*. Essentially, this allows for the incorporation of factors associated with possible influence of one witness on another. We may believe, for example, that W_i told W_j what to testify. If so, there is room in Equation 3 for incorporating such effects and adjusting probative values accordingly.

Measures of event redundancy

For the *cumulative* case, we define the redundancy of event F, knowing event E, as:

$$R_{cum} = 1 - \frac{\text{Log } L_{F|E}}{\text{Log } L_F} \quad (4)$$

where L_F is a likelihood ratio measure of the probativity of event F on facts-in-issue, and $L_{F|E}$ is a likelihood ratio measure of the probativity of event F in light of event E. If the occurrence of E makes F highly probable under both facts-in-issue, then $L_{F|E} = 1.0$. Since $\text{Log } 1 = \text{zero}$, this makes $R_{cum} = 1.0$, its maximum value. If knowing E causes no change in the probativity of F on facts-in-issue, then $L_{F|E} = L_F$ and so $R_{cum} = \text{zero}$; this means that F is not probatively redundant if you knew that E occurred. So, R_{cum} is a number between zero and one which indicates the extent of redundancy in event F if you also knew that event E occurred.

In the *corroborative* case, we define:

$$R_{cor} = 1 - \frac{\text{Log } L_{E|E}}{\text{Log } L_E} \tag{5}$$

and note immediately that R_{cor} *must always equal 1.0*. The reason, of course, is that the second discovery of the same event cannot be probative, $L_{E|E} = 1.0$. Since $\text{Log } 1.0 = 0$, R_{cor} always equals one. In other words, even E is always perfectly redundant with itself. This is why we have said in the text that corroborative redundancy is a special case of cumulative redundancy.

References

Cleary, E. W. (1972). *McCormick's handbook of the law of evidence* (2nd ed.). St. Paul, MN: West.

Cohen, L. J. (1977). *The probable and the provable*. New York: Oxford University Press.
    (1981). Subjective probability and the paradox of the gatecrasher. *Arizona State Law Journal, 1981,* 627–634.

DuCharme, W. M. (1970). Response bias explanation of conservative human inference. *Journal of Experimental Psychology, 85,* 66–74.

Edwards, W. (1962). Dynamic decision theory and probabilistic information processing. *Human Factors, 4,* 59–73.

Edwards, W., Phillips, L. D., Hays, W. L., & Goodman, B. C. (1968). Probabilistic information processing systems: Design and evaluation. *IEEE Transactions on Systems, Science, and Cybernetics, SSC-4,* 248–265.

Egan, J. P. (1975). *Signal detection theory and ROC-analysis.* New York: Academic Press.

Eggleston, R., Sir. (1978). *Evidence, proof and probability.* London: Weidenfeld & Nicolson.

Eils, L., Seaver, D., & Edwards, W. (1977). *Developing the technology of probabilistic inference: Aggregating by averaging reduces conservatism* (Research Rep. 77-3). Los Angeles: University of Southern California, Social Science Research Institute.

Finkelstein, M. O., & Fairley, W. B. (1970). A Bayesian approach to identification evidence. *Harvard Law Review, 83,* 489–517.

Hale, M., Sir. (1971). *The history of the common law of England [by] Sir Matthew Hale* (edited and with an introduction by Charles M. Gray). Chicago: University of Chicago Press. (Original work published 1739)

Hume, D. (1988). *A treatise of human nature.* Book 1, part 3, section 8. New York: Oxford University Press.

Kaye, D. (1979). The paradox of the gatecrasher and other stories. *Arizona State Law Journal, 1979,* 101–109.
    (1981). Paradoxes, gedanken experiments and the burden of proof: A response to Dr. Cohen's reply. *Arizona State Law Journal, 1981,* 635–645.

Keyser, C. J. (1929). On the study of legal science. *Yale Law Journal, 38,* 413–422.

Lempert, R. O. (1977). Modeling relevance. *Michigan Law Review, 75,* 1021–1057.

Lempert, R. O., & Saltzburg, S. A. (1977). *A modern approach to evidence: Text, problems, transcripts, and cases.* St. Paul, MN: West.

Maguire, J. M., Weinstein, J., Chadbourn, J., & Mansfield, J. (1973). *Evidence: Cases and materials on evidence.* Mineola, NY: Foundation Press.

Martin, A. W. (1979). *Cascaded inference and hearsay* (Research Rep. 79-03). Houston, TX: Rice University, Department of Psychology.

(1980). *A general algorithm for determining likelihood ratios in cascaded inference* (Research Rep. 80-03). Houston, TX: Rice University, Department of Psychology.

Peterson, C. R., & DuCharme, W. M. (1967). A primacy effect in subjective probability revision. *Journal of Experimental Psychology, 73,* 61–65.

Pitz, G. F. (1969). An inertia effect (resistance to change) in the revision of opinion. *Canadian Journal of Psychology, 23,* 24–33.

Rapoport, A., & Wallsten, T. S. (1972). Individual decision behavior. *Annual Review of Psychology, 23,* 131–176.

Saks, M. J., & Kidd, R. F. (1980). Human information processing and adjudication: Trial by heuristics. *Law and Society Review, 15,* 123–160.

Schum, D. A. (1977a). The behavioral richness of cascaded inference models: Examples in jurisprudence. In N. J. Castellan, Jr., D. B. Pisoni, & G. R. Potts (Eds.), *Cognitive theory* (Vol. 2, pp. 149–173). Hillsdale, NJ: Erlbaum.

(1977b). Contrast effects in inference: On the conditioning of current evidence by prior evidence. *Organizational Behavior and Human Performance, 18,* 217–253.

(1979a). *A Bayesian account of transitivity and other order-related effects in chains of inferential reasoning* (Research Rep. 79-04). Houston, TX: Rice University, Department of Psychology.

(1979b). *On factors which influence the redundancy of cumulative and corroborative testimonial evidence* (Research Rep. 79-02). Houston, TX: Rice University, Department of Psychology.

(1979c). A review of a case against Blaise Pascal and his heirs. *Michigan Law Review, 77,* 446–483.

(1980). Current developments in research on cascaded inference processes. In T. S. Wallsten (Ed.), *Cognitive processes in decision and choice behavior* (pp. 179–210). Hillsdale, NJ: Erlbaum.

(1981a). *Assessing the probative value of equivocal testimony or no testimony on a relevant issue at trial* (Research Rep. 81-04). Houston, TX: Rice University, Department of Psychology.

(1981b). *Formalizing the process of assessing the probative value of alibi testimony* (Research Rep. 81-05). Houston, TX: Rice University, Department of Psychology.

(1981c). Sorting out the effects of witness sensitivity and response-criterion placement upon the inferential value of testimonial evidence. *Organizational Behavior and Human Performance, 27,* 153–196.

Schum, D. A., & DuCharme, W. M. (1971). Comments on the relationship between the impact and the reliability of evidence. *Organizational Behavior and Human Performance, 6,* 111–131.

Schum, D. A., & Kelly, C. W. (1973). A problem in cascaded inference: Determining the inferential impact of confirming and conflicting reports from several unreliable sources. *Organizational Behavioral and Human Performance, 10,* 404–423.

Schum, D. A., & Martin, A. W. (1980a). *Empirical studies of cascaded inference in jurisprudence: Methodological considerations* (Research Rep. 80-01). Houston, TX: Rice University, Department of Psychology.

(1980b). *On the internal consistency of assessments of the probative value of evidence* (Research Rep. 80-04). Houston, TX: Rice University, Department of Psychology.

(1980c). *Probabilistic opinion revision on the basis of evidence at trial: A Baconian or a Pascalian process* (Research Rep. 80-02). Houston, TX: Rice University, De-ment of Psychology.

(1981). *Assessing the probative value of evidence in various inference structures* (Research Rep. 81-02). Houston, TX: Rice University, Department of Psychology.

Shafer, G. (1976). *A mathematical theory of evidence.* Princeton, NJ: Princeton Univer-sity Press.

Slovic, P., & Lichtenstein, S. (1971). Comparison of Bayesian and regression ap-proaches to the study of information processing in judgment. *Organizational Behavior and Human Performance, 6,* 649–744.

Staniland, A. C. (1966). *Patterns of redundancy: A psychological study.* New York: Cam-bridge University Press.

Stevens, S. S. (1975). *Psychophysics: Introduction to its perceptual, neural, and social prospects.* New York: Wiley.

Swets, J. A. (Ed.). (1964). *Signal detection and recognition by human observers: Contem-porary readings.* New York: Wiley.

Tribe, L. H. (1971). Trial by mathematics: Precision and ritual in the legal process. *Harvard Law Review, 84,* 1329–1393.

(1974). Triangulating hearsay. *Harvard Law Review, 87,* 957–974.

Wigmore, J. H. (1937). *The science of judicial proof, as given by logic, psychology, and general experience, and illustrated in judicial trials* (3rd ed.). Boston: Little, Brown.

Winkler, R. L., & Murphy, A. H. (1973). Experiments in the laboratory and the real world. *Organizational Behavior and Human Performance, 10,* 252–270.

Zadeh, L. A. (1978). Fuzzy sets as a basis for a theory of possibility. *Fuzzy Sets and Systems, 1,* 3–28.

7   Argument structuring and evidence evaluation

David A. Schum

Summary

I have often wondered how many of the subtleties in evidence presented at trial are actually recognized by factfinders and then incorporated in their conclusions. William Twining (1984) goes even farther in wondering how skillful are advocates themselves in recognizing evidentiary subtleties and then in explaining their significance to factfinders. One thing certain is that skillful advocates do not usually offer evidence haphazardly at trial but according to some design or strategy, the objective in such strategies being the presentation of what advocates judge to be the best possible argument on behalf of their clients. It seems likely that, in most cases, advocates spend a significant amount of time before trial in structuring the arguments they will offer. Under the best of conditions, this is not an easy task; given a large mass of evidence it may well be an overwhelming task. That different arguments are possible from the same evidence is one reason why there is to be a trial in the first place. One thing an advocate can be assured of is that his/her arguments will be carefully decomposed or dissected by the opposing advocate. Several current works acknowledge the importance of careful argument structuring by advocates during pretrial preparations and offer various forms of assistance to this process (Anderson & Twining, 1991; Binder & Bergman, 1984).

I am concerned with the process of structuring arguments from evidence to major facts-in-issue, how the evidential subtleties revealed in such structuring might best be exposed for study and analysis, how such subtleties might be explained to factfinders, and how well factfinders can incorporate evidential subtleties in their assessments of the probative value of

Research discussed in this paper was supported by the National Science Foundation under grants SOC 77-28471 and SES 80-24203 to Rice University and grant SES 87-04377 to George Mason University.

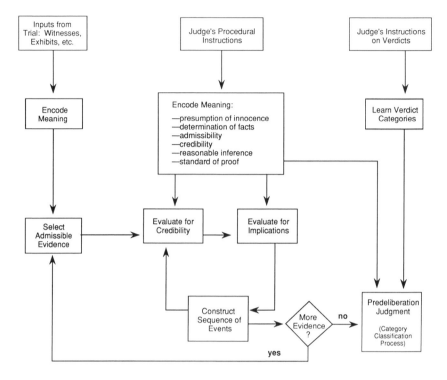

Figure 7.1. Juror subtasks of interest.

evidence. Some of these matters are formal (or logical) in nature, others are empirical. Some of the empirical issues that arise involve various subtasks that Pennington and Hastie have identified in their recent model of the "ideal juror"; the subtasks of greatest concern to me are those labeled "Evaluate for Credibility," "Evaluate for Implications," and "Construct Sequence of Events" in Figure 7.1 (this figure has been adapted from Pennington & Hastie, 1981).

Temporal and relational structuring

There are at least two forms of argument structuring to be considered; each one is important and serves particular purposes. The first one I shall label *Temporal Structuring*, because its major ingredient is the believed ordering over time of events of significance to matters at issue. Temporal structuring is apparent in any effort to present a story or scenario about what happened; identifying a temporal sequence of events is necessary in any assessment of causal relationships of importance. As Figure 7.2 illustrates, there may be several different temporal orderings of interest to an advocate attempting to construct a convincing story or scenario for the purpose of

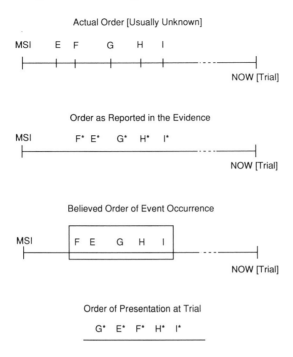

Figure 7.2. Different temporal orderings of interest.

summarizing his/her case. Quite naturally, different stories or scenarios are possible for the same sequence of events. One reason is that there will usually be significant gaps in the event sequence; parties in contention will fill in these gaps in different ways. In addition, of course, there may be controversy about the sequence of events itself; opposing sides at trial may present substantially different event orderings. As Figure 7.2 indicates, the order in which witnesses actually give evidence about events may not correspond to the conjectured temporal occurrence of the events about which the witnesses will testify.

But the presentation of a plausible scenario is not enough. In the first place, as noted, there are always alternative scenarios or explanations possible even when some event sequence is agreed upon. Second, there are always particular points at issue in a trial and advocates will be required to show how their evidence bears upon these specific points. In short, there is another form of evidence marshaling and argument structuring required by advocates on both sides of the matter at issue; for want of a better term I shall label this second form *Relational Structuring*. It is this second form of argument structuring that Wigmore so masterfully describes in his work *The Science of Judicial Proof* (1937). The purpose of relational structuring is to lay bare one's arguments from evidence to major facts-in-issue; that is,

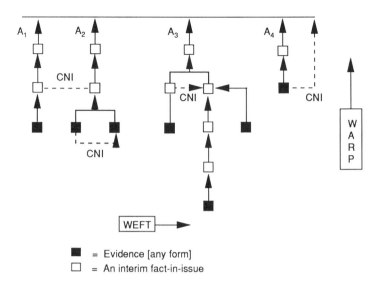

Figure 7.3. The "fabric" of an argument (squares represent evidence and major facts-in-issue).

to show how one's evidence items are related to these facts-in-issue and to each other. Figure 7.3 is an abstraction of a "Wigmore Diagram" that illustrates the typically catenated, cascaded, or hierarchical nature of arguments. Relational structuring allows one to illustrate one's major sources of uncertainty in an argument and it facilitates the tracking of evidential subtleties or conditional nonindependencies (CNI) that are exposed when one marshals evidence on specific points at issue. As this diagram shows, the metaphor of the "fabric" of an overall argument is not such a bad one; as I will discuss, there are discernible vertical or "warp" threads as well as discernible horizontal or "weft" threads.

On one view, temporal and relational structures are two different species of "cognitive models" of an inference problem. I have thought it of some interest to study the formulation of such models and, in the process, to observe how they seem to be related and how one of these forms of structuring may facilitate the other. In a recent paper (Schum, 1986) I gave particular attention to the importance of both forms of argument structuring and how they form a crucial element of the discovery process (see Figure 7.4). The structuring of inference and decision problems has not, until recently, received much attention among inference and decision theorists; in a real sense, Wigmore's work remains state-of-the-art. Surely it is true that the ease with which factfinders can draw conclusions from trial evidence depends in no small way upon the skill of opposing advocates in both temporal and relational structuring. Following is a brief account of the history of attempts to study the process of inferential argument structuring.

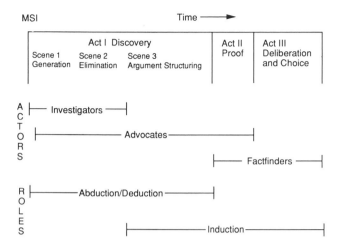

Figure 7.4. The acts and scenes of inference in jurisprudence.

Study of the process of structuring inferential argument

I shall here confine my remarks to scholarship in just two areas, evidence law and probability theory; empirical behavioral research I consider in the next section. Among evidence scholars, Bentham certainly appreciated the catenated or cascaded nature of argument from evidence to major facts-in-issue (Twining, 1985). So did Wigmore, but he did so in a much more elaborate way. Most of us are familiar with his "chart" method for structuring argument and will already have seen examples, such as the one in Figure 7.5, of his process of marshaling a mass of evidence. Unfortunately, as William Twining (1985) discusses, Wigmore's insights into the argument structuring process seem rarely to have been exploited. However, there is now quite a level of interest in argument structuring processes that are quite appropriately labeled "Wigmorean." Within legal evidence scholarship, Anderson and Twining are preparing a major work on argument structuring and evidence marshaling using, as a basis, Wigmore's methods (Anderson & Twining, 1991). In the process, they point out the many practical as well as pedagogical advantages of this form of evidence analysis.

Another valuable contribution to the study of argument structuring is to be found in the recent work of Binder and Bergman (1984). A major emphasis in their work is placed upon careful pretrial argument structuring in which an advocate must determine exactly what each item of evidence to be offered proves and in which the advocate attempts to anticipate counterargument from the opposing advocate. They also emphasize that careful argument structuring actually facilitates the process of discovery; such structuring assists in identifying gaps in one's evidence and may even be suggestive of new or altered hypotheses or theories about the case at

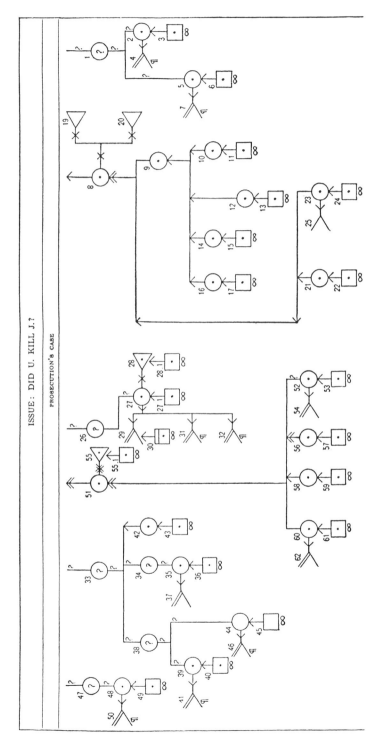

Figure 7.5. A Wigmore evidence chart. Modified version of "Chart Example A: Commonwealth v. Umilian," Wigmore, 1937, p. 872.

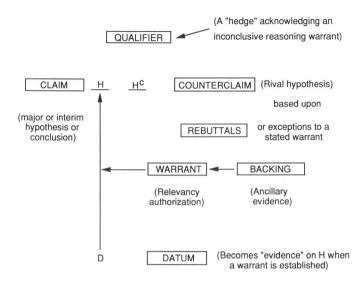

Figure 7.6. Toulmin's scheme for the layout of an argument.

hand. In short, careful argument structuring can facilitate the "generation" and "elimination" stages of discovery as I have identified in Figure 7.4. The actual structuring approach advocated by Binder and Bergman is much less detailed than the Wigmorean approach advocated by Anderson and Twining; however, the two approaches are entirely consistent in their essentials.

Though Stephen Toulmin was not a scholar of legal evidence, he has certainly demonstrated admiration for the adversarial argument process as it is played out at trial and goes on to suggest that such adversarial approaches to inference might well benefit inferential or diagnostic activity in many other contexts (Toulmin, 1964). Toulmin focuses upon the various ingredients necessary to support reasoning from one event to another; his work summarizes, in slightly different terms, the very same ingredients discussed in the work of scholars of trial evidence. Figure 7.6 summarizes the essential elements of Toulmin's scheme for the analysis of a reasoning step.

I believe it is fair to say that probabilists and others who have attempted to apply concepts of probability theory to inference at trial have come rather late upon the argument structuring process. Some of us began, now over 20 years ago, an attempt to extend various probabilistic formulations so that they might capture the wide array of subtleties exposed in careful argument structuring. In my own work, I have taken very seriously the insights of Wigmore about argument structuring and the wide array of evidential subtleties that are exposed in such detailed analysis. Before I discuss some of the work on argument structuring within probability theory, there is a behaviorally interesting controversy brought again to light in some very

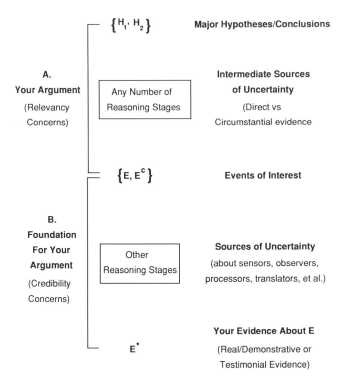

Figure 7.7. Elements of a simple chain of reasoning.

recent work; this controversy concerns the virtue of decomposing inferential tasks.

In most applications of probability to the task of weighing and combining evidence a complex probability assessment is formally decomposed
into a collection of other, presumably more tractable, assessments; these
decomposed assessments made, they are then recombined according to
the decomposition algorithm. It is also true that Wigmore's method for case
analysis is a (nonprobabilistic) species of inference task decomposition.
Stated another way, some holistic judgment is broken down into other
more specific or localized judgments; such decomposition allegedly serves
many ends, among which is a better understanding of the ingredients of
complex judgments and how they "ought" to be combined. Quite recently,
one evidence scholar, M. Abu-Hareira, has made a spirited defense of holistic judgments concerning evidence given at a trial (Abu-Hareira, 1984).
He argues that any rationalist–empiricist focus on decomposed ingredients
of an inference task will lose sight of crucial spatio-temporal and other
characteristics of a collection of evidence when it is examined holistically.
In short, he argues that "the whole is always more than the sum of its

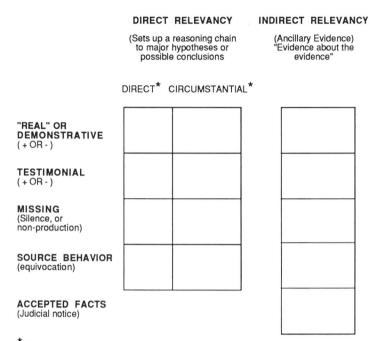

Figure 7.8. An evidence taxonomy.

parts." Under indictment here are any structural decompositions such as Wigmore's and virtually all probabilistic applications I will discuss. I mention this controversy about holistic versus decomposed assessment because some empirical work I will later mention has a bearing on this controversy.

My own formal work on probabilistic inference as it applies to argument structuring has involved attempts to extend conventional or Bayesian representations for the process of evidence weight assessment so that they can incorporate the catenated or cascaded nature of argument (Figure 7.7) and the wide assortment of evidential subtleties revealed in such arguments, examples of which are shown in Figure 7.8 for various identifiable species of evidence and in Figure 7.9 for various combinations of evidence. I am neither unaware of nor unappreciative of the work of L. Jonathan Cohen and Glenn Shafer, both of whom have profound things to say about the process of weighing and combining evidence. I note, in particular, Shafer's recent work on the construction of probability arguments (Shafer, 1986) and Cohen's work on both formal and empirical issues (e.g., Cohen, 1977, 1981). In addition, I note the work of von Winterfeldt and Edwards (1986) on temporal structuring and the many interesting matters that come to light in the process of scenario construction.

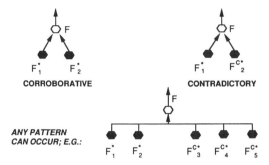

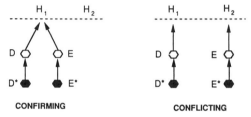

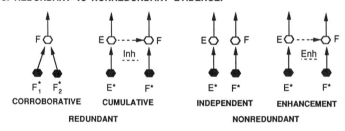

Figure 7.9. Various combinations of evidence.

Empirical research: Inference from structured arguments

Much current behavioral research has painted a "blemished portrait" of human inferential and decisional skills (e.g., Kahneman, Slovic, & Tversky, 1982). Sweeping conclusions about human judgmental bias, suboptimality, and even irrationality are frequently based upon this research. For a variety of reasons, others disagree with such conclusions and offer more charitable views about human inferential skills (e.g., Cohen, 1981; Phillips, 1983; Schum, 1987; von Winterfeldt & Edwards, 1986). Among the arguments against this "blemished portrait" are:

1. There is more than one normative standard against which human probability judgments can be compared.
2. The experiments may simply be demonstrations of lack of formal knowledge rather than cognitive incompetence.
3. Inferential problems presented to experimental subjects are often vaguely or incompletely posed.
4. Subjects are often given vague and incomplete instructions.

But there is another argument I wish to consider, since it has formed the basis for the empirical research I will now tell you about.

As Wigmore emphasized years ago (1937), as well as did John Venn before him (1907), arguments from evidence to hypotheses or major facts-in-issue are necessarily arbitrary; two equally knowledgeable persons may see different reasoning routes from the same evidence to the same hypotheses, or they may, indeed, perceive entirely different hypotheses. Put another way, the structure of an inferential argument has an element of arbitrariness in it. So, when an inference problem is briefly posed for some person whose probabilistic judgments are required, it is to be expected that different persons will structure this problem in different ways. But the trouble is that, in the studies now being criticized, persons are graded against the experimenter's own structure of the problem, something that is almost never revealed to the subjects. Thus, there is no guarantee that any subject even perceives the presented problem in the same way as does the experimenter; the likelihood of this event is increased when instructions given to subjects are vague and incomplete. In some cases, inference problems presented to subjects resemble the ambiguous figures presented by clinicians; many things can be read into them. So, how can we charge a person with being biased, suboptimal, or even irrational, given no knowledge of how this person actually perceived the problem in the first place? I note that this criticism is similar to those made by Phillips (1983) and by Von Winterfeldt and Edwards (1986).

What I shall now tell you about are some of the details and results from a series of empirical studies Anne Martin and I performed and have recently summarized (Schum & Martin, 1982). In these studies we asked our subjects to assess the weight of collections of contrived trial evidence under several different conditions representing increasingly more precise and detailed instructions about the structure of argument from the evidence to the major facts-in-issue in each case. Each one of the 12 contrived collections of evidence or "cases" had a Wigmorean relational structure such as the one depicted in Figure 7.10. For each case, substantive evidence was contrived to fit the logical structure of each case. The collections of evidence we used were contrived to incorporate all of the evidential subtleties shown for combinations of evidence in Figure 7.9. The evidence presented in each case was of two basic species: (A) directly relevant evidence that set up a particular chain of reasoning (e.g., evidence labeled E_2^* in Figure 7.10) and,

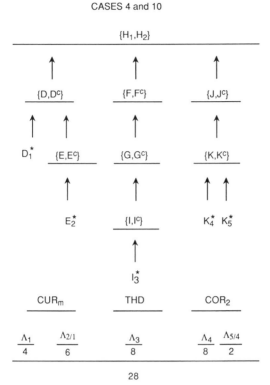

Figure 7.10. Relational structure of an example case.

(B) ancillary evidence that acted either to support or to counteract argument at any reasoning stage. (The actual collections of evidence we used can be supplied by the author.)

Bayesian likelihood-ratio (L) formulations appropriate to the process of "weighing" evidence in each case were developed, examples of which are shown in Figures 7.10 and 7.11. We used such formulations, *not as inferential performance standards,* but as ways of identifying how the evidence weight-assessment tasks could be decomposed to successively "finer-grained" levels. Figure 7.12 is a representation of the three "levels" of weight-assessment task decomposition. These levels range from undecomposed or holistic assessments to a very fine-grained level of assessment. Instructions given to the subjects at each level were increasingly detailed about case "structure"; at the finest level of decomposition, they specified particular probabilistic judgments required at each stage of reasoning depicted in Figure 7.10.

Among the objectives of this series of studies were the following: (A) to observe the degree of weight-assessment consistency across levels of

CASES 4 and 10

$$\Lambda_1 \;=\; \frac{P(D_1^{\bullet}|H_1)}{P(D_2^{\bullet}|H_2)} \;=\; \frac{P(D|H_1) + \left[\frac{h(1)}{f(1)} - 1\right]^{-1}}{P(D|H_2) + \left[\frac{h(1)}{f(1)} - 1\right]^{-1}}$$

$$\Lambda_{2|1} \;=\; \frac{P(E_2^{\bullet}|D_1^{\bullet}H_1)}{P(E_2^{\bullet}|D_1^{\bullet}H_2)} \;=\; \frac{C_1\left[P(E|DH_1) - P(E|D^C H_1)\right] + P(E|D^C H_1) + \left[\frac{h(2)}{f(2)} - 1\right]^{-1}}{C_2\left[P(E|DH_2) - P(E|D^C H_2)\right] + P(E|D^C H_2) + \left[\frac{h(2)}{f(2)} - 1\right]^{-1}}$$

where:

$$C_k \;=\; P(D|D_1^{\bullet}H_k) \;=\; \frac{P(D|H_k)h(1)}{P(D|H_k)\left[h(1) - f(1)\right] + f(1)}$$

$$\Lambda_3 \;=\; \frac{P(I_3^{\bullet}|H_1)}{P(I_3^{\bullet}|H_2)}$$

$$= \frac{P(F|H_1)\left[P(G|F) - P(G|F^C)\right]\left[P(I|G) - P(I|G^C)\right] + P(G|F^C)\left[P(I|G) - P(I|G^C)\right] + P(I|G^C) + \left[\frac{h(3)}{f(3)} - 1\right]^{-1}}{P(F|H_2)\left[P(G|F) - P(G|F^C)\right]\left[P(I|G) - P(I|G^C)\right] + P(G|F^C)\left[P(I|G) - P(I|G^C)\right] + P(I|G^C) + \left[\frac{h(3)}{f(3)} - 1\right]^{-1}}$$

$$\Lambda_4 \;=\; \frac{P(K_4^{\bullet}|H_1)}{P(K_4^{\bullet}|H_2)} \;=\; \frac{P(J|H_1)\left[P(K|JH_1) - P(K|J^C H_1)\right] + P(K|J^C H_1) + \left[\frac{h(4)}{f(4)} - 1\right]^{-1}}{P(J|H_2)\left[P(K|JH_2) - P(K|J^C H_2)\right] + P(K|J^C H_2) + \left[\frac{h(4)}{f(4)} - 1\right]^{-1}}$$

$$\Lambda_{5|4} \;=\; \frac{P(K_5^{\bullet}|K_4^{\bullet}H_1)}{P(K_5^{\bullet}|K_4^{\bullet}H_2)} \;=\; \frac{M_1\left[Y_1 - Z_1\right] + Z_1 + \left[\frac{h(5)}{f(5)} - 1\right]^{-1}}{M_2\left[Y_2 - Z_2\right] + Z_2 + \left[\frac{h(5)}{f(5)} - 1\right]^{-1}}$$

where:

$$M_k \;=\; P(J|K_4^{\bullet}H_1) \;=\; \frac{P(J|H_k)P(K|JH_k) + \left[\frac{h(4)}{f(4)} - 1\right]^{-1}}{P(J|H_k)\left[P(K|JH_k) - P(K|J^C H_k)\right] + P(K|J^C H_k) + \left[\frac{h(4)}{f(4)} - 1\right]^{-1}}$$

$$Y_k \;=\; P(K|JK_4^{\bullet}H_k) \;=\; \frac{P(K|JH_k)h(4)}{P(K|JH_k)\left[h(4) - f(4)\right] + f(4)}$$

$$Z_k \;=\; P(K|J^C K_4^{\bullet}H_k) \;=\; \frac{P(K|J^C H_k)h(4)}{P(K|J^C H_k)\left[h(4) - f(4)\right] + f(4)}$$

Figure 7.11. Likelihood ratios for the structure in Figure 7.10.

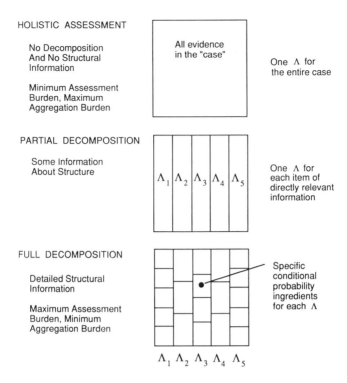

Figure 7.12. Three levels of task decomposition.

1. HOLISTIC EVIDENTIARY WEIGHT ASSESSMENTS

    a.   Applies weakest probative force,
    b.   Least directionally consistent with other methods,
    c.   Most variable across subjects,
    d.   Least degree of concordance among subjects in
        terms of probative value assessments.

2. PARTIALLY DECOMPOSED WEIGHT ASSESSMENTS

    a.   More directionally consistent with other methods,
    b.   Highest degree of concordance among subjects in terms of
        probative value assessments,
    c.   Close agreement with fine-grained assessments,
    d.   Evidential subtleties not captured in assessments,
        e.g., contradiction, corroborative, and cumulative
        redundancy.

3. FINE-GRAINED DECOMPOSITION

    a.   Captured evidential subtleties in assessments, i.e., trapped
        nonindependencies in evidence,
    b.   Most concordance among subjects in ranking probative
        value of individual evidence items,
    c.   Strongest probative force assigned to entire collections of
        evidence.

Figure 7.13. Empirical results summarized.

task decomposition, (B) to observe the level of inter-subject consistency in weight-assessment across these levels, and (C) to observe the extent to which subjects were capable of trapping evidential subtleties in their weight-assessments. The results of this series of studies allowed us to form a much more charitable view of human cognitive capacity than those formed on the basis of research in which very little attention was given to the structure of inferential argument. The essential results, appropriate to the present discussion, are summarized in Figure 7.13.

Some conclusions about argument structuring and evidence evaluation

About the argument structuring process itself

Structuring argument from evidence or, if you prefer, forming a cognitive model of an inference problem, is itself an important and interesting behavioral task and is certainly a worthy subject for research. As noted, there are at least two forms of structuring, one that places emphasis on temporal relations among events of concern and another that places emphasis on the manner in which evidence items bear upon particular issues. It is anything but clear how these two structuring tasks are related and how the performance of one may facilitate performance of the other. The careful laying out of either form of structure provides a visual "forum" for debate on matters at issue and helps to identify the locus of disagreement among the parties in contention. Very few inference problems in law or elsewhere spring forth in well-posed form; essential ingredients in the form of hypotheses, evidence, and assumptions have to be generated or discovered. I believe it true that the careful structuring of an inference problem can be of considerable assistance in the abductive process of generating new hypotheses or possibilities and new classes of potentially relevant evidence.

In many different contexts persons involved in the task of inference must evaluate large masses of evidence. It is certainly true that our methods for collecting evidence far outstrip, both in number and in quality, our methods for the inferential use of it. Confronted with a growing mass of evidence, many persons experience considerable difficulty even in deciding what questions might well be asked of this evidence. My belief is that improvements in our argument structuring capabilities may well enhance this questioning process and help us to uncover more of the subtleties in evidence. In addition, I believe that enhanced structuring capability may also facilitate the manner in which instructions about evidence are conveyed to factfinders. Peter Tillers and I are now embarked upon research on the argument structuring process; one objective in our research is to offer suggestions for the requisites of computer-based systems for facilitating the argument structuring process in very difficult inferential problems involving masses of evidence (Tillers & Schum, 1988).

Argument structuring and the factfinder

I believe it no serious indictment of the cognitive capacity of ordinary persons who serve as jurors that they do not necessarily appreciate the many subtle attributes of inference from incomplete, inconclusive, and possibly unreliable evidence. Both Twining (1984) and Binder and Bergman (1984) argue that many advocates are not always appreciative of these subtleties either, but they argue that this represents a failure of their education or experience and not a limitation on their intellectual skills. I believe we ought to consider a similarly charitable view when considering human cognitive capacities in general and those of experimental subjects in particular. Vague and open-ended posing of an inference problem or the structuring of argument from evidence invites variability in the perceptions of the essentials of this problem among those whose task it is to draw conclusions from the evidence. This we observed in our studies in the case of holistic or undecomposed evidence weight assessment; under such a condition, persons are given no information about how the evidence might bear upon matters at issue and are thus left to their own devices in making such judgments.

I make no recommendation that the deliberation task for factfinders in a court of law be decomposed as we did in our studies; in fact, such decomposition invites inferential paralysis, given the number of possible judgmental ingredients in even "simple" inference problems. What I do suggest is that, if we expect persons to appreciate the many subtle attributes of inference tasks we ask them to perform, we ought to take measures to insure that they are at least aware of the existence of these subtleties and why they are of importance in the inference task at hand. Such instruction must rest on careful structuring of arguments. In fairness, we ought to take such measures whether the persons of concern are actual jurors or experimental subjects in behavioral research.

References

Abu-Hareira, M. Y. (1984). *A holistic approach to the examination and analysis of evidence in Anglo-American judicial processes.* Doctoral dissertation, Law School, University of Warwick.

Anderson, T. J., & Twining, W. (1991). *Analysis of evidence.* Boston, MA: Little, Brown.

Binder, D., & Bergman, P. (1984). *Fact investigation: From hypothesis to proof.* St. Paul, MN: West.

Cohen, L. J. (1977). *The probable and the provable.* New York: Oxford University Press.
    (1981). Can human irrationality be experimentally demonstrated? *The Behavioral and Brain Sciences, 4,* 317–370.

Kahneman, D., Slovic, P., & Tversky, A. (1982). *Judgment under uncertainty: Heuristics and biases.* Cambridge: Cambridge University Press.

Pennington, N., & Hastie, R. (1981). Juror decision-making models: The generalization gap. *Psychological Bulletin, 89,* 246–287.

Phillips, L. D. (1983). A theoretical perspective on heuristics and biases in probabilistic thinking. In P. Humphreys, O. Svenson, & A. Vari (Eds.), *Analysing and aiding decision processes* (pp. 525–543). Amsterdam: North Holland.

Schum, D. (1986). Probability and the processes of discovery, proof, and choice. *Boston University Law Review, 66,* 825–876.

  (1987). *Evidence and inference for the intelligence analyst* (2 vols.). Lanham, MD: University Press of America.

Schum, D., & Martin, A. (1982). Formal and empirical research on cascaded inference in jurisprudence. *Law and Society Review, 17,* 105–151.

Shafer, G. (1986). The construction of probability arguments. *Boston University Law Review, 66,* 799–816.

Tillers, P., & Schum, D. (1988). Charting new territory in judicial proof: Beyond Wigmore. *Cardozo Law Review, 9,* 907–966.

Toulmin, S. E. (1964). *The uses of argument.* Cambridge: Cambridge University Press.

Twining, W. L. (1984). Taking facts seriously. *Journal of Legal Education, 34,* 22–42.

  (1985). *Theories of evidence: Bentham and Wigmore.* London: Weidenfeld & Nicolson.

Venn, J. (1907). *The principles of empirical or inductive logic.* London: Macmillan.

von Winterfeldt, D., & Edwards, W. (1986). *Decision analysis and behavioral research.* Cambridge: Cambridge University Press.

Wigmore, J. H. (1937). *The science of judicial proof, as given by logic, psychology, and general experience, and illustrated in judicial trials* (3rd ed.). Boston: Little, Brown.

8 The story model for juror decision making

Nancy Pennington and Reid Hastie

Introduction

The goal of our research over the past ten years has been to understand the cognitive strategies that individual jurors use to process trial information in order to make a decision prior to deliberation. We have approached this goal with the perspective of psychologists who are interested in how people think and behave. First, we have developed a theory that we believe describes the cognitive strategies that jurors use. We call this theory the story model, and it is described in the first section of the paper. Second, we have conducted extensive empirical work to test the theory. This work is summarized in the second section of the paper. The story model has been developed in the context of criminal trials, so it will be presented and discussed in those terms. In the final section of the paper, we discuss some of our current research directions.

The story model

We call our theory the story model because we propose that a central cognitive process in juror decision making is *story construction* (Bennett & Feldman, 1981; Pennington, 1981, 1991; Pennington & Hastie, 1980, 1981a, 1981b, 1986, 1988, 1992). Although story construction is central in our theory and has been the focus of most of our empirical research, it is but one of three processes that we propose. In overview, the story model includes three component processes: (A) evidence evaluation through story construction, (B) representation of the decision alternatives by learning verdict category attributes, and (C) reaching a decision through the classification of the story

Research reported in this paper was supported by the National Science Foundation, Law and Social Sciences Program.

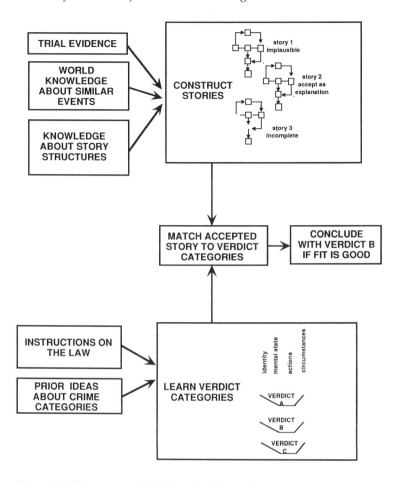

Figure 8.1. The story model for juror decision making.

into the best fitting verdict category (see Figure 8.1). In addition to descriptions of processing stages, one central claim of the model is that the story the juror constructs *determines* the juror's decision. As part of the theory, we also propose four certainty principles – coverage, coherence, uniqueness, and goodness-of-fit – that govern which story will be accepted, which decision will be selected, and the confidence or level of certainty with which a particular decision will be made.

In the next sections of the paper we describe the processing stages proposed in the story model and the certainty principles that govern them. In order to illustrate our ideas with examples, we will draw on one of the simulated trials that we have used in our research, *Commonwealth of Massachusetts v. Johnson*. In this trial, the defendant Frank Johnson is charged with first-degree murder. The undisputed background events include the following: the defendant Johnson, and the victim, Alan Caldwell, had a quarrel early on the day of Caldwell's death. At that time, Caldwell threatened Johnson with a razor. Later in the evening, they were again at the same bar. They went outside together, got into a fight, and Johnson knifed Caldwell, resulting in Caldwell's death. The events under dispute include whether or not Caldwell pulled a razor in the evening fight, whether Johnson actively stabbed Caldwell or merely held his knife out to protect himself, how they got outside together, whether or not Johnson intentionally went home and got his knife, whether Johnson went back to the bar to find Caldwell or went to the bar because it was his habit, etc.[1]

Constructing a story

The story model is based on the hypothesis that jurors *impose* a narrative story organization on trial information. According to the theory, the story will be constructed from three types of knowledge (see Figure 8.1 top left): (A) case-specific information acquired during the trial (e.g., statements made by witnesses about past events relevant to the decision); (B) knowledge about events similar in content to those that are the topic of dispute (e.g., knowledge about a similar crime in the juror's community); and (C) generic expectations about what makes a complete story (e.g., knowledge that human actions are usually motivated by goals). This constructive mental activity results in one or more *interpretations* of the evidence that have a narrative story form (Figure 8.1, top right). One of these interpretations (stories) will be accepted by the juror as the best explanation of the evidence. The story that is accepted is the one that provides the greatest coverage of the evidence and is the most coherent, as determined by the particular juror.

Active story construction. When we hypothesize that jurors *impose* a narrative organization on evidence, we mean that jurors engage in an active, constructive comprehension process in which evidence is organized, elaborated, and interpreted by them during the course of the trial. In part, this activity occurs because comprehension is inherently a constructive process for even the simplest discourse (Collins, Brown, & Larkin, 1980; Crothers, 1979; Kintsch, 1974, 1988). To illustrate this point in general, suppose a listener is told a simple narrative, "Billy went to Johnny's birthday party. When all the children were there, Johnny opened his presents. Later, they sang Happy Birthday and Johnny blew out the candles." Many listeners will infer spontaneously, and most will agree when asked, that there was a cake at the birthday party. Yet, no cake is mentioned in the sentences above; indeed it is not certain that there was a cake. The cake is inferred

---

[1] This trial has been used extensively in mock jury research (Hastie, Penrod, & Pennington, 1983; Ellsworth, 1988) and has been judged by experienced attorneys and trial judges to be a typical felony trial; see Appendix to Chapter 1 of this book for more details.

because we share knowledge about birthday party traditions and about the physical world (the candles had to be on something). Another illustration comes with the comprehension of the sentence, "The policeman held up his hand and stopped the car." Most of us understand this sentence in the cultural context of the policeman's authority, shared signals, a driver watching the policeman but controlling the car, etc. Indeed, this is a sentence that would be puzzling to a person from a different culture.

The constructive nature of comprehension is especially relevant in the context of legal trials in which characteristics of the trial evidence make it unwieldy and unstory-like. First there is a lot of evidence, often presented over a duration of several days. Second, evidence presentation typically appears in a disconnected question and answer format; different witnesses testify to different pieces of the chain of events, usually not in temporal or causal order; and witnesses are typically not allowed to speculate on necessary connecting events such as why certain actions were carried out, or what emotional reaction a person had to a certain event. The attorney's opportunity to remedy the unstory-like form of evidence presentation occurs during the presentation of opening and/or closing arguments, but this opportunity is not always taken.

According to the story model, stories are constructed by reasoning from world knowledge and from evidence. Some potential story elements are accepted as true directly on the basis of their appearance as evidence from one or more credible sources; they are reasonably well established as fact. Which of these events will appear as relevant depends on the interpretation assigned to the fact from its causal relatedness to other events. The inclusion in the story of other evidence, inferred events, and causal relations between them is the result of a wide variety of deductive and inductive reasoning procedures applied to the evidence and world knowledge (Collins, 1978; Collins & Michalski, 1989).

Analyses of inference chains leading to story events reveal that intermediate conclusions are established by converging lines of reasoning that rely on deduction from world knowledge, analogies to experienced and hypothetical episodes, and reasoning by contradiction (Pennington, 1991; Pennington & Hastie, 1980). A typical deduction from world knowledge in the "Johnson case" consists of the following premise (P1 – P3) and conclusion (C) structure:

P1. A person who is big and known to be a troublemaker causes people to be afraid.
P2. Caldwell was big.
P3. Caldwell *was known to be a troublemaker.*
C. Johnson was afraid.

In this example, the juror matches features of Caldwell from undisputed evidence (P2) and a previous inferential conclusion (P3) to world knowledge about the consequences of being confronted with such a person (P1) to infer that Johnson was afraid (C).[2]

Confidence in the conclusion of an inference is assessed by reasoning by analogy to other experiences and by evaluating alternate conclusions that would contradict the initial conclusion. For example, the same juror who provided the premise–conclusion example just mentioned, continued with, "If someone like Caldwell came up to me in a bar and threatened me, I would be afraid." Alternate reactions were also considered, "I don't think Johnson was angry. If he had been angry, he would have gone right back to the bar. He didn't go right back." This alternative is rejected, "No, Johnson was afraid of Caldwell and he took his knife with him because he was afraid."

Different jurors will construct different stories, and a central claim of the theory is that the story will determine the decision that the juror reaches. Because all jurors hear the same evidence, and have the same general knowledge about the expected structure of stories, differences in story construction must arise from differences in world knowledge, that is, differences in experiences and beliefs about the social world. In contrast to the example inference above, another juror might believe that confrontations by bullies are a challenge to manly pride and that as a result, anger is the more likely response. This particular inference may be a keystone in an evolving interpretation of the evidence that is completely different from that of the previous juror.

The structure of stories. Stories involve human action sequences connected by relationships of physical causality and intentional causality between events. In its loosest form, a story could be described as a "causal chain" of events in which events are connected by causal relationships of necessity and sufficiency (Trabasso & van den Broek, 1985). However, psychological research on discourse comprehension suggests that story causal chains have additional higher order structure both when considering the discourse itself and when considering the listener or reader's "mental representations"

[2] It is the certainty of the conclusion C as a function of the levels of certainty of P1, P2, and P3, and the strengths of the relationships between the premises and conclusion that probabilistic (and heuristic) theories of inference were designed to model. It is at this point that Bayesian or fuzzy set calculations could be incorporated into the story model to yield the level of certainty with which a juror believes in any particular proposition (and consequently in the ultimate decision proposition). However, because of lack of empirical support for Bayesian calculations as a *description* of human judgment under uncertainty, we have adopted a set of simple assumptions that will allow us to perform calculations over a network of relationships and that we believe are closer to actual juror judgment processes. The main assumption is that at the time that an inferential conclusion is being considered as a potential story event, it is either regarded as certainly true (and therefore as data, e.g., P2), or as uncertain (and therefore as an hypothesis, e.g., P3, C), or as rejected and therefore certainly untrue. The final level of acceptability of any given proposition is hypothesized to be a function of its role in the story and its relation to relevant world knowledge (we return to the subject of juror confidence in the section on certainty principles).

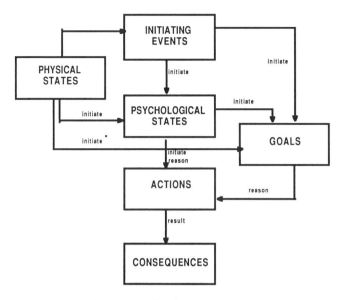

Figure 8.2. An abstract episode schema.

of the discourse. Stories appear to be organized into units that are often called *episodes* (Mandler, 1984; Pennington & Hastie, 1986; Rumelhart, 1977; Schank, 1975; Stein & Glenn, 1979; Trabasso & van den Broek, 1985). We show an abstract episode schema in Figure 8.2 that depicts a typical configuration of events in an episode; an episode should contain events which fulfill particular roles and are connected by certain types of causal relationships. In stories and in episodes, events considered to be *initiating events* cause characters to have psychological *responses* and to form *goals* that motivate subsequent *actions* which cause certain *consequences* and accompanying *states.* An example of an episode in the Johnson case is the following sequence: Johnson and Caldwell are in Gleason's bar. Caldwell's girlfriend, Sandra Lee, goes up to Johnson and asks him for a ride to the race track the next day (initiating events). Caldwell becomes angry (internal response), pulls his razor, and threatens Johnson (actions, note that goal is missing). Johnson backs off (consequence).

Stories may have further structure by virtue of the fact that each component of an episode may be an episode itself. For example, the entire episode above (characterized as Caldwell threatens Johnson) is the initiating event in one version of the Johnson story. In this version, the afternoon "threat" episode causes Johnson to be angry, and want to pay Caldwell back. Thus, a story may be thought of as a hierarchy of embedded episodes (Rumelhart, 1977; Trabasso & van den Broek, 1985). The highest level episode characterizes the most important features of "what happened." Components of the highest level episode are elaborated in terms of more detailed event sequences in which causal and intentional relations among subordinate story events are represented.

The structure of stories, according to our theory, plays an important role in the juror's comprehension and decision making processes. The story constructed by the juror will consist of some subset of the events and causal relationships referred to in the presentation of evidence, *and* additional events and causal relationships inferred by the juror. Some of these inferences may be suggested by the attorney and some may be constructed solely by the juror. Whatever their source, the inferences will serve to fill out the episode structure of the story. Thus, expectations about the kinds of information necessary to make a story tell the juror when important pieces of the explanation structure are missing and when inferences must be made. Knowledge about the structure of stories allows the juror to form an opinion concerning the completeness of the evidence, the extent to which a story has all its parts. Second, the structure of episodes in a story corresponds to the structure of our knowledge about human action sequences in the world. That is, story construction is a general comprehension strategy for understanding human action. Thus the juror can easily compare the structure that is being imposed on the evidence to already encoded prior knowledge. Finally, the hierarchical episode and causal structure of the story provides an "automatic" index of the importance of different pieces of evidence (Trabasso & Sperry, 1985). In the example above, the details of the embedded "threat" episode are subordinate in importance to the details of the top level episode that reveal what Johnson did in order to pay Caldwell back. However, this indexing of importance is something that emerges from the *structure* of the story.

Certainty principles. More than one story may be constructed by the juror. However one story will usually be accepted as the "best" story. And, the juror will have a level of confidence in that "best" story that may be quite high or quite low. The principles that determine acceptability of a story and the resulting level of confidence in the story, we call *certainty principles.* According to our theory, two certainty principles govern acceptance: *coverage* and *coherence.* An additional certainty principle, *uniqueness*, will contribute to confidence.

A story's coverage of the evidence refers to the extent to which the story accounts for evidence presented at trial. Our principle states that the greater the story's coverage, the more acceptable the story as an explanation of the evidence, and the greater confidence the juror will have in the story as an explanation, if accepted. An explanation that leaves a lot of evidence unaccounted for is likely to have a lower level of acceptability as the correct explanation. Poor coverage should lower the overall confidence in a story and consequently lower confidence in the decision.

A story's coherence and level of confidence also enter into its acceptability. However, coherence is a concept in our theory that has three components: *consistency, plausibility,* and *completeness.* A story is consistent to the extent that it does not contain internal contradictions either with evidence believed to be true or with other parts of the explanation. A story is plausible to the extent that it corresponds to the decision maker's knowledge about what typically happens in the world and does not contradict that knowledge. A story is complete when the expected structure of the story "has all of its parts" (according to the rules of the episodic structure, see Figure 8.2 and discussion above). Missing information or lack of plausible inferences about one or more major components of the story structure will decrease confidence in the explanation. Thus, the coherence of the explanation reflects the consistency of the explanation with itself and with world knowledge, and the extent to which parts of the explanation can be inferred or assembled. These three ingredients of coherence (consistency, plausibility, and completeness) may be fulfilled to a greater or lesser degree and the values of the three components will combine to yield the overall level of coherence of a story.

Finally, if more than one story is judged to be coherent, then the stories will lack *uniqueness,* which contributes to confidence in a story and in a decision. If there are multiple coherent explanations for the available evidence, belief in any one of them over the others will be lessened (Einhorn & Hogarth, 1986; van Wallendael, 1989). If there is one coherent story, this story will be accepted as the explanation of the evidence and will be instrumental in reaching a decision. (These principles are elaborated and formalized in Pennington, Messamer, & Nicolich, 1991.)

Summary. Meaning is assigned to trial evidence through the incorporation of that evidence into one or more plausible accounts or stories describing "what happened" during events testified to at the trial. General knowledge about the structure of human purposive action sequences and of stories, characterized as an episode schema, serves to organize events according to the causal and intentional relations among them as perceived by the juror. Specific world knowledge about events similar to those in dispute will determine which particular interpretation is constructed or accepted. The level of acceptance will be determined by the coverage, coherence, and uniqueness of the "best" story.

Learning verdict definitions

The second processing stage in the juror's decision, according to the story model, involves the comprehension and learning of the decision alternatives, which in criminal trials are the definitions of the verdict alternatives (e.g., first-degree murder, second-degree murder, etc.). Most of the information for this processing stage is given to jurors at the end of the trial in the judge's substantive instructions on the law although jurors may also

FIRST DEGREE MURDER

IDENTITY:	Right Person
MENTAL STATE:	Intent to Kill Purpose Formed
CIRCUMSTANCES:	Insufficient Provocation Interval Between Resolution and Killing
ACTIONS:	Unlawful Killing Killing in Pursuance of Resolution

Figure 8.3. Example verdict category represented as a feature list.

have prior ideas concerning the meaning of the verdict categories (see Figure 8.1, bottom).

The verdict definition information in the judge's instructions is usually abstract and often couched in unfamiliar language: A crime is named and then abstract features are presented that define the crime. Features typically describe requirements of *identity, mental state, circumstances,* and *actions* that constitute the crime (Kaplan, 1978). For example, a judge's definition of first-degree murder presented as a feature list is shown in Figure 8.3.

We hypothesize that the juror's mental representation of this information also takes the form of a category label with a list of features. In all respects, this is a difficult one-trial learning task. If the juror has no prior knowledge of the legal categories, then learning of the abstract information is extremely difficult. In the case where prior knowledge is available, it is as likely to interfere with accurate understanding as to help, because jurors' prior exposures to concepts such as first degree murder, manslaughter, armed robbery, etc. are often (mis-) informed by television episodes and other media presentations.

Making a decision

The third processing stage that we hypothesize in the juror's decision making involves matching the accepted story with each of the verdict definitions. In cognitive processing terms, this is a classification process in which the best match between the accepted story's features and verdict category features is determined (see Figure 8.1, middle).

Because verdict categories are unfamiliar concepts, the classification of a story into an appropriate verdict category is likely to be a deliberate process. For example, a juror may have to reason about whether a circumstance in the story such as "pinned against a wall" constitutes a good match to a required circumstance, "unable to escape," for a verdict of not guilty by reason of self-defense.

Although difficult, the classification process is aided by relatively direct relations between attributes of a verdict category (crime elements) and components of the episode schema (see Figure 8.4). The law has evolved so that the main attributes of the decision categories suggested by legal experts (Kaplan, 1978) – identity, mental state, circumstances, and actions – correspond closely to the central features of human action sequences represented as episodes: initiating events, goals, actions, and states. This is not a coincidence; rather, it is a reflection of the fact that both stories and crimes are culturally determined generic descriptions of human action sequences.

The story classification stage also involves the application of the judge's procedural instructions on the presumption of innocence and the standard of proof. If the best fit is above a threshold requirement, then the verdict category that matches the story is selected. If not all of the verdict attributes for a given verdict category are satisfied "beyond a reasonable doubt" by the events in the accepted story, then the juror should presume innocence and return a default verdict of not guilty. We are basing this hypothesis on the assumption that jurors either (A) construct a single "best" story, rejecting other directions as they go along or (B) construct multiple stories and pick the "best." In either case, we allow for the possibility that the best story is not good enough or does not have a good fit to any verdict option. Then a default verdict has to be available.

Certainty principle. A further assessment of confidence occurs in the story classification stage. An evaluation of *goodness-of-fit* between the story and the best-fitting verdict category is based on the extent to which the story includes instantiations of elements of the category. The more missing element matches between the components of the episode schema and the attributes of the verdict category (see Figure 8.4), the lower the juror's confidence in the verdict. As we proposed above, if the goodness-of-fit is not sufficient, then a default decision will be made.

Temporal relations between stages

The processing stages have been presented as though a story is constructed, then the verdicts are represented, and then a decision is reached. A fundamental claim of our theory is that the explanation structure is created a priori and *causes* the decision and is not a structure that is developed as a post hoc justification of the decision. This does not preclude a version of the theory in which there is cycling through the decision phases more than once; in such a case there could be an influence of the tentative decision (initial verdict classification) on an elaboration of the explanation. For example, story construction probably does not stop abruptly at the conclusion of the presentation of evidence. Previous research suggests that jurors' judgments involve much weighing and sifting of evidence as well

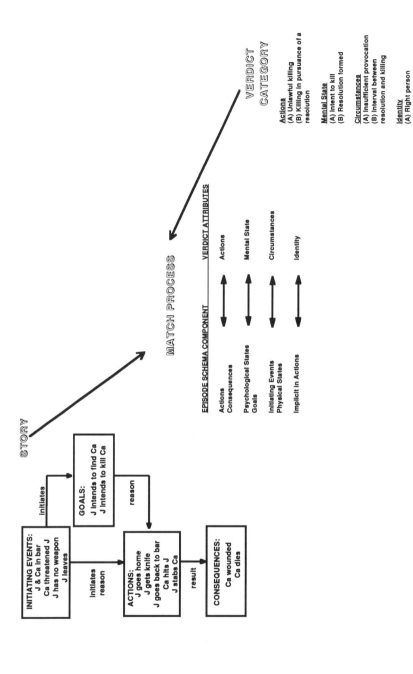

Figure 8.4. The main elements of a story (episode schema) map onto the defining attributes of a verdict definition (verdict category attributes).

as reflection on the meaning of the verdict categories, after the major court-room body of the trial is concluded (Hastie, Penrod, & Pennington, 1983; Pennington, 1981). In addition, story meanings are not static structures. Although many causal and intentional inferences are made during the initial comprehension and encoding of events, causal information processing may not be completed during comprehension (e.g., Kintsch, 1974). Rather, causal reasoning begins then and continues with subsequent attributional inferences influenced by the initial comprehension process. Examining the extent to which processing stages interact is a long-term goal of our research.

Empirical evidence for the story model

The basic claim of the story model is that story construction enables critical interpretive processing and organization of the evidence so that evidence can be meaningfully evaluated against multiple verdict judgment dimensions. The story model provides a psychological account for the assignment of relevance to presented and inferred information.

Other writers have recognized the pervasive role of narrative structures in the comprehension of social events in our culture. Indeed, the story model of juror decision making accrues some support from the popularity of notions of story-telling and narrative structure in the writings of other scholars interested in legal practice: argumentation and persuasion at trial (Mauet, 1988; Moore, 1989; Schuetz & Snedaker, 1988; Twining, 1990); lawyer-client communication (Cunningham, 1989); plea bargaining (Mather, 1979; Maynard, 1988); litigant satisfaction with trial outcomes (O'Barr & Conley, 1985); comparative law (examples in Hamnett, 1977); and juror decision making (Bennett & Feldman, 1981; Holstein, 1985; Lopez, 1984).

The story model is distinctive among "narrative" approaches in the precision of its claims concerning the representational form of the evidence and the central role that is assigned to stories in subsequent decisions and confidence in those decisions. Uncertainty in the decision is based on assessments of the coverage, coherence, and uniqueness of the story and on the goodness-of-fit of the story with reference to the verdict categories. Detailed summaries of empirical studies of the claims of the story model are provided in other reports (Pennington, 1981, 1991; Pennington & Hastie, 1981b, 1986, 1988, 1992). In this section, we summarize the empirical support for the theory.

Interview study

Our initial research on the story model (Pennington, 1981; Pennington & Hastie, 1986) was designed to elicit data that would provide a snapshot of the juror's mental representations of evidence and of verdict categories at one point in time. Three questions were the focus of the empirical analysis: Do the mental representations of evidence show a story structure? Do the mental representations of verdicts show a category structure? Are there systematic relationships between an individual juror's verdict decision and that same juror's evidence representation, verdict representation, or classification procedures? The first study was based on a correlational logic, using an interview to provide structural descriptions of mental representations and then determining whether or not the structures covaried systematically with verdict decisions. According to the story model, if story construction is a central determinant of verdict decisions, then we should find that variability in verdict decisions is correlated with variability in story structures and is not related to verdict category representations or classification procedures.

Twenty-six adult subjects were sampled from volunteers in the Massachusetts Superior Court jury pool and shown a realistic filmed reenactment of a murder trial (the *Commonwealth v. Johnson* case described earlier).

Subjects were instructed that an actual jury had decided the case and their task was to "be one of the jurors" and to try to reach a decision on the verdict. In the trial the jurors chose from among four verdict alternatives in reaching a decision. The defendant Frank Johnson could be judged to be not guilty, guilty of manslaughter, guilty of second-degree murder, or guilty of first-degree murder. A subsample of 16 of the 26 subjects was chosen for extensive analysis so that a range of verdicts was obtained (see Pennington, 1981; Pennington & Hastie, 1986 for details). The verdict distribution for the sixteen subjects was: 5 guilty of first-degree murder, 4 guilty of second-degree murder; 4 guilty of manslaughter; 3 not guilty (self-defense). The major source of data was a verbal protocol obtained in an interview with each experimental juror asking them to talk out loud while making a decision and to respond to questions about the evidence and about the judge's instructions to the jurors.

Verbal protocols from each juror were analyzed by coding all assertions about events and relationships between events that were claimed to have occurred or not to have occurred within the context of the events referred to in testimony. Many of these assertions referred to events and relationships actually mentioned in testimony and many referred to events and relationships inferred by the juror. This coding was transformed into a directed graph designating interrelations between events (Goodman & Hedetniemi, 1979).[3] A graph structure was created for each subject in which the nodes represented event codes and the links represented the asserted connections between events. This structure captured part of each subject's conceptual representation of the evidence as indicated by the protocol events mentioned and assertions regarding relations between events (Graesser &

[3] A directed graph is a structure that includes points (nodes) and arcs (links) between points that have direction. In our application, the nodes will stand for events expressed as single states or actions, such as "Johnson was at the bar," and "Caldwell came over to Johnson's table." The links will stand for relationships between events. An example of one type of directed link would be an enabling causal relationship such as might exist between the two events above: Johnson's being at the bar "enabled" Caldwell to come over and talk to him.

Clark, 1985). To facilitate economy of presentation and to permit comparisons to other experiments, only the results from the two extreme verdict groups, first-degree murder and not guilty, will be summarized in the present report. Analyses of the data for subjects from all four verdict groups are in agreement with this summary (Pennington, 1981; Pennington & Hastie, 1986).

Before reviewing evidence that these graphs had a story structure, we should ask what is the range of plausible structures that we might expect? First, evidence could be stored in memory in an unembellished form as it was presented at trial, in a disconnected question and answer sequence, organized by witness and interconnected largely by referential coherence. This is plausible because we know that when judgments are made on-line[4] (Hastie & Park, 1986; Hastie & Pennington, 1989), memory for evidence is unrelated to the judgment. Second, the evidence could be conceptualized in terms of the structure of the legal argument (see Pennington & Hastie, 1981a, Figure 3, p. 256, for an example of such an evidence structure), as analyzed by legal scholars (e.g., Anderson & Twining, 1991; Wigmore, 1937) and other theorists (e.g., Schum & Martin, 1982). In this conception, evidence is structured in terms of arguments for and against guilt; or for and against a required element of guilt with respect to a particular charge. A third possibility is that the important evidence revolves around the characterizations of the defendant and victim. In this case structures emerging from protocols would show character sketches connected to verdicts. A final possibility is our theory, that the juror organizes the evidence into a story that emphasizes the causal and intentional relations among evidence items.

Our first major conclusion from the interview study was that the mental representations of evidence derived from the interview protocols showed story structures and not other plausible structures. There were several features of the conceptual graph structures that support our claim that these structures had story form and not one of the other plausible forms. First, 85% of all the events referred to in the protocols were causally linked. Thus, subjects were primarily making assertions like, "Johnson was angry so he decided to kill him," (anger initiates goal to kill) rather than assertions like, "Johnson was a violent man. That makes me think he intended to kill him." (The fact that Johnson was violent leads to an inference of intention to kill.) This is strong evidence that subjects were telling stories and not constructing arguments (see Olson, Duffy, & Mack, 1984 for empirical evidence on the psychological differences between narrative forms

---

[4] Making a judgment "on-line" means incorporating the value of a piece of evidence into a judgment as soon as it is encountered. In a legal trial context, this means that a witness testifies, "Johnson was carrying a knife," and the juror immediately increases his or her belief in guilt. If the witness then says, "It was a fishing knife," the juror immediately decrements belief in guilt. Story construction is not an "on-line" decision strategy, but rather a "memory-based" strategy because evidence is organized, elaborated, and interpreted in memory before entering into a judgment.

and argument forms). Second, only 55% of the protocol references were to events that were actually included in testimony. The remaining 45% were references to inferred events – actions, mental states, and goals that "filled in" the stories in episode configurations. This argues strongly against the image of the juror as a "tape recorder" with a list of trial evidence in memory. Experimental jurors did make character inferences (5.4% of story content) but these were integrated into the story structures as reasons for certain behaviors. For example, an inference that Caldwell was a violent man might be given as a reason that Caldwell pulled a razor when provocation was slight or as a reason that Johnson was afraid. Finally, the conceptual graphs can be represented as hierarchies of embedded episodes when rules are applied to identify explicit goals linked to actions leading to final consequences (see Pennington, 1981). Examples of these structures are illustrated in Figure 8.5.

The second major conclusion from the interview study was that story structures differed systematically for jurors choosing different verdicts. In order to analyze this, a measure of shared features (Tversky, 1977; Tversky & Gati, 1978) was used to develop a central story for each verdict group. We call these *verdict stories;* for example, the central story for the jurors choosing first-degree murder is the first-degree murder verdict story. A network was assembled containing only those event codes and links shared in common by 80% of the members of the verdict group. An episode structure was imposed on the causal chains by applying rules to identify explicit goals linked to actions leading to the final consequence (Pennington, 1981). Verdict stories for first-degree murder and not guilty verdict groups are shown in Figures 8.5A and 8.5B.

The gist of the first-degree murder verdict story (Figure 8.5A) is that an argument and threat by Caldwell (the victim) so enraged Johnson (the defendant) that he decided to kill him. He got his knife, found Caldwell, got in a fight and stabbed him to death. In contrast, the gist of the not guilty story (Figure 8.5B) is that Caldwell started a fight with Johnson and pulled a razor on him. Johnson pulled a knife in order to protect himself and Caldwell ran onto the knife.

The episode structures of the two stories map neatly onto their respective verdict category attributes. For example, in the not guilty verdict story (Figure 8.5B), there are three episodes, two of which are embedded. The main episode is the fight, and the initiating events are all Caldwell's actions during the fight. The afternoon episode serves to fortify not guilty subjects' conclusions about Johnson's psychological state, leading first to a goal to show the knife and then to actively protect himself. The not guilty story shows the knife going into Caldwell as a consequence rather than as a goal-directed action. These features correspond to the verdict features of not guilty by reason of self-defense: under immediate attack, unable to escape, intent to defend, and reasonable retaliation. First-degree murder requires

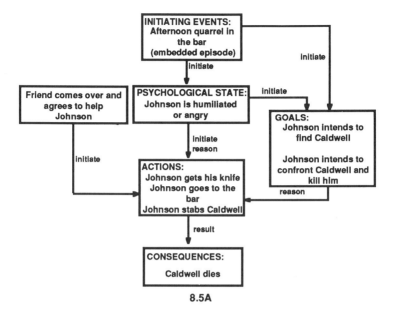

8.5A

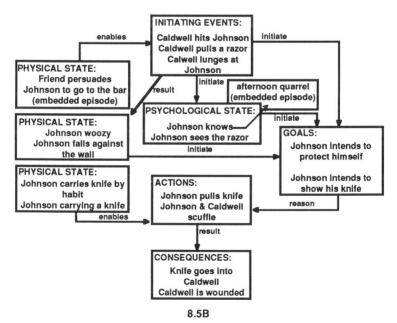

8.5B

Figure 8.5A (top). First-degree murder verdict story (central story for jurors choosing first-degree murder). Figure 8.5B (bottom). Not guilty verdict story (central story for jurors choosing not guilty by reason of self-defense).

premeditation, that is, a resolution formed to kill, an interval of time, and a killing in accordance with the resolution. The subjects' emphasis on the initiation of an intent-to-kill goal is expressed through the elaborated afternoon events (Figure 8.5A). Thus, being hit is not an initiating event, it is part of a sequence of acts that follow from behavior directed by a goal to kill.

Verdict representations were coded and compared across different verdict groups. The majority of references to verdicts during the talk aloud portion of the interview were to particular category features such as "premeditation" and "malice." When asked to tell what the verdicts meant, jurors provided lists of features although they were usually far from complete. Jurors also elaborated their category definitions in some cases by constructing ministories to illustrate. For example, "First-degree murder is premeditated. There is a plan. That would be if he had gone back to the bar looking for him."

There is considerable variation among jurors in the accuracy and completeness of their representations of the verdict category information. If these variations are systematically related to the jurors' verdict choices, then the hypothesis has to be retained that differences occurring in the verdict learning stage determine the verdict choice. For example, if jurors favoring first-degree murder verdicts were also jurors who did not remember the judge's instruction concerning premeditation, it would be plausible that the memory failure affected the verdict choice. To the contrary, analyses of the answers to questions about verdict category definitions showed that juror verdict choice was not related to memory for verdict-element relations. Other analyses (Pennington & Hastie, 1986) showed no content differences by verdict choice. Thus, variance in performance in the verdict learning stage of the juror decision does not appear to determine the juror's decision.

The interview study did not obtain information concerning the juror's notions of presumption of innocence or the beyond reasonable doubt standard. However other research sampling jurors from the same population of jurors and using the same stimulus trial (Hastie et al., 1983) did obtain direct ratings of subjects' estimated values for the beyond reasonable doubt threshold and the presumption of innocence principle. Analyses conducted on these ratings did not find significant differences among the subjects when they were classified by verdict choice. The implication for the present work is that variation in performance in the story classification stage is not associated with variations in verdict choice.

In this research, two key results were established that were necessary conditions for pursuit of the story model as a viable theory of decision making in the juror context. First, the evidence structures constructed by jurors had story structure (not other plausible structures) and verdict structures looked like feature lists. Second, jurors who chose different verdicts had constructed different stories. Thus, decisions covaried with story structures, but not with verdict representations or story classification processes.

The interview study served its purpose as our initial investigation and played a role in our theory building. Moreover, it provides a strong empirical foundation for the story model using a realistic stimulus trial and a range of adult citizen jurors. However, the interview methodology itself may have created a demand for stories as conversational forms or as justifications. Subsequent experiments addressed this issue and tested additional claims of the theory.

Predicting importance ratings and memory for evidence

A second empirical study (Pennington & Hastie, 1988) was conducted to test the conclusions of the interview study using conventional laboratory research methods with college student subjects. In this study subjects' responses to sentences presented in a recognition memory task were used to identify subjects' postdecision representations. The major motivation for this study was to test whether or not stories were constructed spontaneously in the course of the juror's performance. A second goal of the study was to test our claim that the position of an evidence item in its verdict story would predict the importance rating for that item according to verdict choice.

Stimulus materials were constructed based on the content analysis of interviews from the first study. This yielded a 119-sentence written version of the *Commonwealth v. Johnson* case. The written case was carefully constructed so that its constituent sentences included propositions from each verdict story that were not also present in any other verdict story. For example, the proposition "Johnson stabbed Caldwell" was a part of the first-degree murder verdict story, but not included in the not guilty verdict story.[5] In addition, sentences were prepared for the recognition test that were not presented in the stimulus case, but which were parts of the verdict stories identified in the interview study (that is they were frequently inferred by the jurors choosing a particular verdict). Thus, a recognition test could be constructed with *old* (true) target sentences from each story that had been presented as evidence, and with *new* (false) lures from each story that had not been presented as evidence (but were frequent inferences).[6]

[5] This is an empirical observation. This particular statement could have, in principle, been in any of the verdict stories. We described earlier how verdict stories were determined empirically: The graph of events and links for each juror choosing the same verdict were compared. Those events and links in the stories of 80% of the jurors in the verdict group were retained as part of the verdict story. Some of the constituent events and links were evidence items and some were inferences shared by jurors in the verdict group. A particular verdict story would contain only part of the total body of evidence and only part of the total body of inferences that various jurors drew.

[6] Examples of each type of recognition memory test item are as follows:
Old items (presented as evidence) and empirically determined to be a part of:

Subjects "recognized," as having been presented as trial evidence, sentences from the story associated with their verdict with a higher probability than sentences from stories associated with opposing (rejected) verdicts, for both old and new items. That is, they were more likely to correctly recognize as evidence those evidence items in the verdict story corresponding to their own verdict choices, *and*, they were more likely to falsely recognize as evidence those inferences in the verdict story corresponding to their decisions. Subjects also rated the importance of trial evidence items and these ratings were strongly related to the causal role of the item in the story associated with a subject's verdict. These results corroborated the conclusions about story structure and story-verdict relationships from the initial study. Furthermore, they implied that story representations were constructed *spontaneously*, as part of the natural decision process, and not artificially elicited by the interview task used in the first study.

Even though we demonstrated with this experiment that causal explanations are constructed spontaneously in the course of decision making, we have still not demonstrated that the story constructed by the juror is a true mediator of the decision. It could still be the case that the juror makes a decision and then constructs a story as a post hoc justification. The next experiments address this question.

Predicting decisions and confidence in decisions

Two experiments were conducted to test our claim that stories cause decisions. We reasoned that if we could manipulate the ease of constructing a particular story and thereby influence the likelihood of the corresponding decision, then this would be strong evidence for our claim of causal mediation. In both studies, we manipulated the ease of constructing a particular story by varying the presentation order (but not the content) of the evidence.

In our third study (see Pennington & Hastie, 1988), using the abbreviated *Commonwealth v. Johnson* stimulus trial, we varied presentation order to influence the ease with which a prosecution (guilty of murder) or defense (not guilty by reason of self-defense) story could be constructed. Stories were considered easy to construct when the evidence was ordered in a temporal and causal sequence that matched the occurrence of the original events (*story order*). Stories were considered difficult to construct when the presentation order did not match the sequence of the original events. We based the nonstory order on the sequence of evidence as conveyed by

Not guilty verdict story: Johnson held his knife out in front of himself.
Murder verdict story: Johnson stabbed Caldwell in the chest.

New items (not presented as evidence) but empirically determined to be a frequent inference in:
Not guilty verdict story: Johnson was trying to protect himself.
Murder verdict story: Johnson was looking for Caldwell.

Table 8.1. *Percentage of subjects choosing a verdict of guilty of murder by prosecution and defense order conditions*

Prosecution evidence	Defense evidence (%)		Means (%)
	Story order	Witness order	
Story order	59	78	69
Witness order	31	63	47
Means	45	70	

witnesses in the original trial (*witness order*). The logic of the experiment was summarized in our hypothesis that (manipulated) ease of story construction would influence verdict decisions; easy-to-construct stories would result in more decisions in favor of the corresponding verdicts.

One hundred and thirty college student mock jurors listened to a tape recording of a 100-item version of the *Commonwealth v. Johnson* evidence (50 prosecution statements and 50 defense statements), followed by a judge's charge to choose between a guilty of murder verdict and a not guilty verdict. The 50 prosecution statements, the first-degree murder story were presented either in story order or witness order. Similarly, the defense statements were presented in one of the two orders creating a four-cell factorial design. In all four order conditions the prosecution evidence preceded the defense evidence as per standard legal procedure. After listening to the tape recorded trial materials, the mock jurors completed a questionnaire indicating their verdict, confidence in the verdict, and their perceptions of the strengths of the prosecution and defense cases.

As predicted, mock jurors were likeliest to convict the defendant when the prosecution evidence was presented in story order and the defense evidence was presented in witness order (78% chose guilty) and they were least likely to convict when the prosecution evidence was in witness order and defense was in story order (31% chose guilty, see Table 8.1). Thus, story coherence, as determined by presentation order of evidence, affects verdict decisions in a dramatic way. (See Smith, 1988, for a replication of this study with different materials comparing story order with an organization of evidence by *legal issue* rather than with witness order.)

Analyses were conducted on the ratings of strength of the defense and prosecution cases and these ratings were influenced by presentation order, with story order evidence rated as stronger than witness order. Furthermore, the perceived strength of one side of the case depended on both the order of evidence for that side and for the other side of the case. This finding supports our claim that the *uniqueness* of the best-fitting story is one important basis for confidence in the decision. We also examined the verdict confidence ratings and found that, regardless of verdict chosen, jurors who heard *both* sides of the case in story order were more confident than jurors who heard one or neither side in story order. This result reinforces our conclusion that alternate story strength is important, although the empirical finding was not predicted.

It should be noted that this experiment was a laboratory experiment designed to test our hypotheses about the presence or absence of certain mental processes and their relationship to the decisions made. The study was not designed to estimate the *size* of order effects in real trials. In real trials, there are many devices that assist the juror in story construction: opening and closing statements, redundancy in presentation of information, a rich visual environment, and so forth. In this particular experiment, we stripped those enhancements away to reveal the effect of making a story very difficult to construct. In order to estimate the size of order effects in actual trials, this type of experiment would need to be repeated with more realistic stimulus materials.

A fourth experiment focused again on the effects of variations in evidence presentation order, allowing us to further examine the relationship between evidence organization, memory organization, recall memory, and judgments (see Pennington & Hastie, 1992). Using case materials developed by Devine and Ostrom (1985), evidence was presented either in *story order* or *legal issue order*. Two cases were used that varied in whether the preponderance of evidence favored guilt or innocence.

Materials were presented to 414 college student subjects in written form. The two evidence organizations resulted in different memory organizations of evidence, as measured by an analysis of clustering in free recall (using an "adjusted ratio of clustering," ARC, discussed in Ostrom, Pryor, & Simpson, 1981).[7] Subjects who heard the evidence organized by story showed high story clustering and low issue clustering in free recall; subjects who heard the evidence organized by legal issue showed low story clustering and high issue clustering. However, total amount recalled was not different for the two evidence organization conditions.

The results replicate and extend our previous results. When stories were easily constructed, and therefore represented more *coherently* in memory, more verdicts were chosen in the expected direction and subjects rated their confidence as higher. Moreover, this effect was obtained in the absence of effects on the overall amount of recall, ruling out the hypothesis that manipulating order merely manipulates memorability of the evidence.

We have now predicted and observed sizeable effects of story coherence on verdict choice and on confidence that are consistent with the story model. Furthermore, the effects appear in two very different sets of case materials.

---

[7] This is computed by counting the number of times two statements in the same "story" are recalled together and expressing this number as a proportion of total recall, with both numerator and denominator adjusted for the expected number of the story items that would occur together by chance if recall were a random sample of items. Similarly, an ARC would be computed for items recalled together that referred to the same legal "issue."

Alternate algebraic models for juror judgment, derived from the Bayesian approach and primacy-recency principles of information integration, cannot account for the particular pattern of order effects we have obtained. In our next experiments, we utilized a new set of experimental materials and tested predictions from the story model, a Bayesian model, and a sequential updating model (Pennington & Hastie, 1981a).

Comparisons with other models

Many psychological and legal analyses of the juror's task postulate that the decision depends on the estimation and combination of probabilities. A variety of important legal concepts make reference to the probabilistic nature of evidence at trial. For example, relevant evidence is defined as evidence that has a tendency to make the existence of a fact that is of consequence to the determination of the action more probable or less probable than it would be without the evidence (Federal Rules of Evidence, Rule 401, 1976; Lempert, 1977).

There is no doubt that the juror's task involves uncertainty, as do all complex decision tasks of the kind we are considering. But, treating the task as a probability assessment task assumes that the uncertainty assessments behave in ways that are consistent with the rules of mathematical probability theory. Within the mathematical (Pascalian) probability system there is a prescription for coherent probability revision in the light of evidence (Bayes' rule). Under this prescription, probabilistic opinion revisions have three basic properties: the combining process is multiplicative, probabilities of alternate hypotheses must sum to one, and a hypothesis that is held at any time with probability of zero cannot be revived (Schum & Martin, 1980). It is generally known that the Bayesian system is an inadequate description of human behavior under most conditions (Fischhoff & Lichtenstein, 1978; Rapoport & Wallsten, 1972; Slovic & Lichtenstein, 1971).

An alternate probability model has been proposed by Cohen (1977), the inductive probability system, in which probabilities have only ordinal properties. Negation is not complementary, zero probabilities correspond to "no reason to believe" and can therefore be revived with further evidence, and the opinion revision process is not multiplicative. Schum and Martin (1980), in a recent test of the descriptive adequacy of both the Bayesian and inductive probability systems as theories for juror judgments conclude: "We can be fairly conclusive in saying that our subjects did not typically respond in accordance with the canons of probabilistic inference in either the Baconian or Pascalian probability systems" (p. 77). (See also Einhorn & Hogarth, 1985; Pennington & Hastie, 1988.)

In general, features of human uncertainty assessment found across many tasks are inconsistent with the rules of one or more of the traditional probability calculi. For example, the subjective probabilities of complementary hypotheses have been found not to sum to one (Edwards, 1962; Einhorn &

Hogarth, 1985; Robinson & Hastie, 1985; Schum & Martin, 1980; van Wallendael, 1989; van Wallendael & Hastie, 1990); if certainty about one hypothesis increases, certainty about alternate hypotheses may remain constant, increase or decrease (Robinson & Hastie, 1985; Schum & Martin, 1980); hypotheses held with subjective certainty of zero are frequently "revived" (Schum & Martin, 1980); the subjective certainty attached to a conjunction of events is frequently overestimated relative to the optimal combination of the component uncertainties (Bar-Hillel, 1973; Goldsmith, 1978); indeed, the subjective certainty attached to a conjunction of events may be assessed to be greater than the certainty of one or more of the component events (Leddo, Abelson, & Gross, 1984; Tversky & Kahneman, 1983); subjective certainty assessments may be too high under conditions where there is a high similarity between the pattern of evidence and a known standard, or when there is high internal consistency of the evidence even though the evidence is known or thought to be unreliable (Saks & Kidd, 1980; Schum, DuCharme, & DePitts, 1973; Schum & Martin, 1982; Tversky & Kahneman, 1974).

The alternative to modeling juror inference as a probabilistic opinion revision process is to consider that the weight of the evidence "accumulates" in some other manner. In this regard, the additive models (Information Integration Theory averaging rule and sequential weighting, reviewed by Pennington & Hastie, 1981a) are more consistent with the anomalies listed above than are the probability formulations.

In our final two experiments on the story construction process, we examined more closely the impact of story completeness on subjects' beliefs in the guilt of the defendant and its effect on evidence evaluation when subjects were asked to respond to the evidence at different levels of aggregation (see Pennington & Hastie, 1992). We expected that more complete stories would produce more verdicts in the direction of the completed story. We also expected that there would be a greater effect of mediating story structures when evidence was evaluated globally at the end of all of the evidence compared to judgments rendered after each item of evidence was presented. We also compared these two decision modes, subjects' *global* judgments[8] (the normal decision mode for legal judgments) and their cumulative *item-by-item* judgments,[9] with Bayesian, sequential updating, and story models of aggregation.[10]

---

[8] A *global* judgment will refer to the condition in which subjects read through the entire body of evidence and made a single evaluation of the likelihood of guilt at the end of that reading.

[9] Cumulative *item-by-item* judgments refer to the judgment condition in which subjects were asked to read a single block of evidence and then make a judgment of the likelihood of guilt, then read the next block, then make a new judgment (based on all evidence up to that point).

[10] We compared these models to subjects' actual judgments by including a third *local* judgment condition in which subjects were asked to rate the probative value of each evidence block independently. We then applied the three model combination rules to these local judgments and compared the model aggregation result to the subjects' actual global and item-by-item judgments. The Bayes combination rule is well known; each evidence block

We directly varied the ease of constructing particular stories by providing or withholding evidence that was of specific relevance to one possible story or another. These "evidence supplements" were designed to instantiate a component of either the defense or the prosecution story by strengthening causal links between certain pieces of evidence and/or weakening others. In this way, we expected to alter the interpretation of the evidence, thus leading to different decisions. The case materials and methods in these two experiments were based on work by Schum and Martin (1982); three evidence conditions were created for two of their cases involving an embezzlement and a burglary: a *convict* supplements version, an *acquit* supplements version, and the original materials from Schum and Martin (*basic* version). For the first experiment, following methods laid down by Schum & Martin (1982), we had subjects respond to the case materials at three levels: a *global* assessment of the entire collection of evidence; *local* assessments of each block of evidence (essentially each witness's testimony); and an item-by-item evaluation where the subject responded after each block of evidence indicating his or her current cumulative judgment.

Because the supplements tied evidence together into a more (or less) coherent story, we expected that their effect would be greater when considered in the context of all the evidence (global judgment) than when their impact was incorporated into the judgment as the evidence was heard (item-by-item judgment). This prediction was motivated by the assumption that when subjects are asked to make a single global judgment after reading the entire body of evidence, they are able to integrate evidence into a unitary summary structure before evaluation, that is, their judgment strategy will be "memory-based" (Hastie & Park, 1986; Hastie & Pennington, 1989). However, when subjects are asked to make a cumulative judgment after each evidence block, the subject is focussed on the adjustment or change in evaluation. This is likely to invoke an "on-line" strategy whereby subjects anchor on the current opinion and adjust for the new evidence confronting them (Einhorn & Hogarth, 1985; Hastie & Park, 1986; Hastie & Pennington, 1989; Lopes, 1982; Robinson & Hastie, 1985). We also expected that neither the global nor the item-by-item judgments would be well fit by a *Bayesian aggregation* of the local evidence evaluations; that global judgments were more likely to have involved story construction; and that the item-by-item judgments would be better described by an anchor-and-adjust process.

Over the two experiments (see Pennington & Hastie, 1992), our prediction that the addition of story supplements would cause subjects to render stronger evaluations of evidence in the story direction was supported,

was considered to be independent (see formal analyses of these stimuli by Schum & Martin, 1980, 1982). The sequential updating model was an anchor-and-adjust model in which the current judgment (which is a summary of all previous judgments) was weighted .45 and the current evidence block was weighted .55. This model predicts large recency effects. The story model combination rule used equal weighting of evidence, that is, the probative evaluation of the item was its effective weight.

with the convict version of the cases eliciting greater odds in favor of guilt than the basic version and the basic version eliciting greater odds in favor of guilt than the innocent version.

Next, we tested our assumptions about the strategies subjects were using at different levels of aggregation. As predicted, the Bayesian model did not fare well as a description of subjects' global or item-by-item ratings in the experiment (also noted by Schum & Martin, 1982). First, consistent with an hypothesis of "conservatism," neither the final item-by-item nor the global ratings show the degree of influence of the evidence supplement manipulation that appears in the Bayesian calculation based on local evidence block ratings. Bayesian aggregates of the local judgments were about 10 times stronger than the global evaluations and about 15 times stronger than the item-by-item assessments. Thus the subject aggregates (global and item-by-item), consistent with previous research (Edwards, 1968; Schum & Martin, 1982), are extremely conservative with respect to a Bayesian aggregation rule. Second, several specific qualitative characteristics of the item-by-item ratings, primarily in the form of non-complementary adjustments, contradict implications of the Bayesian rule (see also Pennington & Hastie, 1988; Robinson & Hastie, 1985; Schum & Martin, 1982). Third, direct comparisons of goodness-of-fit of a Bayesian updating model and an algebraic anchor-and-adjust model (Einhorn & Hogarth, 1985; Lopes, 1982), applied to the item-by-item ratings, clearly favored the anchor-and-adjust model. The mean difference between item-by-item ratings and the anchor-and-adjust model over evidence blocks is not reliably different from zero for either stimulus case. In contrast, the best fitting algebraic description of the global ratings was neither the Bayesian nor the anchor-and-adjust model (differences between global ratings and anchor-and-adjust predictions were reliably different from zero). A configuration of weights consistent with the story model (see Pennington & Hastie, 1992) provided the best-fitting model for the global judgments.

We also predicted that story supplements would have greater impact on global judgments than on item-by-item judgments. This was supported by the fact that subjects' global assessments are stronger in force than the item-by-item final evaluation by a factor of about 1.5, and the predicted interaction between evidence supplement treatments (convict versus acquit) and response modes (item-by-item versus global) on final judgments of guilt was obtained.

In sum, the essential results of the two studies were consistent with predictions from the story model and projections from closely related research. The Bayesian model did not provide an adequate description of human performance on either the final ratings of the global judgment task or the ultimate rating of the item-by-item response sequence. Nor did the Bayesian approach provide an acceptable description of item-by-item ratings across the course of evidence presentation. An anchor-and-adjust algebraic updating model did provide a satisfactory fit to the sequence of item-by-item judgments. The final item-by-item judgment was less polarized (as a function of the presence of acquit or convict evidence supplements) in all conditions than the single global rating, as predicted from our hypothesis that anchor-and-adjust described the item-by-item judgment process, but story construction best described the global judgment.

Summary. The first study used an extensive interview to establish that intervening narrative structures were created by jurors in a realistic mock-juror study; that these structures took the form of a story; that jurors who agreed on the verdict decision shared a common story; and that other traces of the decision process (e.g., estimates of standard of proof, knowledge of the verdict definitions) did not covary systematically with the decision. The second study using a recognition memory task reinforced the first study's conclusions and added the finding that the story structures were created spontaneously, without the demands of communication with the experimenter in the interview situation.

The next two empirical studies provided substantial evidence that the storylike evidence summary is a key causal mediator of the verdict decision. In both studies variations in the order of presentation of a fixed set of evidence had clear effects on verdict decisions. Furthermore, the order manipulations were selected to facilitate or impede construction of conviction-prone or acquittal-prone stories yielding successful predictions of verdicts from evidence order via the story model. The overall pattern of verdict decisions, confidence ratings, and other collateral judgments also supported our hypotheses that completeness, coherence, and uniqueness of the best-fitting story would predict confidence in the correctness of the verdict.

The final empirical studies provided some comparisons of the story model to two traditional computation-oriented models, a Bayesian updating model and an algebraic anchor-and-adjust model. At the most general level, we hypothesized that the Bayesian formulation would not provide a satisfactory account of any of the human judgments; that the story model would describe global judgments based on all of the evidence; and that the anchor-and-adjust model would describe the sequence of judgments when subjects were prompted for cumulative ratings after each witness's testimony had been summarized. The general hypothesis and subsidiary hypotheses derived from the story model and the anchor-and-adjust model were confirmed.

Conclusions

We have proposed a theory, the story model, that describes jurors' cognitive processing during the trial that results in a tentative predeliberation decision. The essence of this theory is that the construction of a causal model of events, a story, is central in understanding the evidence and its implications. Other processes, such as understanding the judge's instructions and matching the story with a decision option are necessary to turn the juror's understanding of the evidence into a decision.

We have also presented substantial empirical evidence supporting our assertions about the cognitive processing of jurors. Our current research addresses aspects of the theory for which we have not provided compelling empirical support. For example, we are currently investigating issues of generalizability – the extent to which the cognitive processes and mental structures proposed in the story model apply to a large range of legal cases and issues related to the generalizability of our theoretical principles to actual trial settings. A second focus of our current research concerns the time course of comprehension during decision making. By understanding which inferences are made when *during* the comprehension of evidence, the judge's instructions and during subsequent decision making, we will know whether jurors construct single or multiple stories; what factors influence the point at which alternative stories cease to be considered; and the extent to which processing stages interact to produce a decision. Another very important direction for development of the story model involves elaborating and formalizing the principles that we suggest determine confidence in decisions: coverage, coherence (completeness, consistency, and plausibility), uniqueness, and goodness-of-fit, and to formalize these principles in order to understand how confidence in a decision can result from a computation across semantic features of a mental representation of evidence.

In sum, we have conducted a long series of investigations on the story model and believe that it has been established as a major candidate to explain and predict juror decision making in criminal trials. Of course it is clear that there are many areas for further theoretical development and empirical research. Perhaps the most satisfying characteristic of the story model approach, for us as cognitive experimental psychologists, is the extent to which it connects important naturally occurring decision making phenomena to accounts from the mainstream of modern information processing theories of the mind.

References

Anderson, T. J., & Twining, W. (1991). *Analysis of evidence.* Boston, MA: Little, Brown.

Bar-Hillel, M. (1973). On the subjective probability of compound events. *Organizational Behavior and Human Performance, 9,* 396–406.

Bennett, W. L., & Feldman, M. S. (1981). *Reconstructing reality in the courtroom: Justice and judgment in American culture.* New Brunswick, NJ: Rutgers University Press.

Cohen, L. J. (1977). *The probable and the provable.* New York: Oxford University Press.

Collins, A. M. (1978). Fragments of a theory of human plausible reasoning. In D. Waltz (Ed.), *Proceedings of the Conference on Theoretical Issues in Natural Language Processing II* (pp. 194–201). Urbana: University of Illinois Press.

Collins, A. M., Brown, J. S., & Larkin, K. (1980). Inference in text understanding. In R. J. Spiro, B. C. Bruce, & W. F. Brewer (Eds.), *Theoretical issues in reading comprehension* (pp. 385–407). Hillsdale, NJ: Erlbaum.

Collins, A., & Michalski, R. (1989). The logic of plausible reasoning: A core theory. *Cognitive Science, 13,* 1–49.

Crothers, E. J. (1979). *Paragraph structure inference.* Norwood, NJ: Ablex.

Cunningham, C. D. (1989). A tale of two clients: Thinking about law as language. *Michigan Law Review, 87,* 2459–2494.

Devine, P. G., & Ostrom, T. M. (1985). Cognitive mediation of inconsistency discounting. *Journal of Personality and Social Psychology, 49,* 5–21.

Edwards, W. (1962). Subjective probabilities inferred from decisions. *Psychological Review, 69,* 109–135.

   (1968). Conservatism in human information processing. In B. Kleinmuntz (Ed.), *Formal representation of human judgment* (pp. 17–52). New York: Wiley.

Einhorn, H. J., & Hogarth, R. M. (1985). Ambiguity and uncertainty in probabilistic inference. *Psychological Review, 92,* 433–461.

Einhorn, H. J., & Hogarth, R. M. (1986). Judging probable cause. *Psychological Bulletin, 99,* 3–19.

Ellsworth, P. C. (1988). Unpleasant facts: The Supreme Court's response to empirical research on capital punishment. In K. C. Haas & J. A. Inciardi (Eds.), *Challenging capital punishment: Legal and social science approaches* (pp. 177–211). Newbury Park, CA: Sage.

Fischhoff, B., & Lichtenstein, S. (1978). Don't attribute this to Reverend Bayes. *Psychological Bulletin, 85,* 239–243.

Goldsmith, R. W. (1978). Assessing probabilities of compound events in a judicial context. *Scandinavian Journal of Psychology, 19,* 103–110.

Goodman, S. E., & Hedetniemi, S. T. (1979). A descriptive introduction to graph theory and some of its applications. In W. A. Sedelow, Jr. & S. Y. Sedelow (Eds.), *Computers in language research: Formal methods* (pp. 19–95). The Hague: Mouton.

Graesser, A. C., & Clark, L. F. (1985). *Structures and procedures of implicit knowledge.* Norwood, NJ: Ablex.

Hamnett, I. (Ed.) (1977). *Social anthropology and law.* London: Academic Press.

Hastie, R., & Park, B. (1986). The relationship between memory and judgment depends on whether the judgment task is memory-based or on-line. *Psychological Review, 93,* 258–268.

Hastie, R., & Pennington, N. (1989). Notes on the distinction between memory-based versus on-line judgments. In J. N. Bassili (Ed.), *On-line cognition in person perception* (pp. 1–17). Hillsdale, NJ: Erlbaum.

Hastie, R., Penrod, S. D., & Pennington, N. (1983). *Inside the jury.* Cambridge, MA: Harvard University Press.

Holstein, J. A. (1985). Jurors' interpretations and jury decision making. *Law and Human Behavior, 9,* 83–100.

Kaplan, J. (1978). *Criminal justice: Introductory cases and materials* (2nd edition). Minola, NY: Foundation Press.

Kintsch, W. (1974). *The representation of meaning in memory.* Hillsdale: NJ: Erlbaum.

Leddo, J., Abelson, R. P., & Gross, P. H. (1984). Conjunctive explanations: When two reasons are better than one. *Journal of Personality and Social Psychology, 47,* 933–943.

Lempert, R. O. (1977). Modeling relevance. *Michigan Law Review, 75,* 1021–1057.

Lopes, L. L. (1982). *Toward a procedural theory of judgment* (Technical Rep. No. 17). Madison: University of Wisconsin, Wisconsin Human Information Processing Program.

Lopez, G. P. (1984). Lay lawyering. *UCLA Law Review, 32,* 1–60.

Mandler, J. M. (1984). *Stories, scripts and scenes: Aspects of schema theory.* Hillsdale, NJ: Erlbaum.

Mather, L. M. (1979). *Plea bargaining or trial? The process of criminal-case disposition.* Lexington, MA: Lexington Books.

Mauet, T. A. (1988). *Fundamentals of trial techniques* (2nd ed). Boston, MA: Little, Brown.

Maynard, D. W. (1988). Narratives and narrative structure in plea bargaining. *Law and Society Review, 22,* 449–481.

Moore, A. J. (1989). Trial by schema: Cognitive filters in the courtroom. *UCLA Law Review, 37,* 273–341.

O'Barr, W. M., & Conley, J. M. (1985). Litigant satisfaction versus legal adequacy in small claims court narratives. *Law and Society Review, 19,* 661–701.

Olson, G. M., Duffy, S. A., & Mack, R. L. (1984). Thinking-out-loud as a method for studying real-time comprehension processes. In D. E. Kieras and M. A. Just (Eds.), *New methods in reading comprehension research* (pp. 253–286). Hillsdale, NJ: Erlbaum.

Ostrom, T. M., Pryor, J. B., & Simpson, D. D. (1981). The organization of social information. In E. T. Higgins, C. P. Herman, & M. P. Zanna (Eds.), *Social cognition: The Ontario Symposium on Personality and Social Psychology* (Vol. 1, pp. 1–38). Hillsdale, NJ: Erlbaum.

Pennington, N. (1981). *Causal reasoning and decision making: The case of juror decisions.* Unpublished doctoral dissertation, Harvard University.

(1991). *A cognitive model of explanation-based decision making.* Manuscript submitted for publication.

Pennington, N., & Hastie, R. (1980, June). *Representation and inference in juror reasoning: Two illustrative analyses.* Paper presented at the annual meeting of the Cognitive Science Society, New Haven, CT.

Pennington, N., & Hastie, R. (1981a). Juror decision-making models: The generalization gap. *Psychological Bulletin, 89,* 246–287.

(1981b, August). *Juror decision making: Story structure and verdict choice.* Paper presented at the meeting of the American Psychological Association, Los Angeles, CA.

(1986). Evidence evaluation in complex decision making. *Journal of Personality and Social Psychology, 51,* 242–258.

(1988). Explanation-based decision making: Effects of memory structure on judgment. *Journal of Experimental Psychology: Learning, Memory, and Cognition, 14,* 521–533.

(1992). Explaining the evidence: Tests of the story model for juror decision making. *Journal of Personality and Social Psychology, 62,* 189–206.

Pennington, N., Messamer, P. J., & Nicolich, R. (1991). *Explanatory coherence in legal decision making.* Manuscript in preparation.

Rapoport, A., & Wallsten, T. S. (1972). Individual decision behavior. *Annual Review of Psychology, 23,* 131–176.

Robinson, L. B., & Hastie, R. (1985). Revisions of beliefs when a hypothesis is eliminated from consideration. *Journal of Experimental Psychology: Human Perception and Performance, 11,* 443–456.

Rumelhart, D. E. (1977). Understanding and summarizing brief stories. In D. LaBerge & S. J. Samuels (Eds.), *Basic Processes in Reading: Perception and Comprehension.* Hillsdale, NJ: Erlbaum.

Saks, M. J., & Kidd, R. F. (1980). Human information processing and adjudication: Trial by heuristics. *Law and Society Review, 15,* 123–160.

Schank, R. C. (1975). The structure of episodes in memory. In D. G. Bobrow & A. Collins (Eds.), *Representation and understanding: Studies in cognitive science* (pp. 237–272). New York: Academic Press.

Schuetz, J. E., & Snedaker, K. H. (1988). *Communication and litigation: Case studies of famous trials.* Carbondale: Southern Illinois University Press.

Schum, D. A., DuCharme, W. M., & DePitts, K. E. (1973). Research on human multistage probabilistic inferences processes. *Organizational Behavior and Human Performance, 10,* 318–348.

Schum, D. A., & Martin, A. W. (1980). *Probabilistic opinion revision on the basis of evidence at trial: A Baconian or a Pascalian process* (Research Rep. 80-02). Houston, TX: Rice University, Department of Psychology.

(1982). Formal and empirical research on cascaded inference in jurisprudence. *Law and Society Review, 17,* 105–151.

Slovic, P., & Lichtenstein, S. (1971). Comparison of Bayesian and regression approaches to the study of information processing in judgment. *Organizational Behavior and Human Performance, 6,* 649–744.

Smith, V. L. (1988). The psychological and legal implications of pre-trial instructions in the law. (Doctoral dissertation, Stanford University, 1987). *Dissertation Abstracts International, 48,* 3451B.

Stein, N. L., & Glenn, C. G. (1979). An analysis of story comprehension in elementary school children. In R. O. Freedle (Ed.), *New directions in discourse processing* (Vol. 2, pp. 83–107). Norwood, NJ: Ablex.

Trabasso, T., & Sperry, L. L. (1985). Causal relatedness and importance of story events. *Journal of Memory and Language, 24,* 595–611.

Trabasso, T., & van den Broek, P. (1985). Causal thinking and the representation of narrative events. *Journal of Memory and Language, 24,* 612–630.

Tversky, A. (1977). Features of similarity. *Psychological Review, 84,* 327–352.

Tversky, A., & Gati, I. (1978). Studies of similarity, In E. Rosch & B. B. Lloyd (Eds.), *Cognition and categorization* (pp. 79–98). Hillsdale, NJ: Erlbaum.

Tversky, A., & Kahneman, D. (1974). Judgment under uncertainty: Heuristics and biases. *Science, 185,* 1124–1131.

(1983). Extensional versus intuitive reasoning: The conjunction fallacy in probability judgment. *Psychological Review, 90,* 293–315.

Twining, W. (1990). Lawyer's stories. In W. Twining, *Rethinking evidence* (pp. 219–261). Oxford: Basil Blackwell.

van Wallendael, L. R. (1989). The quest for limits on noncomplementarity in opinion revision. *Organizational Behavior and Human Decision Processes, 43,* 385–405.

van Wallendael, L. R., & Hastie, R. (1990). Tracing the footsteps of Sherlock Holmes: Cognitive representations of hypothesis testing. *Memory and Cognition, 18,* 240–250.

Wigmore, J. H. (1937). *The science of judicial proof, as given by logic, psychology, and general experience, and illustrated in judicial trials* (3rd ed.). Boston: Little, Brown.

Part II

Commentaries

9　Notes on the sampling of stimulus cases and the measurement of responses in research on juror decision making

Robyn M. Dawes

Phoebe Ellsworth fails to find much effect of attitude on verdict. Having been personally involved in over 150 similar judgments of "guilt or innocence" by serving on two separate professional ethics committees, I was astounded. Why might Professor Ellsworth's correlations between attitudes and judgment be so low?

My first reaction was that she may have looked at the wrong variables; specifically, I would have suggested looking at age (the everyday observation that old people tend to be more conservative than young people is borne out by surveys) and occupation. She did.

But then I thought of the analogy of the single legal case to the single item on an intelligence test. Certainly, we would not expect to predict success in an intellectual endeavor very well from the response to a single intelligence test item. If we were to find – analogous to what Ellsworth found – a very low correlation between one item and the task performance, there are two possible explanations. The first is that even if intelligence were assessed with multiple items, it would not predict performance well; the second is that the number of items sampled was too small.

The only way to distinguish between these two possibilities is to use many items. Analogously, the only way to distinguish failure due to using a single case from the possibility that attitude does not predict verdict in general is to investigate many different verdicts on many different trials. Moreover, we should avoid using single items for attitude assessment as well. For example, support of the death penalty or support for its abolition may be the best *single* attitudinal predictor of verdict (and my understanding is that it has been shown to predict at least mock-jury verdicts, reliably and weakly), but many other specific attitudes are in fact also assessed by it. What is needed are multiple indicators of the hypothesized general attitudinal predisposition toward guilt or innocence. Such a general orientation may also be challenged on logical grounds (after all, the juror's problem is to determine what happened, not to create social policy), but in the past, general attitudes – multiply assessed – *have* been found to be remarkably good predictors of behavior in such contexts as voting in Congress or reaching judicial decisions on the Supreme Court (cf. Poole, 1981; Schubert, 1961; Spaeth, 1965).

My plea for the use of multiple cases and multiple indicators brings up the problem of how to allocate experimenters' and subjects' time. Ideally, it would be nice to have a larger number of subjects respond to multiple attitudinal items and then reach verdicts on many trials presented in as much detail as possible. That clearly can't be done. My suggestion is that the past efforts directed toward studying process and verdicts in a *very few* realistically presented cases should be supplemented by studies in which multiple cases are used at the expense of realism. My apologies for thinking up work for others to do; it's a dubious privilege of a self-labeled "methodologist."

I believe, moreover, that the history of our field indicates that concentration on single stimuli does not work too well. The "case history" method in clinical psychology, however fascinating its output, has essentially failed. In contrast, statistical analyses across multiple instances have tended to yield insights. In legal decision making itself, for example, it would not have been possible to discover that a decision to execute a convicted murderer is related to the race of the victim by scrutinizing a small number of cases involving black and white murderers and black and white victims, no matter how careful the scrutiny. Statistical analysis, in contrast, did establish this relationship (Gross and Mauro, 1984). In the history of experimental work as well, focusing upon single cases has not been fruitful. For example, the "risky shift phenomena" – by which groups appeared to advocate more risky choices than did the individuals within them prior to group discussion – appears to be an artifact of the selection of problems used in the research; in most of these problems, individual opinion was oriented toward choosing the riskier of two alternatives, the group opinion was more polarized in this direction. In contrast, in those scenarios in which the initial individual opinion was more conservatively oriented, the group judgment was even more conservative. Thus, what was originally believed to be a "risky shift" when only a few cases were studied was in fact a "polarization effect" (Cartwright, 1973). That distinction could become clear only after sampling many situations involving risk. And if, as here, only two had been sampled, it is quite likely that the phenomenon would have been known as either a "risky shift" or as a "conservative shift" depending on which two.

My concern with single stimuli extends to the evaluation of single models. In fact, all the "model evaluation" I have read in the juror decision area concerns how well a single model of decision fits the data. But the problems are "noisy" to begin with, and there is no reason to expect a very tight fit. Thus, a model may fit for the wrong reasons, or it may fit adequately when another model fits better. Perhaps an emphasis on qualitative distinctions between model predictions might be more appropriate. For example, a strict Bayesian model implies that the order in which information is presented is not relevant to the final judgment, while an Information Integration model (N. H. Anderson, 1981) implies strong order effects. Are there order effects? (Answer, yes; see Pennington & Hastie, 1987, 1988.) Of what nature? (Again, see Pennington & Hastie.)

In fact, are we really concerned with model fits anyway? For example, most of us recognize the concepts of "satisficing" and "bounded rationality" (originally termed "approximate rationality") without being able to recognize the algebraic model presented in Simon's *Psychological Review* paper (1956) whose structural characteristics were described by these terms. Isn't it in fact such structural characteristics in which we are really interested?

Finally, I would like to suggest that deliberately choosing cases that are "ambiguous" may not be the best way of studying judgment, particularly not in the jury decision context. In clinical psychology, for example, the Rorschach blots were deliberately chosen to be ambiguous, under the assumption that the ways in which the subjects structured such visual ambiguity would be representative of the way in which they structure the ambiguity in their "worlds." Such structuring was believed to follow from psychodynamic factors, which could therefore be assessed by Rorschach responses. In fact, the few enduring characteristics of Rorschach responses that appear to predict anything are those concerning the "quality" of the responses, which can be assessed only by assuming that certain blots *do* correspond better for some people than for others (i.e., are *not* ambiguous).

So why not use trials where there is a criterion of truth or correctness? Certainly there are cases in which learned jurors would agree that one verdict is "right" and another "wrong." Moreover, jurors assess their task – in part, anyway – as obtaining the *right answer* concerning the commitment of a crime. So why not have right answers? If, for example, a certain attitudinal dimensional could be shown to be systematically related to *incorrect* decisions of one type or another, then we would have very good cause to be concerned about jury selection procedures that lead to a biased selection of attitudinal predispositions among the jurors. In general – and I cannot present a complete supporting argument in this comment – investigations of human judgment on tasks with a criterion (e.g., an actual disease, actual success or failure at staying out of jail or in graduate school) has led to greater insight about the judgmental process than have investigations of tasks without one (e.g., aesthetic preference).

References

Anderson, N. H. (1981). *Foundations of information integration theory.* New York: Academic Press.

Cartwright, D. (1973). Determinants of scientific progress: The case of research on the risky shift. *American Psychologist, 28,* 222–231.

Gross, S., & Mauro, R. (1984). Patterns of death: An analysis of racial disparities in capital sentencing and homicide victimization. *Stanford Law Review, 37,* 27–153.

Pennington, N., & Hastie, R. (1987). Explanation-based decision making. *Proceedings of the Ninth Annual Meeting of the Cognitive Science Society* (pp. 682–690). Hillsdale, NJ: Erlbaum.

(1988). Explanation-based decision making: Effects of memory structure on judgment. *Journal of Experimental Psychology: Learning, Memory, and Cognition, 14,* 521–533.

Poole, K. T. (1981). Dimensions of interest group evaluation of the U.S. Senate, 1969–1978. *American Journal of Political Science, 25,* 49–67.

Schubert, G. (1961). A psychometric model of the Supreme Court. *The American Behavioral Scientist, 5*(3), 14–18.

Simon, H. A. (1956). Rational choice and the structure of the environment. *Psychological Review, 63,* 129–138.

Spaeth, H. J. (1965). Unidimensionality and item invariance in judicial scaling. *Behavioral Science, 10,* 290–304.

10 Sausages and the law: Juror decisions in the much larger justice system

Joseph B. Kadane

My personal experience as a consulting statistician in legal hearings and trials and my exposure to research from a variety of intersections of social justice and the law have led me to view juror decision making as a small part of our legal institutions. When viewed from this broader perspective it is not clear that research on juror decision making should have the highest priority in our agenda of studies of legal decision making or of decision making in general.

First, I am impressed that juror decision making as an institution is designed to be opaque to the scrutiny of social scientists, the citizenry, and even legal authorities. It is not an accident that the instructions to jurors are sometimes vague, incomplete, and difficult to understand. In fact, there is a cliché that jurors frequently set aside these instructions and decide the case on its merits according to the dictates of their consciences and not according to written statutory law. I'm also impressed by the resistance of legal authorities to opening courthouses to exploration of social scientists. Again, I think it is no accident that we have federal laws forbidding social scientists and other reporters from penetrating into the mysteries of the jury room for a direct look on how the decisions are made. I'm reminded of the old aphorism admonishing us that people who love sausages (and the law) should never watch their being made. Contrary to the rampant curiosity of most social scientists, I wonder if those who love the institution of jury decision making should not also avoid watching it being done.

There are also a host of reasons to question the value of research on jury decision making from a purely rational consideration of how we should invest our scientific energies in studying legal institutions. First, I am troubled with the problem of establishing the criterion for a proper verdict: It is a fact that we will never know that any particular jury, experimental or actual, has reached the right answer. This is in contrast to the tasks that are studied in many other domains of research on decision making. When subjects in psychological experiments are asked to solve math problems, physics problems, to make predictions in well-defined gambling situations, or even predictions of naturally occurring events such as elections and sports contests, the researcher has the advantage of knowing the right answer. In juror decision making tasks some people have suggested we can solve the problem of finding a criterion for a correct answer by relying on the judgments of experts, the modal judgment of several juries, or the verdict that is supported by evidence found after the trial occurs. But this solution is not as unambiguous and satisfactory as the case in mathematics, physics, or gambling tasks where the right answer is demonstrable and everyone agrees on it.

There is a second aspect of juror decision making that I want to explore that has to do with the inherent complexity of legal decisions. Social scientists often want to refer to actual trials as a motivation and a target for generalization of their research on jurylike tasks. In order to properly understand what data describing the behavior of jurors in real trials might mean, we have to understand how events come to be cases and how citizens come to be jurors.

Let me start by examining the manner in which a dispute or an allegedly criminal action reaches the status of a case at trial. There is no well-defined natural population of possible cases. Instead, there is a sequence of discretionary decisions made by a number of different parties with various motivations that jointly determine whether an event becomes a case. The police and prosecutors make initial decisions about what kinds of behavior ought to be looked into and whether to seek an indictment. But, notice that these authorities do not start with a list of potential cases and then sample in some well-specified manner from an identifiable part of the population.

Next in the sequence, the case is taken to a grand jury and a sample of citizens exercise their discretion about whether or not it is to go to trial. I should note that most experts do not believe that grand juries exercise a great deal of discretion. The received wisdom is that grand juries usually do what the prosecutors ask them to do.

If an indictment is handed down, as it almost always is, the next step is a series of negotiations between the defense and the prosecution sides of the case. My impression is that this is probably the most important stage and that these are the most important decisions in the path of events on the way to trial. I understand that more than 90% of the cases that reach this "plea bargaining" stage in the process are diverted by a settlement between the two parties without moving on to a trial. So, even of cases that go beyond the grand jury to indictment, 90% of these do not go to trial. This stage is not only the most influential in selecting the 10% sample of cases that move on to trial, but it is probably also the most complex and least understood. The negotiation process is full of tactics, revelations, and the vicissitudes of individual judgments. There is some speculation that the defense will settle for a plea bargain agreement in all but the strongest and the weakest defense cases (Penrod & Hastie, 1979). The reasoning behind this speculation is that when the defense has a very weak case it will not be offered a "good deal" no matter what, so the defendant might as well go to trial; and when the defense has a strong case, the defendant and his attorney are likely to say, "We can prove innocence, nuts to any deal, let's go to trial." But let me emphasize that this is just somebody's guess about what happens; no one really knows very much about the distribution of strengths of prosecution and defense cases that actually do go to trial. The message for social scientists who want to study jury decision making is that they should be concerned about a process that eliminates 90% of the cases that might have gone to trial; a process, moreover, that we know very little about.

There is a final filter in this sequence of discretionary choice points that exerts an ultimate influence on whether cases go to the jury. Of all the cases that actually go to trial, only a fraction of them go to the jury; a large number of criminal trials are bench trials in which a single judge decides on guilt or innocence. Once again the process is poorly understood. Most of the discretion lies in the hands of the defendant because of the constitutional guarantee to a jury trial. Nonetheless, a large proportion of defendants choose a bench trial rather than a jury trial.

So we have a sequence of complicated decisions made by a varied cast of players at several points in time in the justice system route from the streets to a jury trial. It is important to note that many of these decisions are conditioned on the players' predictions of what would happen if their case did go to a jury trial. Obviously, prosecutors will not bring cases to trial that they do not believe will result in a conviction, even if they know the law has been broken. A clear example is available in cases involving charges of possession of a small amount of marijuana in this country. Similarly, projection to what will happen in a jury trial exerts a large effect on the form of the offers and deals that are made in the plea bargaining process.

Now, if we consider the manner in which a citizen becomes a juror we see a second, unrelated sequence of uncertain processes. The juror selection process is probably a little better understood and more sharply constrained by explicit rules and procedures. First, the selection process starts with a list of candidates to be called to serve as jurors. In the United States the source list is usually the list of registered voters in a jurisdiction. This basic list is frequently supplemented by other sources of names of eligible citizens; many states use drivers' license lists and Alaska even uses the list of licenses for hunting and fishing (Kairys, Kadane, & Lehoczky, 1977). Although the source list can usually be clearly identified in any particular jurisdiction, the sources vary considerably across jurisdictions and there is always additional complexity introduced when source lists are combined to yield a single list of citizens in a venue. An obvious problem is introduced by a failure to eliminate duplicate names when lists are merged. Many jurisdictions fail to thoroughly eliminate duplicates and so some citizens will be double-counted and have a higher chance of being selected for service. There is a recent example of two counties in New Jersey in which the problem of duplications in juror sample source lists was one of the grounds for a legal injunction that prevented these counties from using jury trials until their method of combining source lists was repaired.

A number of well-documented problems are introduced by using a source list that yields biases in the distribution of demographic characteristics. For example, voter registration lists typically underrepresent younger citizens, older citizens, poor people, black people, etc. Supplementation with driver license lists and other sources helps but does not completely eliminate these sampling biases.

Next there is a process in jury selection in which jurors apply to be excused from jury service. Some jurors simply do not return the juror questionnaire that calls them to service, and across jurisdictions there is a great diversity in the grounds for an acceptable excusal from service. There is a general trend nationally to shift to "one day or one trial systems," in which almost no one is excluded from service. Of course, this method broadens the base and increases the representativeness of the sample of jurors, but even under these systems the yield of jurors is still only a fraction of the total. For example, in the two counties in New Jersey with which I am acquainted, a typical yield from the original jury source list is approximately 30% with a "one day or one trial" call. Again, we see a dramatic effect on the sample that eventually goes into the jury box; 70% dribble out of the sample, but the general nature of these excuses and their effects on the representativeness of the final sample are largely unstudied and mysterious.

Next, once our jurors are in the courthouse and in the jury pool and called to a courtroom for impanelment on a jury there is a further step in which attorneys for the two sides of the case exercise challenges to eliminate jurors from the final panel. There are two types of challenges, challenges for cause and peremptory challenges. A review of trial tactics textbooks, attorneys' memoirs, or experience as a potential juror gives one a direct and dramatic sense of arbitrary and confusing decisions at this stage of the process. For the most part, attorneys' strategies in specific cases are obscure, sometimes even to the attorneys themselves. Furthermore, for strategic reasons and because of the threat of reversal on appeal, specific strategies are rarely if ever revealed to public scrutiny. Complications are also introduced by the institutional structure in which these challenges are exercised. There are several procedures commonly used in state and federal courts (one-by-one individual challenges; group challenges in which a jury-sized group plus alternates is seated and challenged individuals are replaced until a final panel is left; and the "struck jury" system in which an initially large sample is winnowed down to the final panel through the application of challenges) and the structure of the procedure interacts with the strategy pursued by each attorney, the distribution of jurors of various types in the panel, and random or quasi-random factors that determine the order in which jurors are brought into the jury box in the voir dire selection sequence. Some of the subtlety (and confusion) inherent in this selection process is revealed by the fact that attorneys from *opposing* sides of the case often *agree* on which jurors should be eliminated from the jury (for example, both defense and prosecution attorneys frequently attempt to eliminate highly educated jurors). Again, this process is poorly understood and little studied by social scientists.

The point of my lengthy exploration of the vicissitudes that underlie the creation or selection of the case that goes to trial and the selection of jurors to decide it is to emphasize the complexity of these processes, the low degree of understanding we have of these processes, and to point out that the jury decision process which occurs at the end of a sequence is probably not the most important decision in determining the impact of our criminal justice system on the defendant or on citizens in the society at large. It is also obvious that we do not have a good grasp of the type of case and type of juror to which we want to generalize the results of controlled laboratory research. The procedure of grabbing a sample of experimental subjects and exposing them to a single, abbreviated case in the laboratory lacks ecological validity. As a statistician, my impression is that psychologists are too quick to assume that just about anyone will do the jury task in the same way and too quick to assume that they have created a representative task in the laboratory without carefully checking both these assumptions.

I would like to conclude by raising another set of issues concerning the complexity of events that occur once the trial begins. First, there is the question of the strategic presentation of arguments and information by the attorneys. Schum (this book) has addressed some of these issues, but his research only begins to illuminate the variety of trial tactics employed by experienced attorneys.

Strategic representation is further complicated by the fact that attorneys design the manner in which they present their evidence to appeal to the particular jurors whom they know are on the final jury after the voir dire selection hearing. Attorneys will frame their arguments differently depending on who is on the jury and who they think will influence whom on the jury. The attorneys have their own conceptions of the varied processes of jury decision making, and these conceptions have a second-order effect on the evidence that actually reaches the jurors through the vehicle of the attorney's strategic decisions about the presentation of his or her arguments. Obviously, this introduces a complex reflective cycle of decisions by the attorney conditioned on the nature of the jurors, conditioned on the attorney's juror selection strategies, and so on. For the social scientist researcher, it means that a stimulus case is not a stimulus case independent of the jurors to whom the case is presented.

Finally, after all the complexity that I have briefly addressed above, the juror makes his or her decision and then the jury as a group attempts to integrate the individual decisions into a consensus verdict. These last stages involve many fascinating questions for social science research, and most of the chapters in the present book are fine examples of research on the process and events in those final stages in the decision.

The ultimate question that I want to raise is simply this: Are juror decisions by themselves so overwhelmingly interesting and important that we should neglect research on the myriad of other decisions that are distributed through the criminal justice system? From a larger perspective it seems there are many other actors on the stage of the criminal justice system, the decisions of these actors are equally or more important than those of jurors, and these decisions are even less understood and less studied than those of jurors. If I had to single out one decision as the most important in the entire system I would point to the decision made by prosecutors fairly early in the sequence about whether or not to prosecute at all.

References

Kairys, D., Kadane, J. B., & Lehoczky, J. (1977). Jury representativeness: A mandate for multiple source lists. *California Law Review, 65,* 776–827.

Penrod, S. D., & Hastie, R. (1979). Models of jury decision making: A critical review. *Psychological Bulletin, 86,* 462–492.

11 A rational game theory framework for the analysis of legal and criminal decision making

Ehud Kalai

Game theory is a branch of mathematics developed to rigorously treat questions concerning the optimal behavior of participants in situations of uncertainty, conflict, and strategy. In these situations, called games, each participant attempts to maximize his advantage in circumstances where the outcome depends not only on his actions or on those of the natural world but also, most importantly, on the behavior of other participants whose interests are sometimes opposed and sometimes coordinate to his own interests. Most applications of game theory are in the field of economics, but important insights have been provided concerning social behavior as studied by all of the social sciences and, recently, even in evolutionary biology.

Let me start my remarks with an interesting observation on the nature of the decision confronting a juror as I would analyze it in game theory terms. First, I start with a representation of the situation confronting a juror trying to discriminate between cases in which the defendant is guilty as charged and cases in which he or she is innocent. I have picked a representation of the situation that is similar to the signal detection theory–inspired representation introduced by Kerr (this book). In Figure 11.1, I conceptualize cases as lying along a unitary dimension that I will label (as did Kerr) weight of evidence. There are two types of cases, hence two distributions corresponding to states guilty and innocent. I will let the shape of these distributions appear to be Gaussian unimodal, but it would turn out that this simplifying assumption does not have a big effect on the outcome of the analysis. I have, optimistically, pictured the distribution of values for weight of evidence for the guilty state as lying higher than the distribution for the innocent state. The two states are represented as distributions because presumably the juror cannot be certain of the exact value of the weight of the evidence; if there were certainty, it would be a waste of time to go through the decision theory analysis.

Now to proceed with the analysis I want to assume that the person being tried, the defendant, has made a choice about whether or not to commit a

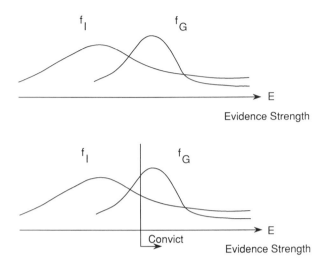

f_I = distribution of Evidence for an innocent person

f_G = distribution of Evidence for a guilty person

$P(I|e \ \varepsilon \ C) = F_I(C)$

$P(G|e \ \varepsilon \ C) = F_G(C)$

Figure 11.1. A picture of the relationships between distributions of evidence generated by innocent defendants (f_I) and guilty defendants (f_G). The ordinate represents the strength of evidence for guilt (E); the vertical line C represents a hypothetical criterion on the strength of evidence dimension which indicates the threshold to convict a defendant.

criminal act; that is, whether or not to represent the innocent or the guilty state. Let me also assume that a person deciding whether or not to commit a crime considers what society will do to him and this has an effect on his choice. So, in game theory terms the defendant's strategic choice is whether to commit a crime and draw a weight-of-evidence value at trial from the distribution for the guilty state; or, on the other hand, to not commit the crime and then at trial to draw a value from the innocent state distribution.

The other half of the game theory analysis concerns what society's agent – in our example a juror – will do when he or she gets the value of the weight of evidence that is sampled from the distribution subsequent to the defendant's choice to be guilty or innocent. The juror's decision is whether or not to convict the defendant.

Another way to represent this situation is to draw a game tree that depicts the sequence of strategic choices that can be made by the two participants in the game. The game tree shows the three steps I have already described: the defendant chooses to commit or not to commit the crime; an

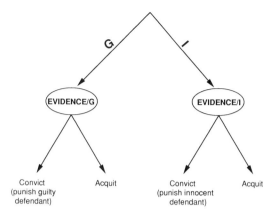

Figure 11.2. A decision tree depicting the conditional dependencies between defendants' and jurors' decisions.

apparent weight of evidence value is drawn from the distribution corresponding to the defendant's choice; and the juror decides to convict or acquit the defendant (see Figure 11.2). Once the game is represented in this form I can proceed to compute the equilibrium (the Bayesian "Nash equilibrium") that determines where along the weight of evidence continuum the decision maker (juror) should place a cutoff criterion to use in the decision to convict or acquit.

Let me start analyzing the game in terms of the preferences of society's agent, the juror. What this analysis yields are four utilities (U_S), one for each of the four possible states depicted as the leaves on the bottom of the game tree; corresponding to acquitting an innocent defendant, acquitting a guilty defendant, convicting an innocent defendant, and convicting a guilty defendant. I have depicted these four states in a third game theory representation, a payoff matrix, and I have simplified the analysis by considering only the rank order of preferences that the juror might have when the outcome falls in each of the four cells (Figure 11.3).

It is obvious that the most preferred situation would be to acquit an innocent defendant, the least preferred situation would be to convict an innocent defendant, and the other two cells fall between these two cases. Perhaps the simplest solution is to treat the two cases associated with guilty defendants as equal in preference. This means that I have eliminated consideration of a vengeance motive that would make the juror prefer to punish the guilty defendant rather than not punish him. This assumption may be unrealistic, but for the sake of the analysis, let me begin with the simple case where the values of the two guilty state cells are equal.

The next ingredient in the analysis, that allows me to compute the equilibrium, is a term describing the defendant's choice, probability P_i that he has chosen to be innocent and probability $(1-P_i)$ that he has chosen to be

DEFENDANT

		Guilty $(1\text{-}p_I)$		Innocent (p_I)
STATE (Juror)	Punish	$U_S(P,G)$	$>$	$U_S(P,I)$
		$\shortparallel$		$\wedge$
	Not Punish	$U_S(NP,G)$	$<$	$U_S(NP,I)$

(NB: U_S (P,G) must be greater than U_S (NP,G) to choose to punish—one interpretation of such a relationship would be a "taste for vengeance.")

Figure 11.3. A payoff matrix depicting the alternative courses of action available to defendants and jurors; the entries in the cells of the matrix represent the utilities of outcomes associated with each pair of defendant and juror actions. The example analysis in the text assumes that the utilities are ordered: $U_S(NP, I) > U_S(NP, G) = U_S(P, G) > U_S(P, I)$.

$$U_s(C;P_I) = (1-P_I)\int_0^C f_G U\,(NP,G) + P_I \int_0^C f_I U\,(NP,I) +$$

$$(1-P_I)\int_C^{\infty} f_G U\,(P,G) + P_I \int_C^{\infty} f_I U\,(P,I)$$

Figure 11.4. An equation for the utility of the juror's decision. The juror wants to choose a location for C on the strength of evidence dimension that will maximize this value. The surprising result is that C should be equal to infinity – the juror will never convict.

guilty. Now, what happens when I calculate the Nash equilibrium characterized by value C which is the weight of evidence cutoff above which the juror should convict and below which the juror should acquit? The calculation of this value begins by laying out a Bayesian equation for the overall utility produced by the decision and then seeking a value that will maximize the equation (Figure 11.4).

Although these assumptions are simplified, they give us a rough idea of what the incentives should be for a juror deciding a criminal case. I want the juror's utility associated with the cutoff point (C) to be as large as possible which implies that he or she should choose a cutoff point, value for C, as high as possible. Surprisingly the result of this derivation is that the cutoff point for C should be infinity. Under this analysis a rational juror would never vote to convict the defendant.

A simpler explanation of the result is to examine the values in the payoff matrix (Figure 11.3) and to note that the action of the decision maker to acquit dominates the action to convict. In game theory terms, a dominating action is always valued equally or better than all other actions available to the participant. It is obvious looking at the four cells in the payoff matrix that acquital is equally or more preferred for all possible states of the game (i.e., whether the defendant has chosen to be guilty or innocent).

Let me review the assumptions of the analysis that produces this surprising outcome. First, I have assumed that one mistake (conviction of an innocent person) is very costly to the juror. Second, I have assumed that there is no satisfaction in convicting and punishing a defendant other than strategic considerations derived from the structure of the game itself (i.e., no vengeance motive).

Well, what are we to do with this analysis? It seems that it must be deficient in some respect as a description of actual judicial decisions because jurors do convict defendants. What the analysis does is to focus our attention on additional considerations that need to be added to the simple representation to make it plausible. Let me explore some of the possible additions to the current assumptions that would make it possible for the social agent, the juror, to decide to convict as well as acquit.

I think the critical weakness of the analysis is in its ordering of the sequence of decisions by defendant and juror across time. The basic problem, as I have represented the game, is that the juror decides last. He or she can only dispose of the single case and make the best of the utilities after the defendant has made his choice about whether or not to be guilty or innocent. What is missing is deterrence; our hypothetical juror does not make a move before the defendant's choice. I think the appropriate elaboration of the game would be to add a mechanism that commits the social agent to punish, at least some of the time. This commitment to punish in some cases becomes a deterrent to defendants when they make their choice at the beginning of the sequence as we have represented it for a single case.

I think there are some clear examples of commitment mechanisms elsewhere in the trial surrounding the juror's decision. For example, the judge is often committed to assign a penalty to a defendant once he has been convicted of a particular crime. Sentencing guidelines that commit the judge to a certain range of severity of penalties are built in to the statutes for some crimes in some jurisdictions. I would even suggest that the manner in which legal institutions break up the total decision task, separating it into one part performed by the judge and one part performed by the juror, is designed to build in certain degrees of pre-commitment to the decision by each of the parties.

A completely different possibility, outside of institutions that build in commitment mechanisms, is to simply raise citizens in our society so that they do have a vengeance motive. I want to emphasize that the consideration here is to build in a satisfaction that is directly linked to punishing guilty people, a satisfaction that does not derive from pure strategic considerations.

Another possibility, which I believe does not apply to jury decisions, is to treat them as examples of repeated games. Recent developments in game theory have demonstrated that repeated games, where the same players repeatedly choose interdependent actions, may have solutions that derive from each player's ability to punish and reward the other player in response to previous actions. This analysis in terms of repeated play probably does not apply in the jury decision situation: The defendants and the jurors are different on each play of the game, so there is no conditioning of response on one play of the game dependent on earlier actions in the game.

I know that some analysts might suggest that the analogy to repeated play games applies because juries represent samples from a fixed population of jurors with similar values; thus, a jury is a jury is a jury. Similarly, criminals represent populations of criminals and so one bank robber and his fate serve as a general deterrent for all members of the class of potential bank robbers. However, here again the game theory analysis suggests that the analogy to repeated play breaks down.

Let me start with the case where the analogy does work, a single agent (perhaps a parent) punishes or doesn't punish another agent (a son). It is obvious that the parent would like to punish the son every time there is sufficient evidence that the son has done something wrong in order to deter the son from performing the bad behavior. Here the parent reveals his strategy to the other player. Now, if we turn to the jury decision case, we already have different people in the role of jurors and different people in the role of defendants. Let's suppose that there is a system in which every time the weight of the evidence exceeds a specific cutoff criterion the jury decides to punish the defendant. This goes on for years and years and now we consider the case of a new juror who decides a new case. What should this new juror do when confronted with a value of weight of evidence for a particular defendant, if he wants to decide optimally? He knows about the consistent habit of other juries to punish when the weight exceeds a criterion, but this really has no effect on his personal decision about whether or not to punish the defendant. In fact, this new juror, to behave optimally, should defect and not punish no matter what (i.e., using a criterion value of an infinite weight of evidence). This juror does not expect his behavior will affect the behavior of jurors who follow him, and in essence he reasons, "Why not let them do the punishing, I want to avoid that extremely aversive error of convicting an innocent man." This is really a "free rider" issue; the juror would rather have other people do the punishing than take a chance on making an error if he punishes.

Let me finish with a general comment on the role of the Bayesian decision theory as a source of understanding of human decision making. It seems to me that there is a big difference between the Bayesian approach and the approach taken by most psychologists who want to describe human decision behavior. The general philosophy of the Bayesian approach is to assume the highest possible level of rationality on the part of the players and perfect communication of information among the players, and then to attempt to solve for this "frictionless case" to see how optimally rational agents would behave. Then, after the ideal case has been solved, we'll start to bring in additional considerations that make the situation more realistic and change it from a "frictionless case" to a case in which all sorts of naturally occurring frictions are present. Obviously, this agenda of beginning with the ideal case means that the theory will not be immediately useful as a tool to understand everyday human decision making. However, there are valuable benefits from proceeding with this agenda that derive from its completeness, logical consistency, and mathematical eloquence. I would like to note that some of the recent developments in game theory introduce assumptions that yield a bounded or finite rationality. One direction in which this work has gone is to combine results from computer science with game theory so that we can understand what strategies are computable under assumptions of finite computational power. As an example of where this analysis might lead, I have an intuition that the order of evidence presentation will be predicted to have an effect on the ultimate judgment under a finitely bounded Bayesian calculation.

12   Why do jury research?

Richard O. Lempert

I want to focus my remarks on the question, "Why do people conduct jury studies?" After all, as Kadane (this book) has noted, jury decisions affect only a small fraction – far less than 10% – of the cases that enter the criminal or civil justice systems. There are arguably four or five other decision points in the criminal justice system and several in the civil justice system that are more important in terms of processing cases and affecting the lives of individual citizens.

To improve the law

First, people conduct studies of juror and jury decisions to influence the law and to improve jury performance. People with this goal want their social science to be relevant to their lives by offering ways to make the world a better place. Studies that reflect this urge embody the belief that social science research is most worthwhile when it tells us directly something about the solution to a real-world problem or elucidates an issue of popular concern. For example, when the U.S. Supreme Court in *Williams v. Florida* (1970) appeared to rely on four seriously flawed empirical studies for the proposition that six-member juries were constitutionally permissible, social scientists – chiefly psychologists – responded with a flood of research on small groups and juries.

For those interested in affecting the law, there is always the question of what institutions to target for influence. Occasionally, as in the work by Ellsworth and her colleagues on the death qualification issue (e.g. Cowan, Thompson, & Ellsworth, 1984; Fitzgerald & Ellsworth, 1984) the courts, and ultimately the Supreme Court, must be the target, and whether or not it must be there is a sense of accomplishment in being cited by the nation's

I am grateful to Phoebe Ellsworth for her comments on an earlier version of this paper.

highest court. Occasionally, as in *Lockhart v. McCree* (1986), the death qualification case, the research is the center of judicial attention. More often,
however, if influence is the goal, a sense of accomplishment at being cited
by the Court is misplaced, for most social science research is only cited in
footnotes, and these footnotes are seldom essential to court opinions. Indeed, they may have been added by law clerks long after the decisions they
support in fact were reached, and the Court's reading of the cited social
science is frequently imperfect if not downright wrong. Too often the best
work, like that of Ellsworth and her colleagues mentioned above, persuades
only the dissent. It is easy for a court that wants to reach a particular result
to ignore social science research, and when research is cited by the majority the chances are that the same result would have been reached had the
social science work never been done. Thus for social scientists seeking an
impact on the law, it is usually a mistake to let appellate court decisions,
especially Supreme Court decisions, set the agenda, and it will often be
equally misguided to make appellate courts the implicit audience for one's
findings.

If jury researchers seek to influence the law, reaching other audiences
may yield higher profits. Perhaps the highest payoff comes, as Kalven (1968)
suggested 25 years ago, from research that changes the common sense
understandings – or at least the understandings of educated elites – about
how the jury system operates and the ways in which various system features, such as jury size or the type of permitted voir dire, affect the quality
of the justice that juries deliver. When research affects such understanding,
all decision making reflects that research in the taken-for-granted conception of reality from which decision making proceeds. From this perspective jury researchers may affect the law more through articles in *Psychology
Today* and references to their findings in *The New York Times* than they do
by publishing in the *JPSP* or being cited in a leading law review. However,
personal credit for influencing how people perceive the world is elusive.
Not only is there seldom an equivalent to the Supreme Court citation, but
often individual credit cannot be given, for the effects of social science on
popular views of reality are ordinarily traceable to a cumulative body of
scholarship rather than to particular studies with names attached.

An alternative to targeting research at the appellate courts is to target it
at members of legislatures, legislative committees, and administrative commissions (Tanford, 1991). While some researchers, like those investigating
rising tort verdicts, have a legislative audience in mind, this is less common
than it should be if influencing the law is the goal. Legislatures are, generally speaking, better equipped than courts to use research intelligently.
They have professional staffs, some members of which may have graduate
social science training, and they are better situated than courts to make
systematic studies of issues. Legislatures have the additional advantage of
setting their own agendas, which not only can make social science relevant
but may also be influenced by social science research in the first place.

Research may also influence legislators more than courts because legislators are less constrained than courts by such considerations as respect for precedent or concern for the federal system. I have, for example, heard that the research following *Williams v. Florida*, which never led the Supreme Court to reconsider that decision, did affect several state legislatures that were considering a move to six-person juries.

To influence courts, legislatures, or commissions, jury research should speak to issues that currently concern them. Too often researchers who look to courts for a sense of what is relevant cannot expect to influence what courts do because they are gathering evidence after a matter has been decided. This is certainly true of the research that responded to the Supreme Court's decisions on jury size and nonunanimous verdicts, although the research on the former issue may have had some influence in *Ballew v. Georgia* (1978) when the Court decided that criminal juries could not go below size six. The task for those who would influence judicial or legislative law making is to decide what jury related problems are likely to be addressed in the near future. For example, it is likely that the Supreme Court will eventually address the question of whether a party has an absolute right to a jury trial in complex civil litigation and that the Court's judgment on this matter will to some extent reflect the jury's ability to deal rationally with complex, lengthy trials. While the possibility of a Court judgment has been obvious for a decade, few psychologists have attempted to gather relevant empirical evidence (for notable exceptions see Bermant et al., 1981; Diamond & Casper, 1992; Horowitz & Bordens, 1988, 1990).

But even when researchers anticipate empirical issues that are likely to confront the High Court, there is no guarantee the research will be influential. In *Witherspoon v. Illinois* (1968), for example, the Court refrained from holding that death-qualified juries could not fairly resolve guilt or innocence because they thought the available evidence was inadequate to establish the point. Several researchers saw in this refusal to decide the issue an invitation to provide evidence on which the Court could rely. The general import of their work, particularly of the careful studies of Phoebe Ellsworth and her students (see Cowan et al., 1984; Fitzgerald & Ellsworth, 1984), was that death-qualified juries were more prone to convict than juries that had not been restructured by the death qualification process. This research was important in setting the Supreme Court's agenda, for it is unlikely that the Court would have reconsidered the issue *Witherspoon* reserved had the research never been done. However, the research did not shape the final outcome. Justice Rehnquist, writing for the majority in *Lockhart v. McCree* (1986), treated the *Witherspoon*-inspired studies as if he were an advocate concerned with scoring points rather than a judge interested in what social science could tell him. He never evaluated the studies collectively; he criticized those studies that could be criticized; he ignored the research that was least vulnerable to challenge; and he concluded by defining the legal issue so as to make the studies cited, his criticisms, and any future research responding to his criticisms irrelevant to the constitutional issue as the Court defined it.

The outcome of this empirically oriented campaign against the death-qualified jury does not mean that it was a silly enterprise from the outset. One can easily imagine a differently – and by no means radically differently – constituted Court accepting the empirically based argument and outlawing the death-qualified jury even while reaffirming the general constitutionality of the death penalty. However, one can also imagine a different use of the evidence than the Court-oriented uses for which some of it was almost immediately employed. It might have been used to try to shape and educate public rather than judicial opinion.

Instead of a campaign to present the research to the courts, there might have been a campaign to disseminate the same message broadly through journals such as *Scientific American,* mass media like *The New York Times,* and specialty journals like law reviews to persuade both the ordinary people and legal elites that death penalty procedures made the determination of guilt in capital cases suspect. The goal would have been to define the issues as fairness, propriety, and justice; rather than the accuracy of empirical research. My speculation is that even the Court that decided *Lockhart* might have been responsive to a systematic long-term campaign of this type, as, for example, the Court was in *Batson v. Kentucky* (1986) to repeated claims that the exclusion of black jurors by prosecutors through peremptory challenges was racist and unfair. But there was no time for the results of the best of the *Witherspoon*-inspired research to percolate through the legal community – people were facing death and could not wait until general attitudes were changed. Moreover, educating the public or even elite segments within it is easier said than done.

Casper's research in this book seems similar to the *Witherspoon*-inspired research in certain respects. It also focuses on a specific type of case, in this instance Section 1983 civil suits claiming illegal police behavior, and suggests that our treatment of juries may cause the results in such cases to fall short of the legal ideal. The specific issue that Casper investigates is whether when an individual sues the police for constitutionally impermissible conduct that includes an allegedly illegal search, the jury should be informed of the results of that search. Casper's data suggest that judgments of illegality and the damages due to illegal activity are affected by knowledge of whether the search in fact turned up contraband or other evidence of illegal activity. This effect persists even when jurors are instructed that they must judge the situation as of the time the police entered the plaintiff's premises before it was known what might turn up. Taking his cue from the law, Casper suggests that if his results generalize then juries in 1983 actions should not learn the results of illegal searches, since legally such searches should have no effect on verdicts but behaviorally they do.

However, by taking the formal law so seriously Casper misses larger issues that might motivate judges considering whether to keep outcome information, like the results of illegal searches, from juries. First, although outcome information should not have an influence under a formal legal analysis, it may in fact lead to better jury decisions. Consider, for example, two close cases, in one of which the search was without probable cause and the police found nothing and in the other of which there was probable cause and drugs were turned up. Although the jury in each instance is to judge the situation as it appeared when the search commenced, juries with outcome information may do a better job of sorting out close cases than those without. Of course, it may be that a search without probable cause turns up drugs and an illegal search turns up nothing, but in the long run results should correlate with legality.

Even an inappropriate influence of search results on damage awards in cases that are not close may be easily tolerated by the legal system. Whatever the formal law provides, people may sense that the "innocent" victim of an illegal search is damaged more than the "guilty" one. Moreover, society may wish to deter police more from the aggressiveness that results in illegal searches in situations in which no illegal activity is going on than from undue aggressiveness in situations where the suspect had in fact broken the law. If an illegal search turns up a million dollars worth of cocaine, that cocaine will not be sold even if the possessor escapes conviction. Moreover, the outcome of an allegedly illegal search is an important part of the search story. If jurors are not given outcome information, they may speculate on the reasons why. It is better that a verdict reflect a true state than an outcome which an imaginative juror mistakenly assumes.

Judges, in short, are often motivated by more than the formal implications of the law. Social science research which seeks to induce legal change by arguing that the fit between law (taken as given) and reality (as shown by scientific research) requires a particular rule or way of proceeding often fails to persuade because judges are motivated by more than the formal doctrine the researcher considers and need not accept the scientists' portrait of reality when so motivated.

To sum up this section, jury researchers who seek to improve the law directly through their investigations should be prepared for disappointment, particularly if their aim is to affect judicial law making. Even if jury research addresses value issues that are legally important, it seldom addresses the full range of values that influence courts, and the value issues that are ignored – often because they cannot be addressed empirically – may carry more weight with courts than the values that underlie the empirical issues that are illuminated. Even where an empirical issue has been defined by a court as core, if a court does not like the direction in which the data point then it can, as in *Lockhart*, ignore some studies, pick holes in others and, to be sure that no further empirical objections are raised, reconsider the legal issues in the case. Because the jury system entails important values in addition to accurate factfinding and because so many settled expectations may be threatened by systematic deficiencies in the ways juries are treated, jury studies may be even more likely than other types of social research to be purposely distorted or ignored.

I do not mean, however, to suggest that jury studies cannot affect the law, or that courts are necessarily immune to their influence. Most often the influence of jury studies on judicial law making will be indirect. Where the empirical assumptions underlying prior decisions are questioned by criticism or new research, a court is unlikely to overturn prior precedent on that account, but it may make wiser use of empirical data in the future. Where the cumulative knowledge from jury studies shapes popular or elite understandings of the jury system, the influence of jury research is likely to be more profound because it will have shaped the taken-for-granted understandings from which judicial law making proceeds. If, however, the goal is to influence the law more directly, researchers should consider the possibility that legislatures or specialized commissions more than courts may be receptive audiences. Researchers should also consider the possibility that influencing the law is the least important reason to do jury research.

Influencing lawyers

A second reason for doing jury research, but a reason that receives short shrift from many social scientists, is to influence lawyers. More specifically, social scientists through original research or syntheses of what is known can assist attorneys in their preparation and delivery of cases to the jury. There is an irony here. Lawyers, unlike courts, seem eager to gobble up any advice from social scientists that promises to make them more effective at trial, yet academic social scientists who have no qualms about drawing broad implications for legal reform from limited studies that courts properly ignore appear reluctant to conduct research directed at lawyer's needs. Even studies that are relevant to lawyer's concerns, such as studies of the order which makes for the most effective argument, often conclude with advice to courts about how to make their processes more balanced rather than with advice to lawyers about how to win cases. It appears almost as if there is a sense that research is crass and mercenary if it is not directed at improving the jury system but aims instead at simply furthering a party's chances in the adversary process. My feeling is that academic social scientists should be more responsive to the practical concerns of lawyers and less concerned with possible contributions to jury reform. Lawyers search out research that can help them, and when quality research is not easily available oversimplifications and downright trash are consumed. Moreover, there is a lot to be learned about juries from working with lawyers in the context of actual cases. Much of this knowledge is today possessed by private companies formed to aid lawyers in litigation and, except insofar as tales are told for publicity purposes, it is treated by these companies as proprietary information. As such it neither informs the work of other researchers nor is subject to the criticism and correction that attends publication.

The research by Pennington and by Schum (this book) seem to be directed more to the concerns of lawyers than to those of courts although neither study was done with the goal of aiding lawyers specifically in mind. The implications of these studies are not simply general conclusions, such as "Arguments should be structured in a Bayesian form," but they are steps to understanding how jurors comprehend information and make inferences, and as such can aid lawyers in structuring their cases. Both studies, but Schum's in particular, will require translation before lawyers will fully appreciate the implications of their findings, and Pennington's work appears closer to the point where lessons for lawyers can be easily drawn. It is not, of course, necessary that researcher and translator be the same person, but if they are, new gates to knowledge might open. Pennington's idea of the story model, for example, will not surprise many lawyers, who commonly describe their cases in terms of the stories they will tell. They may, however, not appreciate how jurors make stories of their stories and the systematics of what is going on. At the same time lawyers might alert Pennington to types of stories that she has not considered or constraints on advocacy that affect the kinds of stories that juries put together. Both practice and theory might be enriched by more concern with application.

Understanding juries for their own sake

A third general motivation for social science research on juries is to better understand the way juries behave. This motivation has particular appeal for social scientists who in general subscribe to the "knowledge for its own sake" dictum. Clearly greater knowledge about juries may have implications for the law, but I have already noted my concurrence with Kadane's (this book) observation that if our goal is to improve the legal system, the jury may not be an appropriate research priority. Research on prosecutorial decisions or the attorney–client relationship, for example, might yield bigger payoffs in terms of affecting larger numbers of cases. Thus the best motive for jury research may be that the jury is of considerable interest in its own right.

Scholars interested in studying juries for their own sake do not, however, necessarily adopt the most efficient paths to knowledge. This is because jury research often proceeds on the assumption that if understanding juries is the primary goal, research should be focused only on the behavior of actual jurors and juries or, if actual juries cannot be studied, on individuals or groups in simulated jury situations. It does not, however, follow from the goal of understanding juries that jury researchers must exclusively study jurylike groups or people dealing with jurylike problems. Jurors are individuals and juries are small groups, and there may be tasks and situations that are facially unlike jury decision making but are none the less better suited to the study of the social psychological processes that govern behavior in juries than much of what now passes for jury simulation. Often faster progress may be made by first studying decision processes that are not shaped to resemble a jury's and then, when hypotheses are well-established, exploring the issue in actual or simulated jury situations (consider, for example, the group polarization literature).

An indicator of the importance of overarching theoretical perspectives is that we rarely see an article on jury behavior in a major journal that does not tie its results to principles of behavior that apply beyond the jury decision context. However, many jury researchers seem to have become so interested in the jury that they leave the generation of theories that may generalize to the jury to individuals working outside the jury paradigm. While these jury specialists often borrow theories from cognitive or social psychology, too many jury studies seem unconcerned with contributing to more general theory in these areas.

The research by Kerr in the current volume on judgment thresholds and evidence tradeoffs seems to me to be an example of work that would ultimately have more to offer jury researchers had it been less focused on the jury in the first instance. Suppose that rather than focusing on jury decisions, Kerr had started by studying a variety of situations in which the decision maker has to balance evidence evaluations and judgment thresholds. He could then have designed his jury simulations with more refined hypotheses about the importance of these factors. For example, it is likely that we would gain greater insight into criterion–evidence relationships by looking at a variety of tasks and cases than we can gain from a restricted focus on the guilty versus not guilty verdict. These insights might in turn have suggested further hypotheses to test in simulated jury situations. The message, in short, is that when we pursue the general goal of understanding jury behavior, we should not assume that our research must be restricted to jury tasks.

Understanding beyond juries

A fourth motivation for jury research is to better understand the way individuals make decisions on nonjury tasks and behave in groups other than juries. Even psychologists with no special concern for understanding jurors may find that the study of simulated jury decision making has certain attractive features. For example, jury decision making is more involving than many psychological research tasks and subjects appear highly motivated to perform to the best of their abilities. Indeed juries are so involving that some social psychologists who come to study juries because they are interested in more general psychological processes end up fascinated with the jury as an institution or the field of psychology and the law more generally. Such people face both the danger and the challenge of trying to serve two masters: They seek to add to our knowledge about the jury while at the same time trying to contribute to the social psychological understanding of social life. Ironically the researcher who is less interested in generalizing to actual juries and so is free from pressures to emphasize external validity may, by focusing on a problem for its social psychological significance, learn more in the long run about juries than the researcher who deliberately makes compromises between a research design that allows the most efficient test of a psychological theory and a research task that from the point of view of learning about juries is more externally valid. But ultimately psychological theories, if they are to inform jury research, must be tested in externally valid settings.

The potential utility of the jury paradigm for illuminating theoretical issues that have little to do with juries is, I think, nicely illustrated by Casper's research in this volume. Indeed, although Casper might not agree, I believe that his research is potentially most important for what it might tell us about basic psychological processes underlying the hindsight bias, and that it has only peripheral and relatively unimportant implications for understanding or reforming the institution of jury decision making. What is most interesting in Casper's research is that he has not simply replicated the classic hindsight research paradigm. Rather than asking his subjects to make judgments about outcomes in hindsight, he has asked them to make judgments about other matters. Thus we see another way in which perseverance effects operate (cf. Hawkins & Hastie, 1990), and Casper's research adds to our understanding of psychological processes that seem to be involved in hindsight phenomena of the traditional type. Moreover, Casper's statistical methodology could be used to elucidate the causal relationships that underlie other hindsight type phenomena.

A focus on juries and legal decision making can also stimulate more general social-psychological inquiry. A researcher interested in the hindsight phenomenon might from this perspective focus on dimensions that are missing from the early hindsight research of Fischhoff and others. One such dimension, that is obvious in the context of legal judgments, has to do with the costs of the decision. It is possible to use mock-jury research to study this general theoretical issue, just as it is possible to investigate this issue in contexts quite unlike jury decision making, and come up with findings that have clear implications for the jury. Thus, even if one is not interested in juries for their own sake but is only concerned with general issues of individual or group decision making, programmatic research might be stimulated by contemplating the situation of the jury and it might employ studies that examine mock or real juries doing jury type tasks.

Understanding legal systems

The final motivation for research on juries that I wish to discuss is not to understand juries per se, but to understand law and how the legal system operates. For example, we might examine juries in an effort to learn more about citizens' perceptions of law or their relationship to the legal system. With this motivation, knowledge about juries may turn out to be incidental.

Let me again use Jay Casper's research as an example. His study may or may not tell us something fundamental about the manner in which jurors assign damage awards in a Civil Rights Act case. But even if we learned nothing useful about the topic that concerns him, his research might still tell us something about why the exclusionary rule is controversial and important. We can, through research like Casper's, learn how ordinary people relate to legal rules. We will learn more, of course, if researchers have this concern consciously in mind.

To this point I have been suggesting that both jury researchers and social psychologists with other interests can build on the presumed similarities between juries and other small decision making groups to advance knowledge in both spheres. But when one examines juries for what they may tell us about law or the legal system, the key issue is not how jury decision making might be like other decision making but rather, and perhaps more importantly, how the two types of decision making differ. How do people take responsibility for themselves and for other people when they must apply the law as jurors and how does this differ from taking responsibility in other contexts for interpersonal judgments? Many aspects of the jury's task make jury decisions different from decisions in other spheres: the tremendously important consequences for individuals, a very strong sense of normative order, explicit instructions on how the decision making task is to be performed, a highly authoritarian relationship with a judge, and so forth. Here the problem of external validity is not a problem to be wished away, but rather it is an important focus of inquiry. What is it that makes for external validity in jury research or the lack thereof? How does decision making change when it is legally consequential?

By way of example, consider the implications of class or attitudinal differences on juries. We may treat such differences as predictors of verdicts or we may ask and examine in the jury context what class and attitudinal differences portend for how people react to the legal system. When the latter question is our focus, issues are raised concerning individual feelings of control and efficacy and differences in people's sense of belonging to the legal system. What distinguishes "scrupled" jurors who could not vote for the death penalty but could convict a defendant of a capital crime from "nullifiers" who even if they have no role in sentencing will not convict if death is a possible sentence? Answers to questions like these should tell us something about what "respect for the law" means and how legal values fit into a person's larger hierarchy of values. For some people, legal values may head a value hierarchy; other people who profess allegiance to the same values may nonetheless accord legal values a subordinate place; and still others may reject certain legal values altogether.

This last point, that perhaps a primary motivation for research on juries should be to understand the legal system and ordinary people's relationship to it, was stimulated by reading a book by a colleague of mine. Thomas Green (1985) provides a fascinating historical survey of forces and events that helped shape modern Anglo-American juries. He explores not only the political and historical roots of the institution of jury trial but also the relationship of juries to medieval and early modern society and to the cases they had to decide.

In reading this book I was particularly struck by Green's sampling of justifications for the decisions provided by petit juries in fourteenth-century England. The following is an example of a jury decision agreeing with a defendant's claim of self-defense:

William Childerle returned home from the fields and met Richard on the stairs of his apartment where a struggle ensued and the intruder was slain. At the trial the petit jury assured the court that William had fled to a wall near the door of the house where he was finally cornered and forced to strike back in self defense. (quoted in Green, 1985, p. 41)

Now consider some excerpts from Nancy Pennington's research on jury decision making in twentieth-century America. The excerpt is the prototypical summary of the "self-defense story" from the *Commonwealth v. Johnson* case:

Caldwell and Johnson were in Gleason's bar one afternoon when a woman named Sandra Lee asked Johnson for a ride somewhere the next day. Caldwell suddenly became violent, pulled out a razor and threatened to kill Johnson. Thinking it best to get out of Caldwell's way, Johnson left the bar. Later that evening Johnson's friend came over to Johnson's house and suggested they go to Gleason's for a beer. Johnson didn't want to go but agreed to, if they checked first and Caldwell wasn't there. At the bar they saw that Caldwell was not there so they went in. However, Caldwell came in later and asked Johnson to step outside. As soon as they went outside Caldwell punched Johnson unexpectedly, knocking him back hard against the wall of the building. Johnson was woozy from the punch and he knew that Caldwell had a razor because Caldwell had threatened him with it earlier. Johnson was carrying his fishing knife, so he pulled it out to show the knife and keep Caldwell from coming after him. As he came back from the wall he saw that Caldwell had his razor and was coming at him. Remembering Caldwell's earlier threats, he thought he had better protect himself so he held his knife out in front of him. Either Caldwell lunged on to the knife or as Johnson put the knife out he thrust a little and the knife went into Caldwell wounding him.

What strikes me about these two jury summaries is the remarkable continuity of elements that constitute self-defense, similarities that carry across six centuries. Now consider a second example that makes a slightly different point. From a fourteenth-century English jury:

John Doughty came home at night to the house of Robert in the village of Laghscale as Robert and his wife lay asleep in bed in the peace of the King, and he entered Robert's house; seeing this, Robert's wife secretly arose from her husband and went to John and John went to bed with Robert's wife; in the meantime Robert awakened and hearing noise in his house and seeing that his wife had left his bed rose and sought her in his house and found her with John; immediately John attacked Robert with a knife . . . and wounded him and stood between him and the door of Robert's house continually stabbing and wounding him and Robert seeing that his life was in danger and that he could in no way flee further, in order to save his life he took up a hatchet and gave John one blow in the head. (quoted in Green, 1985, pp. 42–43)

What is remarkable here is not the similarity to current decisions, although I believe that is present as well, but the relationship of this account of the petit jury and the prior account of an inquest jury:

Robert Bousserman returned home at mid day, to find John Doughty having sexual intercourse with his wife. Bousserman forthwith dispatched Doughty with a blow of his hatchet. (quoted in Green, 1985, p. 42)

Note the contrast between the accounts of the inquest jury and the petit jury that rendered the ultimate verdict concerning Robert Bousserman. I suspect the inquest jury provides the rendition of the fact that is closest to what really happened: Bousserman came home at midday and found his wife in bed with Doughty and he killed Doughty. The petit jury tells a more convoluted story, but a story that supports an acquittal of Bousserman on grounds of self-defense. Why the discrepancy between the two accounts? If the petit jury had found the same facts as the inquest jury, Doughty would have been sentenced to death. So, the only way the jury could exercise its duty to do justice was to reconstrue the facts to admit a verdict of self-defense. Contrary to the facts, the petit jurors constructed, in Pennington's terms, a "not guilty story" after the fact, to support their verdict.

There is remarkable continuity in what constitutes a proper or just verdict. There is also remarkable similarity in the elements of an appropriate "not guilty" verdict justification. And, I wonder if Pennington's jurors and the fourteenth-century jurors may not have been engaged in the same activity; constructing a representation of the facts to justify the verdict that they believed was just.

I do not want to make too much of these continuities; in fact, I'm not sure what all of the implications should be. However, the remarkable similarity in stories constructed by jurors across the span of 600 years leads me to believe that research on jury decision making may yield its most important fruit in what it can tell us about how the legal system works and about how citizens relate to it.

There is nothing wrong (and much that is right) with seeking to improve the jury system, or to aid lawyers, or to better understand the jury as a small group, but approaching the jury with any of these concerns may blind one to much that we can learn from this unique form of democratic self-government. The jury should be appreciated in its entirety. When we investigate the jury, it is not just another small group we are studying.

References

Ballew v. Georgia, 435 U.S. 223 (1978).
Batson v. Kentucky, 90 L.Ed. 69 (1986).

Bermant, G., Cecil, J. S., Chaset, A. J., Lind, E. A., & Lombard, P. A. (1981). *Protracted civil trials: Views from the bench and the bar.* Washington, D.C.: Federal Judicial Center.

Cowan, C. L., Thompson, W. C., & Ellsworth, P. C. (1984). The effects of death qualification on jurors' predisposition to convict and on the quality of deliberation. *Law and Human Behavior, 8,* 53–79.

Diamond, S. S., & Casper, J. D. (1992). Blindfolding the jury to verdict consequences: Damages, experts, and a civil jury. American Bar Foundation, Working Paper No. 9127, Chicago, IL.

Fitzgerald, R., & Ellsworth, P. C. (1984). Due process vs. crime control: Death qualification and jury attitudes. *Law and Human Behavior, 8,* 31–51.

Green, T. A. (1985). *Verdict according to conscience: Perspectives on the English criminal trial jury, 1200–1800.* Chicago, IL: University of Chicago Press.

Hawkins, S. A., & Hastie, R. (1990). Hindsight: Biased judgments of past events after the outcomes are known. *Psychological Bulletin, 107,* 311–327.

Horowitz, I. A., & Bordens, K. S. (1988). The effects of outlier presence, plaintiff population size, and aggregation of plaintiffs on jury decisions. *Law and Human Behavior, 12,* 209–229.

(1990). An experimental investigation of procedural issues in complex tort trials. *Law and Human Behavior, 14,* 269–285.

Kalven, H., Jr. (1968). The quest for the middle range: Empirical inquiry and legal policy. In G. C. Hazard, Jr. (Ed.), *Law in a changing America* (pp. 56–74). Englewood Cliffs, NJ: Prentice Hall.

Lockhart v. McCree, 106 S. Ct. 1758 (1986).

Tanford, J. A. (1991). Law reform by courts, legislatures, and commissions following empirical research on jury instructions. *Law and Society Review, 25,* 155–175.

Williams v. Florida, 399 U.S. 78 (1970).

Witherspoon v. Illinois, 391 U.S. 510 (1968).

13   Two conceptions of the juror

Lola Lopes

Two contrasting theoretical conceptions have developed in recent research on jury decision making. I call these two alternate views of what goes on inside jurors' heads the "meter model" and the "story model" (Figure 13.1). The meter model is based on the conception that inside the head are one or more mechanisms that continuously track, and can read out, one or more values that reflect the juror's current evaluation of the evidence. This view is probably the more popular theoretical position (subscribed to by Schum, Kerr, Casper, Dawes, Kadane, and Zabell, this book).

Usually the meter is conceived of as a unitary mechanism that reads out a quantity measuring the perceived guiltiness of the accused. However, the model can be easily elaborated to include separate meters, for example, for each of the elements of a criminal charge; a meter for identity, a meter for state of mind, and so forth. For Kerr (this book) the measure is the "quantity" of guilt that has accumulated in the juror's mind. For Casper (this book) it is the measure of convictability predicted by a linear regression equation. For Schum (this book) the meter actually generates probabilities or likelihood ratios measuring the goodness of evidence for alternate hypotheses (e.g., the defendant is guilty versus the defendant is not guilty).

In the story model (Pennington and Hastie, this book) the juror is depicted as having a cognitive structure that organizes individual facts (or things that the juror believes to be facts) and the relations among facts into a causal structure that explains how the events in question came about. This structure is constructed "on line" and it pieces together an overarching picture of the evidence, indicates what is missing and what inferences need to be made to produce a complete structure. In the simplest version of the story model a fact or a relationship is either in the structure or not in the structure; in other words, the individual elements are discrete. These structures are built by the juror and at some point (or several points in time)

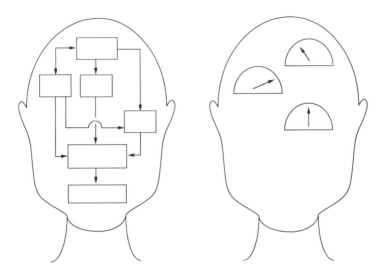

Figure 13.1. A whimsical rendering of the two concepts of decision making mechanisms referred to in this comment.

compared with "verdict structures" that represent the alternate verdicts in the choice set, and the fit of the two structures (story and verdict) to one another is assessed. The judgment of guilt or innocence is therefore a pattern-matching process.

In my opinion both of the models are correct. Each represents a real facet of the psychological process. Jurors are almost always ready after hearing testimony to state their opinions as to guilt or innocence and presumably they are also able to assess their level of confidence. Their assessment of guilt and confidence may, of course, change over deliberation, but probably at most points in time jurors are able to respond with an opinion about the verdict. However, despite the fact that people may have aggregated measures of guilt and innocence at any time during the trial process, this does not imply that they do not also have a propositional structure into which they integrate new pieces of testimony. Furthermore, it is almost certain that a juror's propositional structure representing the testimony is at least in reasonable correspondence with his or her "meter reading." For example, one would not expect a meter reading of "guilty" in the absence of at least some substantial structural support. (Even in the most blatant case of bias, the structure would entail a stereotype to support a meter reading.)

How do meters respond to evidence?

Movements of single meters to successive pieces of evidence

Let me start with the observation that most jurors have a value in mind that represents their strength of belief concerning the defendant's guilt or innocence toward the end of the testimony and at most points in time from then on. The issue I want to focus on is how do meters move as evidence comes in? Two subsidiary questions can be asked: In what direction does the meter move? And, how far does a meter move? The various algebraic models (e.g., averaging models, Bayesian probability models, Thomas & Hogue's and Kerr's evidence accumulation models) make strong predictions about exactly how the meter will move in response to an item of evidence. However, if we consider that language is vague and that subjects in jury decision tasks without technical training may not assign the same meanings as we do to the scales we use in obtaining estimates of guilt or innocence, we may find that subjects' meters do not even move in the appropriate direction in response to an item of evidence (relative to a model's predictions) much less in the appropriately sized quantitative step.

Most of the meter models (Kerr's evidence accumulation model is probably an exception) construe evidence as coming in packets that are all conditionally independent of one another and that vary in strength. These two conditions may confuse readers, so let me develop an example. Consider Schum's analysis in terms of Wigmore evidence support diagrams. Schum has several complex units of evidence located along each line of support for a contention or a verdict. Each unit has a complicated internal structure, but the separate units in each diagram are not connected. This is what I mean by independent. The lack of connection between two complex units implies that the values in one of the units have no implications or impact on the values in the other unit.

The second characteristic of a unit of evidence is its importance to the ultimate judgment, sometimes labeled "probative impact" in legal discussions, or "strength" in psychological contexts. Within the Schum diagram it is the location of a unit of evidence with reference to the top or bottom of the diagram that indexes its importance. Units near the top of the diagram are more directly relevant to the verdict hypotheses and therefore are more important in terms of their support or impact on the strength of belief in the verdict. The fewer inferential steps between a unit of evidence and the ultimate hypothesis, the stronger the evidence, everything else being equal.

I want to talk about a specific situation in which two packets of evidence come into the span of the juror's attention, one packet that is relatively strong and the other relatively weak. We might imagine two prosecution witnesses, one of whom presents evidence that weakly implies the defendant is guilty followed by a witness who provides strong evidence for guilt. Now, I want to consider two possible orders for these witnesses, the weak witness followed by the strong versus the strong followed by the weak. It will turn out that one critical test between two conceptions of the meter mechanism derives from predictions about how the meters will move successively as the two pieces of evidence are presented.

In Bayesian models the meter is constructed to read either posterior odds ratios or probabilities of particular hypotheses. Presumably "reasonable doubt" in the Bayesian model corresponds to some criterial odds ratio or probability value. In the Bayesian model, meters aggregate probabilities and should always move in the direction of the hypothesis that is more favored by the evidence. Thus, if two items favoring the same hypothesis but to differing degrees are presented, both weak–strong and strong–weak orders should produce two meter movements, both movements toward the supported hypothesis.

On the other hand, according to an averaging model, the meter is constructed to read the average strength of the evidence. This means that the meter moves from its current position toward the position indicated by the new packet of evidence. This is what it means to average. Thus, an average will always lie between the current value and the new value of presented evidence. When evidence comes in the weak followed by strong order, both meters – Bayesian and averaging – would shift in the same directions: The weak piece of prosecution evidence would shift the juror slightly toward conviction and the strong piece would shift the juror even further toward conviction. But, consider what happens when the reverse order of presentation occurs, strong evidence followed by weak evidence. Under the Bayesian model a large shift toward conviction would occur as the strong evidence comes in followed by a further shift in the direction of conviction as the weak evidence comes in. But the averaging model, with the strong then weak order, does something surprising. The strong packet of evidence shifts the meter from neutral fairly far in the direction of conviction. However, the weak piece of evidence, pointing toward conviction, lies between the value of the meter set by the strong piece and the neutral position; thus the shift is back toward neutral.

In fact, recent work of mine (Lopes, 1985, 1987) plus older work of Shanteau's (1970, 1972) on Bayesian judgment tasks (cf. Edwards, 1968) has shown that the averaging model best describes what subjects are doing when they make judgments serially. Note, this occurs even when subjects are instructed "judge probability" since to subjects "probability" is just a word that labels a scale and their ratings seem to follow the averaging meter, not the normative Bayesian probability meter.

This finding raises an interesting point when we consider the manner in which jurors are instructed. In both our "probability instruction" judgment experiments and in the situation of jurors who have been given instructions by the trial judge on how to decide the case, we do not really know what kind of mechanism the subject or the juror has in mind as a result of hearing the instructions. The implication of the Lopes (1985, 1987), Shanteau (1970, 1972), and Pennington and Hastie (1992) results is that subjects in psychology experiments and jurors at trial are making their judgments in keeping with the mechanism implied by an averaging process rather than a probability process. It may be that special instructions or training could induce jurors and judges to follow the rules of probability theory when updating their beliefs. However, it seems that in most dynamic, sequential updating judgment tasks the averaging mechanism describes the mental meter's natural behavior.

An interesting development in this research (Eils, Seaver, & Edwards, 1977) has taken subjects' averaging behavior as a starting point and tried to devise training procedures and task constraints that will encourage subjects to at least approximate the normatively proper probability updating rules. One potentially useful observation from this work is that averages of likelihood ratios can be artificially transformed to odds ratios that are very close to the optimal cumulative likelihood ratios.

The point I want to make in the present context is that it is imprudent to simply assume without careful examination that a subject who is instructed to follow certain rules (e.g., the laws of probability) will naturally be able to do so. In fact, in my own research I have found that people do not even make their judgments in a manner that is qualitatively (directionally) appropriate in response to certain patterns of evidence.

How is evidence integrated from two or more meters?

Pennington and Hastie (1981) point out that juror decisions, at least if they follow the judge's instructions, are not assessed on a single unidimensional scale that might correspond to a single meter. Rather, each verdict is defined as a complex logical structure comprising several sub-units or subdimensions connected by logical operators such as *and* and *or*. For example, first degree murder is defined by the conjunction of actions (unlawful killing, killing in pursuance of a resolution), mental state (intent to kill, purpose to kill formed), circumstance (insufficient provocation, interval between resolution and the act of killing), and identity (the defendant was the agent of the victim's death). The meter model can be adapted to a multidimensional case by supposing that the juror has meters in his or her head corresponding to each of the features or dimensions composing the verdict. Here I think we can improve the meter model by combining it with the manner in which categories are represented in "fuzzy set theory" (Zadeh, 1965). By fuzzy category I mean that each of the elements (e.g., intent to kill) is not represented mentally as a discrete present-or-absent value but rather each element is "more or less" present in a given case. The juror's ultimate task is then to integrate several "fuzzy" meter readings into a composite meter reading.

At this point I want to raise the question of what do we mean by reasonable doubt in the multidimensional case? If one conceptualizes the multidimensional case in terms of a set of probability meters jointly associated with a single hypothesis (e.g., first degree murder), we could define reasonable doubt as present whenever any one of the individual meters falls below a criterial value. This would be equivalent to the minimum rule in Zadeh's formal expression of fuzzy set theory; or in more common decision theory terms, it would represent a noncompensatory conjunctive decision rule.

A second conceptualization is to define reasonable doubt as a criterion value on a unitary composite judgment. One possibility for the composite judgment would be to use a multiplicative rule such as Oden (1984) has applied to Zadeh's fuzzy logic. As it happens Oden has shown that people seem to follow the multiplicative rule when making simple category classification judgments. The multiplicative rule is of special interest in the present context because it suggests that complex verdict definitions (comprising several elements) would be likely to generate low values almost by necessity, since the products of probability truth values (lying between 0 and 1) get small very quickly.

A third view, which seems to follow from the Bayesian point of view, is that the composite meter reads and integrates ratios of meters defined as a guilt versus innocence quotient. All three views, but especially the last, raise a question in my mind concerning what is the normative legally proper method for combining several meters' values. The combination of meter values seems fairly straightforward when, for example, we see a strong prosecution case pitted against a weak defense case or the opposite of a weak prosecution and a strong defense. However, it is less clear what to do in cases where both prosecution and defense have presented a strong case, or perhaps more common, where neither prosecution nor defense have presented a strong case. In such conditions the integration of meter values may not discriminate between both strong, both weak, or even some combinations of strong and weak; but these differences may be very different subjectively and perhaps of significance from a normative legal perspective. Presumably jurors do not convict simply because of a relativistic sense that the evidence of innocence is weaker than the evidence of guilt. It seems obvious that if both are weak then the accused should go free.

Some comments on the story model

One immediate reaction I had to Pennington's paper (this book) was to suppose that given the adversarial nature of trials, it is likely that subjects would initially generate two structures, one representing the defense and the other the prosecution. If this is true, several questions are raised: First, how are facts placed in the stories? Do some facts appear in both stories and some in only one? Second, how do story construction processes change over time? Is the preliminary prosecution story constructed in the same manner as the defense story? Is direct testimony incorporated into a story in the same fashion as information produced on cross-examination? Does the subject frequently switch between alternate stories or is one story available and under construction for long segments of time (e.g., first the prosecution then the defense)? Third, what happens to a rejected story after the juror reaches a preliminary verdict judgment? Is it destroyed, does it simply fade away, or is it less accessible, but still available? Fourth, how is goodness of fit between the story model of events and the verdict model of verdict elements assessed? Note, this is where the issue of meters and the integration of meter values reappears. Part of the assessment of confidence in the verdict may derive from the presence of micrometers associated with specific molecular elements within the stories. For example, the juror may include a confidence assessment of the event, "Caldwell had his razor out during the fight," and somehow dozens of micrometer values will be integrated to yield an overall strength of belief or confidence in the story structure taken by itself. Another issue is raised by the story-to-verdict pattern matching process, which again is amenable to representation in terms of multiple meters. Oden (1984) has developed a version of the fuzzy set theory propositional model that applies to both confidence in a propositional structure's internal components and a confidence derived from the fit of the propositional structure to a generic category.

Individual differences

I was struck by some commonalities in the work I have been conducting during the past few years on individual differences in risky choice and the findings reported by Ellsworth (this book) and Casper (this book) on individual differences as predictors of jurors' verdicts. Individual juror variables such as personality traits, generalized attitudes, and demographic attributes do not seem to work well in predicting either verdicts or choices among gambles. Individual differences that appear to work better as predictors of voting on the jury are attitudes specific to the task (e.g., attitudes toward the death penalty) and, in the case of gambles, attitudes toward risk or preferences for "sure things" versus "gambles." Another successful predictor in the juror task is the form of evidence evaluation structures (story structures) and the analog in risky choice is the representation of the gamble (e.g., as a gain or loss) or the goal aspired to by the subject (e.g., the subject attempts to maximize the probability of winning *at least* $50).

In my work on risky choice I have found that a subject's taste for a sure thing versus a gamble in a very simple two outcome bet has great power to predict the same subject's preferences among much more complicated gambles with multiple alternatives in the choice set. I've also found that subjects' attitudes toward goals in the gambling context, attitudes that they bring with them into the experiment, are powerful predictors of choices. In general terms, my work suggests that there are two types of people: people who try to avoid bad outcomes, "risk-averse" people, and people who seek to obtain good outcomes, "risk-seeking" people. To end on a speculative note I wonder if there is a simple analogy from my work on risk attitudes to types of jurors in the context of deciding a case. For example, is there a class of jurors who focus, like my risk-averse subjects, on avoiding the serious error of convicting the innocent? On the other hand, is there a class of jurors who focus, like my risk-seeking people, on obtaining the just outcomes, thereby appearing to be conviction prone in their desire to punish the guilty? Moreover, I wonder if such a principle might be generalized; to wit, are these two types of people (supposing they exist) associated with different general orientations toward the legal system. Could it be that at the heart of a distinction like Casper's due process versus crime control ideologies, is the same kernel of risk adversity and risk seeking that figures so prominently in subjects' behavior in my gambling experiments?

References

Edwards, W. (1968). Conservatism in human information processing. In B. Klein-muntz (Ed.), *Formal representation of human judgment* (pp. 17–52). New York: Wiley.

Eils, L., Seaver, D., & Edwards, W. (1977). *Developing the technology of probabilistic inference: Aggregating by averaging reduces conservatism* (Research Rep. 77-3). Los Angeles: University of Southern California, Social Science Research Institute.

Lopes, L. L. (1985). Averaging rules and adjustment processes in Bayesian inference. *Bulletin of the Psychonomic Society, 23,* 509–512.

(1987). Procedural debiasing. *Acta Psychologica, 64,* 167–185.

Oden, G. C. (1984). Integration of fuzzy linguistic information in language comprehension. *Fuzzy Sets and Systems, 14,* 29–41.

Pennington, N., & Hastie, R. (1981). Juror decision-making models: The generalization gap. *Psychological Bulletin, 89,* 242–287.

(1992). Explaining the evidence: Tests of the Story Model for juror decision making. *Journal of Personality and Social Psychology, 62,* 189–206.

Shanteau, J. C. (1970). An additive model for sequential decision making. *Journal of Experimental Psychology, 85,* 181–191.

(1972). Descriptive versus normative models of sequential inference judgment. *Journal of Experimental Psychology, 93,* 63–68.

Zadeh, L. A. (1965). Fuzzy sets. *Information and Control, 8,* 338–353.

14   A mathematician comments on models of juror decision making

Sandy Zabell

In this comment I will briefly address three topics. First, some comments on the aptness of the Bayesian model as a description of the way people think; in particular, how jurors think. Second, a comment on the application of mathematical models in general to the behavioral sciences. Third, some suggestions for specific directions in jury research that would be of particular interest to mathematicians and statisticians.

The Bayesian model

Let me start with a few remarks on the Bayesian picture of belief and belief revision. Specifically, I want to talk about some of the goals a researcher might want to accomplish when using a Bayesian model. First, the researcher might want to use the model descriptively; as a description of the mental processes and behavior of an actual decision maker. Unfortunately, it has become increasingly clear that human behavior does not approximate the prescriptions of a Bayesian model. Work by Tversky and Kahneman (1974) and others has shown that people exhibit substantial violations of the laws of probability in making assessments of probability. In a sense this conclusion has positive implications for the Bayesian enterprise. If the mathematical theory of probability corresponded to our intuitions at all points, we wouldn't need it. It is precisely because the theory on occasion tells us things that seem initially counterintuitive (e.g., revealing errors of judgment in problems such as the "birthday paradox," the "regression fallacy," and reasoning about conditional probabilities) that it is useful.

Another use of the theory might be as a normative model, a model for optimal or proper reasoning. I distinguish between two versions of the normative application. One version assumes that the model prescribes how people should act and think on a day-to-day basis. Here again, I think the goal is impractical, because no one really thinks in strictly Bayesian terms. The second version, which seems more realistic and useful, is to think of the theory as a model of normative consistency. I find it useful here to think of the analogy between probability theory and formal logic. In the case of logic, we know the formal model does not describe the way people actually think, and no modern logician has proposed that people should be trained to think from day-to-day in that precise mode. But as a theory of consistency it helps us to police our beliefs.

As I see it, the major use of subjective probability is as a partial analysis of rational belief. That is, although it does not capture all the elements of rational belief, it does give us some important corrective insights into our thinking. For example, I find it helpful, when I get confused trying to think through some of the paradoxes mentioned above, to have the theory at my disposal and be able to use representations such as sample spaces and probabilities to analyze what is going on and to remove some of the confusions and obscurities that arise.

As a practical, technical tool probability theory has many uses in theories of statistics and data analysis. It is important to realize that this is a fairly narrow domain of applications. But within that narrow domain there are some dramatic success stories. (For example, during World War II the mathematician Alan Turing was able to apply the theory in his research on cryptanalysis and his group broke several enemy codes of significant value to the British war effort.) However, even with such examples in mind, I do not want to argue that probability theory be employed as a serious tool in too many natural contexts. A case in point is the proposal by Finkelstein and Fairley (1970) that jurors use Bayes' theorem to aggregate pieces of information in some cases to evaluate identification evidence. Their proposal was subjected to heavy, and I think reasonable, criticism, on the grounds that the technical Bayesian approach is more likely to mislead than to assist a lay jury.

The gap between what probability theory prescribes and how people actually think suggests that we might try to revamp the theory and make it into one that more closely approximates the way people actually think. Such theories, designed to be closer to everyday human thought, have been proposed by Cohen (1977), Shafer (1976), and Zadeh (1978), among others. But I believe these efforts fall short and that none of them succeed in adequately describing human thinking about uncertainty. I think that Tversky and Kahneman's work in particular, especially their results on the conjunction fallacy (1983), show that all of these alternatives to traditional probability theory will be violated by the way people think about probabilities.

Let me make a few additional comments on the system proposed by Cohen. Cohen as a philosopher raises some valid questions about human violations of traditional probability theory principles (cf. Cohen, 1981). For example, he has raised several questions about how subjects in psychological experiments interpret the instructions or questions of experimenters, and the scales on which they respond. The gist of his criticism is that experimenters have often misinterpreted their results and do not realize that their subjects are responding to questions different from those that experimenters believe they have put. These criticisms have some merit, but they are scarcely original. Furthermore, my conclusion on reading the empirical research, even considering Cohen's criticisms, is that the effects concerning errors in judgment and violations of probability theory are robust across variations in the experimental tasks and instructions. The findings from psychological research represent a fundamental mode of thought in the subjects, and are not simply artifacts of the experimental methods employed.

Cohen's claim that traditional normative models (probability theory models) are incorrect and should be replaced by an alternative probability calculus that he proposes is also unconvincing. Let me simply refer to an exchange in the journal *Behavioral and Brain Sciences* (1981) in which the errors in Cohen's arguments are exposed by several of Cohen's critics.

This comment extends to many of the arguments in criticism of Bayesian probability theory that Cohen makes in his book *The Probable and the Provable*. For example, he criticizes the Bayesian model because of its use of prior probabilities, which imply consideration by the juror of information external to the trial. But, obviously, a decision maker always draws on background knowledge in assessing the implications of information obtained at trial: e.g., the demeanor of a witness, the meaning of an exhibit, and so forth. A second example is Cohen's criticism of the Bayesian model based on an interpretation of the standard of proof, "preponderance of evidence," as referring to a probability greater than .50. Cohen notes that making a decision, perhaps to award a large sum of money, on the basis of a probability of .51 does not seem fair. But, if we look at the situation he posits, the decision maker has to decide for A or B, and if there is a close call, the decision is still required. So the dilemma arises from the constraints imposed by Cohen's hypothetical situation and not from something inherent in the Bayesian analysis. In summary, although I agree that Cohen raises some important questions, I do not find them especially problematic for the Bayesian model.

Another set of phenomena that have been cited as problematic for the Bayesian model concern the effects of order of evidence on the ultimate judgment. For example, the Greek rhetoricians thought that the strongest manner in which to order a series of arguments was the "Nestorian order," in which the evidence is presented starting with the strongest argument, then the third strongest, the fourth, and so on, concluding with the second strongest. There is in fact a fair amount of evidence in the literature on jury decision making that the order of presentation of arguments, witnesses, or exhibits does influence the ultimate decision. The law tries to deal with inequities that might be introduced by order effects with conventions that prescribe and balance the order of arguments and also with instructions to jurors to reserve judgment until all of the evidence has been heard. There is no claim that the law approaches some platonic ideal of perfect equity; obviously it has evolved over time and has a long history which has not been driven by some underlying rational principle. Legal procedures such as the order of argumentation at trial, the rules governing when instructions are presented, whether information about past crimes can be introduced, and many other legal practices have developed for reasons; but these reasons are not exclusively concerned with an ideal, rational decision process.

In summary, the Bayesian theory is a reasonably successful, partial analysis of rational belief; and I do not think at present there are serious challenges to it. Nonetheless, I do not believe it provides a useful description of how people actually think in legal decision making.

The role of mathematical models

Now let me turn to some remarks about the general practice of using mathematical models in the behavioral sciences. Consider the example of the Poisson process model introduced by Thomas and Hogue (1976; see Kerr, this book). At the heart of the model is an unknown quantity (x) that represents the weight of the evidence against the accused as arrived at by the juror as a result of the trial. I am willing to believe that an individual can partially order his degrees of belief based on the weight of evidence so that, for example, if he heard several trials he could order the trials according to the strength of evidence he perceives against the accused in each trial. I am also comfortable with the notion that the theorist can take a set of ordered outcomes like these and attach a numerical quantity to each to yield at least an ordinal scale. However, it is a major leap of faith from these assumptions to the notion that there is some kind of common scale for *different* jurors. What I am uncomfortable with is the notion that a 56 on my scale somehow bears a definite relationship to a 58 on another juror's scale.

The fundamental problem I see arises from the absence in this research of an operational definition of the term, "weight of evidence," one that could be applied to a single juror to obtain the number from that juror for a particular case. Another way to state my concern is to note that this coefficient for weight of evidence is a value on an ordinal scale, but the theoretician can always use a monotone transformation of the underlying scale to produce another similarly ordered scale. This is especially troublesome when one thinks of aggregating individual jurors' weights of evidence into a common scale.

My discomfort is compounded when we turn to a scale of confidence, because now we have a second numerical variable piggy-backed on the first and, again, we have to make the assumption of a common scale of confidence across jurors. In the particular applications by Thomas and Hogue and by Kerr, I am troubled by the lack of a theoretical motivation for the choice of the favorite model from the set of several candidate variations on a basic formulation. My concern about the justification for a common scale of weight of evidence and of confidence makes me suspicious of selection based on a simple goodness-of-fit competition among the candidate models; and my concern is increased by the flexibility introduced by monotone transformations of the hypothetical, but unoperationalized, individual values of weight of evidence and confidence.

What I mean by a theoretical motivation would be some type of psychological justification for why one mathematical distribution or another would be appropriate for the weight of evidence and confidence variables. For example, in other domains of psychological research, the exponential or geometric distributions are frequently used to represent learning and forgetting processes that are generated by mechanisms similar to those that are known to produce variables with these distributions. In the case of the Poisson process model, such justifications have not been developed.

This set of concerns arises from my understanding of the utility of using mathematical models in science. The early successes of mathematical models in the physical sciences in the seventeenth and eighteenth centuries encouraged social scientists to attempt similar applications (Stigler, 1986). If we look at early examples of mathematical models in mechanics, for example a model that predicts that a cannonball will follow a parabolic trajectory, we can see that repeated uses of the model fit the phenomena. Then, insights into the component processes producing the phenomena and predictions of future phenomena were derived from fundamental components of the mathematical formulation. These initial qualitative successes then led to further elaborations of the model which eventually provided highly accurate quantitative predictions of the behavior of objects in uniform gravitational fields. In contrast, in the case of the models currently applied to juror decision making, I do not feel that fundamental qualitative properties of the behavior of the individuals under study are well understood, that the simple models employed are motivated by such properties, or that quantitative developments are built on this foundation. Rather, I have an impression of premature quantitative development and I suspect that many of the conclusions are highly model-dependent. At the same time I do not feel that the basic models have been grounded solidly on empirical phenomena. So, without a substantial theoretical rationale or models robust across plausible transformations of their basic variables, I view conclusions such as Kerr's with a great deal of caution.

Future research

I conclude with a few suggestions concerning directions for future research on juror decision making. Given my own interests in statistics and the law, especially statistics concerning employment discrimination, I am curious about how juries handle technical evidence. For example, how do jurors handle statistical and probabilistic information presented by experts in employment discrimination cases? Tribe (1971) has made a number of arguments opposing the use of statistical evidence in jury trials. Some of his arguments involve legal values. For instance, he asserts that if the uncertainties involved in evaluating evidence were exposed and made prominent at trial, it would undermine the jury's and society's belief that proof "beyond a reasonable doubt" could be achieved. Consequently, Tribe argues that any efforts to quantify standards of proof, such as preponderance, "clear and convincing," and "beyond reasonable doubt," will erode fundamental values associated with jury trials by underlining the uncertainty inherent in any decision.

Another set of Tribe's criticisms are based on his assumption that juries are incapable of properly using this type of evidence. Since the publication of Tribe's paper, this assertion has been called into question by the increasing use of statistical evidence in jury trials. An important landmark here is the *Griggs v. Duke Power Co.* case in the early 1970s, in which it was established that if the plaintiff could show that an employment practice had a disparate impact on a protected class of citizens (e.g., women, minority group members), then the burden of proof (to demonstrate "nondiscrimination") shifts to the defendant (employer). Thus, in such cases the statistical evidence puts the burden of justifying a hiring or promotion practice on the employer, entirely independent of the issue of intent, creating a purely statistical category of discrimination. Subsequent decisions (e.g., *Castaneda v. Partida*, 1977; *Hazelwood School District v. U.S.*, 1977) continued this trend toward the increasing use of statistical evidence, and the Supreme Court has even on occasion cited statistical formulas in some of its decisions. Following these opinions, lower courts have begun to accept complex statistics with increasing frequency. Thus an important and interesting question concerns the extent to which juries can handle such information. Some subtle statistical issues, for example, the determination of confidence intervals for multiple comparisons or the interpretation of Simpson's paradox type patterns in cross-classified frequency data, increasingly face modern juries.

As a final comment I think that it is good that much of the research on juror decision making is focused on empirical studies of psychological processes. The Bayesian probability model provides certain consistency constraints on probabilities that may help us police our beliefs, but the theory says nothing about where probabilities come from in the first place. I find that current research on juror decision making gives me insights into how people think about probabilities and generate beliefs in complex natural situations.

References

Castaneda v. Partida, 430 U.S. 482, 496 n. 17 (1977).
Cohen, L. J. (1977). *The probable and the provable.* New York: Oxford University Press.

(1981). Can human irrationality be experimentally demonstrated? *The Behavioral and Brain Sciences, 4,* 317–370.

Finkelstein, M. O., & Fairley, W. B. (1970). A Bayesian approach to identification evidence. *Harvard Law Review, 83,* 489–517.

Griggs v. Duke Power Co., 401 U.S. 424, 91 S. Ct. 849, 28 L. Ed. 2nd 158 (1971).

Hazelwood School District v. U.S., 433 U.S. 301 (1977).

Shafer, G. (1976). *A mathematical theory of evidence.* Princeton, NJ: Princeton University Press.

Stigler, S. M. (1986). *The history of statistics: The measurement of uncertainty before 1900.* Cambridge, MA: Harvard University Press.

Thomas, E. A. C., & Hogue, A. (1976). Apparent weight of evidence, decision criteria, and confidence ratings in juror decision making. *Psychological Review, 83,* 442–465.

Tribe, L. H. (1971). Trial by mathematics: Precision and ritual in the legal process. *Harvard Law Review, 84,* 1329–1393.

Tversky, A., & Kahneman, D. (1974). Judgment under uncertainty: Heuristics and biases. *Science, 185,* 1124–1131.

(1983). Extensional versus intuitive reasoning: The conjunction fallacy in probability judgment. *Psychological Review, 90,* 293–315.

Zadeh, L. A. (1978). Fuzzy sets as a basis for a theory of possibility. *Fuzzy Sets and Systems, 1,* 3–28.

Index of names

Index of subjects